ORGANIZATIONS IN A CHANGING SOCIETY:

Administration and Human Values

RICHARD H. VIOLA, Ph.D.

Professor of Management
College of Business Administration
Temple University
Philadelphia, Pennsylvania

1977
W. B. SAUNDERS COMPANY
Philadelphia, London, Toronto

W. B. Saunders Company: West Washington Square
Philadelphia, PA 19105

1 St. Anne's Road
Eastbourne, East Sussex BN21 3UN, England

1 Goldthorne Avenue
Toronto, Ontario M8Z 5T9, Canada

Library of Congress Cataloging in Publication Data

Viola, Richard H

Organizations in a changing society.

1. Organization.   2. Management.   3. Social values.
   I. Title.

HD31.V55   658.4'08   76-27062

ISBN 0-7216-9055-6

Organizations in a Changing Society:
Administration and Human Values   ISBN   0-7216-9055-6

Last digit is the print number: 9   8   7   6   5   4   3   2   1

This book is dedicated to
Lucy, Francesca, Elise, Christa, Richard, and Maria

PREFACE

Our society is going through a time of turbulence that is characterized by the loss of credibility in our institutions. Business and government, most especially federal government, are two of the most important of these institutions. The influence of business and government on our lives is so great and so widespread that every American citizen is affected by them in one way or another. Both business corporations and the large government agencies are feeling the impact of this credibility gap. The crisis of confidence that business and government organizations are undergoing is a serious problem precisely because it will have an effect on the future of the private, profit-making sector of our society as well as the public sector.

This book suggests that the business corporation is at a crossroads in America. It must address itself to its lagging credibility and begin to monitor society for relevant signals that are being given. The business corporation as well as the bureaucratic government agencies must see that in engaging in any surveillance of society, the most important factor in the society is the human being. This book argues for organizations in America to put man at center stage in our society. Man is the central actor, the protagonist, in the turbulent environment of business and government. Since he is the central figure, business and government organizations would do well to analyze the major social forces that are affecting man. These social forces are affecting him inasmuch as they are influencing and changing his values. In examining the linkage between social forces and human values this book takes a step beyond most of the literature now being written in organizational behavior and management.

It is the purpose of this book to ascertain how man's values are changing, where they are taking him, and perhaps most important, how changing human values will affect the management of the business corporation and government bureaucracy. Managers should keep in mind that the employees of business and government are also members of society and are affected by what is happening in society. These employees carry their values into the organizations where they work, and these values are very influential in determining and guiding their behavior on the job. Managers and administrators can ignore this fact only at great danger to the effectiveness of their organizations.

Organizational effectiveness is linked to organizational survival. This book argues that survival of the business corporation is increasingly going to be a matter of how effectively it contributes to the quality of the lives of the millions of Americans it affects. This is where the future is. What does the American business corporation do for the quality of life in our society? Since we human beings *are* society, and since we are so much affected by business, we have a stake in the business corporation. The corporation's employees are undergoing a shift in the direction of their values. Values are choices, and the following chapters stress the ways in which these new choices are affecting managers and the actions managers must take to keep their corporations viable, effective, and indeed adaptive to society's changes. How can the business corporations close the credibility gap? Since organizations exist only at the sufferance of the society in which they operate, survival means continued concern with society's well-being. This translates into the well-being of its members, who are also the business corporation's members. The connection is clear. We have now reached the point where it is not at all hard to see that what is good for society is good for the business corporation. The new social responsibility of business lies in its obligation to improve society, and understanding the changing values of its workers is the essential first step. For those managers who do not like the notion of obligation, the book will suggest that it is more a matter of necessity. Private business enterprise is probably one of America's two or three most important institutions. It therefore has to assume its rightful responsibilities and obligations if it is to continue as a free institution in a democratic society.

This book is divided into seven chapters. The first chapter outlines the problems faced by business and its managers in terms of work in the organization. The following five chapters are devoted to discussion of social forces the author considers important, considering the impact they are having on human values. The final chapter addresses itself to the changes in organizational structure and managerial philosophy needed to help the business corporation and government bureaucracy effectively cope with and adapt to this turbulence in our society. The new leadership and motivational strategies that are part of the managerial philosophy proposed here are also discussed in the last chapter.

Finally, though this book deals with the role of work organizations in society and is appropriate for such courses as Social Issues in Business, Business and Society, and Industrial Sociology, it can also be used in courses in Organizational Behavior, Organizational Development, and Industrial Psychology. Its use as a supplementary text in any number of Management, Industrial Relations, and Personnel courses also is appropriate. In addition, practicing managers should find this book helpful.

RICHARD H. VIOLA

ACKNOWLEDGMENTS

In writing this book I received much help. I should first of all like to thank John C. Neifert, my editor, for his encouragement and consideration. An author could not ask for a finer editor. In addition, special thanks go to those colleagues at Temple University with whom I discussed the manuscript and from whom I received invaluable suggestions: Dr. Richard Leone, Dr. Arvind Phatak, and Dr. Jugoslav Milutinovich. Graduate students and research assistants also were most helpful in gathering data.

I am grateful to Dennis Kennedy, Charles Patterson, Neal Pollock, Andrew Erlanger, Cindy Handler, Vivian Seely, Marie McGrath, and Grace Tappert for their help. Finally, I owe deep appreciation to Dr. Ruth Johnston, Department of Economics, The University of Western Australia, who read the manuscript and gave many helpful comments.

RICHARD H. VIOLA

CONTENTS

CHAPTER

I

WORK: A MODERN DILEMMA

INTRODUCTION

In this last quarter of the twentieth century, the United States is beset by many problems. The energy crisis, strained international relations, economic problems, crime, and persistent crises of national leadership are but a few of the difficulties facing us. The ability to manage and resolve these problems will test the mettle of the United States as the twenty-first century approaches.

One problem not mentioned above is the problem of work in the United States. It is not a problem that has suddenly beset us; rather, it has been developing over the past several years and has blossomed into a full-blown national problem which easily ranks with those mentioned above and, depending on one's point of view, may be among the most crucial facing us. The problem should not come as a surprise to astute observers of American life, because much has been presented about it in the various media. Those of us in academia who are concerned about the problem have attended scholarly meetings which have devoted varying portions of their agendas to the problem. Usually the presentations made and the papers delivered deal with relevant topics, such as leadership, motivation, and other aspects of organizational behavior. These subjects are also part and parcel of any modern executive development program.

The writer regularly receives notices from professional consulting organizations regarding conferences and seminars which deal with such subjects as "the quality of work in America," "the work ethic," "job enrichment," and "the meaning of work." The U.S. Department of Commerce has published a lengthy study called *Work in America* (1973). The federal government has a National Productivity Council to investigate the problems of motivation, job design, the behavioral implications of work, and other related issues.

An interesting booklet entitled "What's Wrong With Work?" published by the National Association of Manufacturers best sums up the points being made here (Beckhard, 1973). A full-page advertisement in *The New York Times* is revealing in that it illustrates this problem from a broader perspective (Thursday, Nov. 1, 1973). The advertisement is a picture of a distinguished-looking businessman who has had eggs splattered all over his face. Under the picture is the caption "American Business is Under Attack." The advertisement is announcing the sponsorship by *Industry Week* magazine of a National Teleconference called "The Selling of American Business." This national closed-circuit teleconference was held in ten major American cities in order to "raise questions, answer questions, provide valuable insights into why the public disapproval of business is growing—and how it can be countered." The panel of discussants was a prestigious group which included an educator, business executives, a politician, a consumer affairs representative, and a national union official. Each person attending this teleconference received a "Business Missionary Kit" which was designed to help him spread the gospel of American business.

Many American businessmen have accused academicians of concocting a problem where none really exists. Other businessmen have suggested that *if* there is a problem, the academicians have exacerbated it by discussing it so much. If it were not discussed, it would go away; perhaps the employees of large work organizations would not have even known thay had a problem. That a very reputable organization like the National Association of Manufacturers would publish the aforementioned booklet and that *Industry Week* saw fit to have a teleconference to sell American business point up the fact that the problem of work in the United States and the part business plays in this problem are not make-believe or the result of some conspiracy. The *Industry Week* advertisement underscores this when it says that the "attack" is coming from the college campus, the pulpit, the media, the politicians, and your own employees. This is a very extensive cross section of American society which hardly leaves any other sector to consider. Finally, the advertisement very frankly states, "American business and industry are plainly in trouble." This says it as clearly and succinctly as any academician could.

This first chapter will briefly outline some of the symptoms of the problem, i.e., in what ways is the problem manifesting itself at various levels in the hierarchy of large-scale business and government organizations? Following this, a diagnosis of the problem will be made, and based upon this diagnosis, an approach to the problem will be put forth. The approach is rather different from the ways in which the problem has traditionally been attacked, and it is hoped that a fresh approach will provide some insights to help resolve the difficulties we are facing.

SYMPTOMS OF THE PROBLEM

Symptoms at the Blue-Collar Level

Physical Escape Mechanisms. The problem of *absenteeism* in many sectors of American business corporations is a crucial one. The automobile industry provides a good example. Many of the younger employees on the automobile assembly line will only work three days a week, given the monotomy, the boredom, and what they describe as the "dehumanizing" nature of the work. This coupled with relatively high pay (about $13,000 annually) causes a situation in which they will not spend five days a week in the auto assembly plants. In some of these plants the annual rate of absenteeism is 13 per cent, compared to 3 per cent a few years ago. In one of the major auto companies an average of 5 per cent of the hourly workers are absent each day (Gooding, 1970). There is a joke about never buying a car from that company that was made on a Monday or a Friday because the rate of absenteeism doubles on those days. This requires the utilization of part-time workers who attend nearby colleges. The quality of their work cannot be expected to reach that of the regular "full-time" automobile assembly workers.

Another symptom is the *turnover rate*, perhaps best illustrated again by the auto industry. One of the major automobile manufacturers has an annual quit rate of over 25 per cent.

The absenteeism and the turnover represent escape mechanisms. We have been witnessing a phenomenon whereby workers are not overly concerned with regular attendance at many jobs, nor are they so "turned on" by the work that they stay on the job. Why? Because they find the work difficult to tolerate. When a shipyard worker was asked by a reporter if he would want his son to work in the shipyard, the worker replied "Would you want your son to go to prison?"

Psychological Escape Mechanisms. These are physical escape mechanisms. Just as critical and damaging to the worker as well as to the corporation are the psychological manipulations workers use to escape the job mentally. One of these "escape hatches" can be found in the form of *alcoholism*. An alcoholic is anyone whose drinking interferes frequently or continuously with any of his important life adjustments and interpersonal relationships (Clapp, 1971). Certainly, one of the important life adjustments is the ability to cope with work. If adjusting to one's work is difficult, alcohol enables a worker under its influence to regress backward in time and recapture feelings that he experienced in childhood.

Alcoholism on the job is a major problem in American industry. Many automobile workers go out to the parking lot, sit in their cars, and sip a little whiskey each day during their lunch break. This helps them to get through the day. Not only is alcoholism destructive to those addicted to it, but also it takes a toll on their families and on the companies for whom they work. The cost of alcoholism to industry, on a national basis, has been estimated at anywhere from $4 to $10 billion per year. Problem drinkers miss work about twice as often as those workers who do not have this problem. Their tardiness is greater, and they have more lost time accidents.

Drug abuse is yet another problem that is on the increase in industry. More and more workers are turning to the use of narcotics as a means of escaping the realities of their jobs. The drug user is blind to the self-destructive nature of his action; rather, he views it as a method of coping with his work. A survey of 222 firms (131 manufacturing and 91 non-manufacturing), ranging in size from 250 to 250,000 employees, in a cross section of American industry revealed some interesting findings:

1. About one-fourth of the firms state that drug abuse is already a problem in business, and an additional two-fifths predict it will become a problem.

2. Of the 117 companies reporting some experience—whether as a widespread problem or in terms of isolated instances—15 per cent specified that "hard" addictive drugs have been involved almost exclusively.

3. Size of company (number of employees) makes little difference in the extent of the drug problem.

4. Analysis of responses by geographic location indicates little difference in the extent of the problem of drug abuse.

5. Many different drugs are used by employees of the surveyed firms; however, use of "soft" drugs is most common.

6. More than 111 of the firms surveyed anticipate more extensive drug abuse problems within their own organizations (see Rush and Brown, 1971).

Some workers use *prayer* to establish some means of adjustment to the work they must do. One example reported involves an automobile worker who "goes to the assembly plant about an hour before his shift every day and takes out his worn Bible to read and meditate before he faces his job" (Salpukas, 1972). This employee said that he had to do this to prepare himself mentally.

Another symptom of the problem facing the blue-collar worker is *aggression* on the job. This aggression comes about as a result of frustration with the work and the inability to make any changes in it. To show management that they will make an impact on the organization, many workers resort to sabotage. In the automobile industry it has taken the form of scratched paint, slashed upholstery, tool handles welded into fender compartments, and screws left in brake drums (Gooding, 1970).

Erich Fromm has suggested that one of the major causes of aggression is boredom. Certainly the automobile assembly line epitomizes the boredom that is related to many types of jobs in the United States. In their attempt to alleviate this boredom, the workers, among other things, engage in sabotage not only as a result of anger and frustration but also as a kind of game to make the work a bit more interesting. This is especially true when they leave screws in brake drums and weld tool handles into fender compartments. They derive great pleasure from knowing that new car buyers and new car dealers will not easily find the funny noises and solve the constant problems caused by this sort of game playing on the part of the worker.

This has further ramifications inasmuch as poor workmanship is also involved. The recall of automobiles because of safety hazards caused by defective workmanship is almost commonplace. Nor is it confined to the automobile industry.

These problems of sabotage, shoddy workmanship, and lack of interest in work are affecting the ability of the United States to compete in world markets. The devaluation of the dollar cannot continue to be this country's solution to improving its trade deficit picture. We must begin to get greater productivity from our workers through a more beneficial mutual adjustment of the problems existing between management and the worker. Otherwise how can automation be productive? Joseph A. Livingston, an economic columnist for the *Philadelphia Evening Bulletin*, reported in 1972 that Undersecretary of the Treasury Charls E. Walker said to him, "If we don't get increased productivity in this country, we might as well put up a sign, saying 'Going out of Business.' Our economic survival is at stake." The point here is that if we in the United States cannot get the kind of productivity from our technology that other high-technology nations such as Japan and West Germany are getting, capital investment in the country will dwindle. Many American companies are building plants abroad to meet this problem.

One of the more tragic problems associated with our complex, highly technological work organizations is that of *mental illness*. John MacIver, (1971), a psychiatrist in one of America's major corporations, reported that: "as many as 25 per cent of the work force at any given time has emotional problems of some magnitude, but there is considerably more in the lower echelons. An estimated 15 per cent of the work force has emotional problems which are moderately severe or severe at any given time" (p. 4). Not all of these cases of emotional illness are job-induced. The pertinent questions are, however, what are the conditions in the work environment which promote mental illness, and what is management doing to alleviate such conditions? In other words, when emotional problems do have their root causes in work organizations, corporate management is faced with a serious situation which demands a more sophisticated and creative approach to these problems than management has hitherto applied. This will be discussed in more detail later.

Symptoms at the White-Collar Level

Most of the points made thus far concern the blue-collar worker. However, the white-collar worker is also experiencing work-related problems.

Alcoholism has no respect for the hierarchical position one occupies in the corporation. For example, Alcoholics Anonymous, in a study of 200 members, reported that 30 per cent of those studied held professional and managerial jobs. A major American corporation which has a program for rehabilitating its alcoholic workers found that 30 per cent of the cases involved white-collar workers.

Mental illness, moreover, is not solely a blue-collar problem. As Dr. MacIver has pointed out, emotional illness merely "takes on different forms at different levels [of the hierarchy]" (p. 4). He goes on to suggest that in middle management, manic-depressive illness is more common than in the other levels of the organizational structure. At the highest levels of the management hierarchy, "complex personality disorders and depressive disorders are the types of illness found" (p. 4).

The *rebelliousness* of young executives may have a more profound effect than any other symptom of the problem. These young executives are articulate and well-educated and do not perceive themselves as organization-man types. They are questioning corporate policies and corporate goals—the profit motive in particular. "Today's junior managers . . . reflect the passionate concerns of youth in the 1970's—for individuality, openness, humanism, concern and change—and they are determined to be heard" (Gooding, 1971, p. 101). Anthony G. Athos (1970), writing in the *Harvard Business Review*, quoted George Kich, president of the Grocery Manufacturers Association, as saying, "Within five years, a president of a major corporation will be locked out of his office by his junior executives" (p. 49). Of great interest here is the idea that should the corporation be the next to "fall" among American institutions (university, church, and family), it will not be as a result of large masses of blue-collar workers storming the executive suite. Rather it will result from an internal revolt or "palace coup."

This leads us to ask whether the younger members of corporations are really committed to their organizations as were their predecessors. The identification with and commitment to the company just is not as great today as it was in the 1950s or even in the 1960s. Professor Harry Levinson, a psychologist at Harvard, suggests that people need attachments for growth, that they *want* to work for companies in which they can be effective. Being effective means many things to the younger members of organizations. It means doing something the individual considers important, a degree of autonomy, freedom to make mistakes, participation in decision-making processes, and working in the kind of corporate environment which allows them an enhanced sense of self-esteem. The latter, in the view of many humanistic psychologists, is what being an *effective* human being, in terms of psychological growth, development, and fulfillment, is all about.

Business may be letting young people down, and the result is that the younger generation does not view business and government organizations in a very favorable light. Many students in colleges and universities around the nation find business boring, decadent, not attuned to the pressing societal problems of the 1970s, and a profession in which it is very difficult to find the kind of self-expression that promotes psychological growth and development.

DIAGNOSIS OF THE PROBLEM

Can these symptoms of the problems facing our work organizations be identified by our modern bureaucracies? The answer, of course, is yes. The symptoms can be seen, but they are only surface manifestations of more deeply rooted problems. Management may be treating symptoms and not getting to the heart of the problem. The reason for this may lie in our approach to the study of organizations.

Modern Organization Theory

One of the more modern ways in which to view the organization is as an organismic whole operating on a total systems basis. However, as today's organizational theorists know, the organization does not operate in a vacuum and therefore must be viewed as an open system. Thus there is a great deal of literature discussing the open systems approach to organizational analysis. What is the organization "open" to? The organization interacts with its environment, exerting certain pressures on it but also being constrained by it. This concept is not new. What may be needed, however, is for organization theory to re-think what is entailed in the word "environment."

Need for a New Focus in the Open Systems Concept

A new conceptualization of "environment" may be necessary to get at the root causes of some of the major problems facing complex work organizations. A new approach to the open systems concept should consider that the central factor in the environment is still man. Since he is the focal point of society, man's values will be one of the important elements shaping society. Modern organizational theory analyzes man's behavior within the context of the organizational sys-tem of which he is a member. Most of the literature on organizational behavior is concerned with the relationship between man and organi-zation and how these two elements interact to affect one another.

Modern business school courses, as well as those executive de-velopment programs concerned with human behavior, mainly devote themselves to the ways and means of understanding man and organi-zation so as to modify the behavior of each in order to make them more compatible. In other words, what is sought in organizational behavior courses, seminars, and programs is the optimum mutual adjustment between man and organization so that the goals and objectives of each will be simultaneously achieved.

It is not that this has been the wrong approach but rather that it has been a nearsighted approach, one that is not as encompassing as it might be. This approach does not go far enough because it does not seek this mutual adjustment through a genuine understanding of man's changing values *as a member of society*. The present focus is primarily on man's needs as they are exhibited within an organiza-tional context. The organizational behavior approach of today fails to recognize in an adequate way that man moves in and out of the organi-zation as a member of society. He is not just a member of the ABC Corporation, and his values are not shaped by the corporation only. Modern management must look at man as a carrier of values. The organizational employee carries into the organization values which may have been shaped *outside* the organization by major forces at work in society.

Consequences

This failure on the part of management to see man as the central factor in society and as a carrier of values has had a number of consequences for business and governmental organizations. These consequences affect both the organization and the individual. The organization is affected because it is not achieving its goals as efficiently as it could. Business as well as government must be concerned with the dual concepts of efficiency and effectiveness. Any good manager knows this. When man's changing values are not monitored and considered, the human being in the organization cannot realize or "play out" newly acquired values within the framework of the organization. The result is less efficiency and effectiveness for the individual and, since he is also the central factor at work, less efficiency and effectiveness for the organization.

The inefficient utilization of human resources is the result, and the cause may well be management's inability to provide a channel through which individuals can maneuver on their way to the goal of full expression of their values at work. Business in the United States is one of the nation's dominant institutions, and the dominant institutions of a society have always reflected the dominant ethos at any point in time. For example, in the United States the concept of private property has had very significant implications for whether or not there will be something called "business"; it has also influenced the *mode* of organization through which business is conducted. In the Soviet Union and the People's Republic of China the absence of the autonomous business corporation is a result of the philosophical systems of the societies themselves. Organizations, then, must satisfy the needs of the society in which they exist. We know, however, that needs are dynamic, and since they are based upon values, organizations must be concerned with shifts in values.

Thus if business is one of the United States' dominant institutions, dependent to a large extent on the dominant ethos of the times, it must be an adaptive institution in order to be viable and, more importantly, to survive. Business must then provide a channel for man through which he can express newly acquired values. Bureaucratic organizations are subcultures in which millions of people spend a large part of their lives. The old values that spawned these bureaucratic institutions, however, are under fire. Important questions are being asked not only by college students but also by businessmen themselves and by executives in government. The questions revolve around how to live real lives in the corporate state and how to be an individual in the face of society's increasing institutionalization with its deadening conformity. The absolutism of rational efficiency is being challenged, as well as the ethic of materialism which was so strongly fashioned by an overorganized technocracy. Values that are contradictory to the purest form of pragmatism are beginning to emerge. Values are shifting toward "personalism," with a concomitant emphasis upon the primacy of the individual who is trying to discover his identity not only as a member of society but also as a member of a bureaucratic work organization. Some of the most eminent philosophers have questioned the pro-Western, static notion of man's nature and the relevance of man's relationship to the world, which must include the organizations in which he works. Teilhard De Chardin, the Catholic philosopher-anthropologist, suggests that man is only an embryo of what he will become. Man, therefore, must maintain an unlimited openness to an unlimited future. More significantly, the Jewish existentialist, Martin Buber, argues that man finds his identity only in knowing other men and being known by them. According to Buber, man's authentic existence comes into being only when a personal "I" meets the personal "Thou" and accepts the other as a human being. In meeting another, man meets himself.

We must now ask to what extent such ideas and the values they represent find expression in our modern complex organizations. Do large bureaucratic organizations by an overemphasis on competition, immediate results, and profit set up barriers between people as they work? Or do they create an environment in which Buber's ideas can come to fruition through a more humanistic management? Are complex organizations the media through which human potentialities can be developed or stunted? To become productive media, work organizations will have to investigate the needs of their environments and the demands of society, both of which are based upon value systems. If we in academia are going to continue to describe complex organizations as "open systems," then we had better get on with the task of environmental surveillance and analysis. Any positive, forward-looking changes that are going to come in organization structure, leadership, and management will result primarily from our ability to monitor and understand the meaning of shifting values and the philosophical systems upon which they are based.

Where do we begin? With society and man who is at its center. The difficulty in measuring values and predicting demands based on them should not deter us. Loren Eisley (1969) tells us:

> I think we worship predictability too much. Men in the hard sciences frequently speak as though predictability, sureness of prediction, were the primary object of science. It may be, under certain circumstances. But I think we should remember we are dealing with a creature who . . . transcends himself, looks at himself, has in a sense a mirror in him, and changes even as we look at him, because of ideas and styles and fashions. Therefore, trying to lay down some precise physical-social laws about him is a very dangerous procedure. (pp. 177, 178)

The work organization has been defined in many quarters of the academic world as a problem-solving system. Insofar as this is an accurate description, a shift in society's values may cause a shift in the definition of organizational success. The criterion of the future may be the organization's ability to maximize societal values, not just the ability to solve intraorganizational problems. Institutions which in the past were not designed primarily to meet broad social needs, as exemplified by shifting values, may have to undergo changes in order to continue as effective organizations that will prosper and survive. The shift in values is now causing some questioning. Should complex work organizations address themselves to newly defined needs? Indeed, can they? The point of departure for any attempt to reexamine our managerial strategies may well be provided by stressing the role of values.

The important role values are playing in our lives must be brought into clear focus, because the failure of the American corporation and government organizations to satisfy higher-order psychological needs and to consider human values important in the world of work has placed business and government organizations at a crossroads. The effective manager should realize that the development of one's self-concept can only be enhanced if the organization understands that man's values, attitudes, and beliefs which are shaped in society must be allowed their continued expression in the organization. This is essential to management if it is to induce man to participate in and truly identify with the organization.

AN APPROACH TO THE PROBLEM

What, then, can be done? One of the most fruitful approaches for the manager to take is to attempt to understand the intimacy of the relationship between organizations and society. A necessary first step is for the manager to analyze the dominant forces which are rapidly and radically changing man, the focal point of society. These forces are changing man because they are contributing to changes in his values. There are, of course, many factors related to the shifting values we are witnessing in man; in this book five dominant forces have been chosen: (1) the emergence of changing concepts of morality, (2) man's increasing understanding of human behavior, (3) education, (4) technology, and (5) affluence. Each social force will be examined individually, and the interrelationships among the various environmental factors will be discussed. Moreover, an attempt will be made to ascertain the impact of these variables on man's values and on his behavior at work. Finally, the implications for the organization in terms of its survival in a turbulent and dynamic environment will be examined. For example, how will organizational design, managerial and leadership style, work methodology, and corporate goals, objectives, and strategies be affected?

New Concepts of Morality

The present-day influence of organized religion in molding the nation's ethos has been declining. Not only is man becoming more realistic and gaining a new awareness of himself, but also, more significantly, he is developing a new ethic as the influence of organized religion diminishes. Whatever it may be—i.e., situation ethics, a new personalism, the primacy of the individual conscience—man is becoming increasingly hesitant to use a legalistic code to judge whether his acts and those of others are right or wrong. We might say that it is love, not law, that is becoming more important apropos the decision to do or not to do. As man perceives himself to be free from the dominance of ecclesiastical organizations, he may expect a new freedom as he interacts in other organizations such as the business corporation and the government agency. Rollo May has suggested that "the old morality was essentially a superego morality . . . now we are getting an organismic human being who feels his way into the standards he is going to live by" (Dempsey, 1971, p. 98). This statement by May provides us with an important insight into the change we have been witnessing in beliefs regarding moral behavior. Whereas at one time Western civilization was heavily influenced by Descartes' profound statement "I think, therefore I am," we are now seeing a shift to "I feel, therefore I am." This accentuates the experiential aspect of man. What does man experience, what kinds of feelings does he get from his experiences, and what does it all mean with reference to his existence as a man?

Along these lines, the complex work organizations of today and of the future must give serious consideration to the value of creative participation of the worker in social life, because work is social behavior and ties him to the mainstream of society. Is work moral insofar as it contributes to the moral well-being of the individual? To what extent do the activities of our work organizations provide for the expression of creative imagination? This is an important question, because freedom to be is one of the most important preconditions for creativity. Can the business corporation survive in a globally competitive market without creativity?

Wrestling with philosophical questions can have very practical and relevant implications. There has been much discussion in recent years about man being only a cog in the organizational process. If this is true in our bureaucratic, overly specialized, highly technological society, then man has only instrumental value. What this means is that man begins to feel he has no reason for being at all, or he is unable to fathom the meaning of his existence, especially from the experiential nature of his work. So man is beginning to ask questions, and these questions are arising from a new concept of morality which is personalistic in nature. That is, the emphasis is on the uniqueness of the person who must be respected in the fullness of his humanity. The new morality, then, stresses authenticity in human relationships, which means being true to one's self and open and honest with others. What effect these values have on the work organization will be explored in more detail later.

Greater Knowledge of Human Behavior

The exponential growth in research under the generic heading of Behavioral Sciences has resulted in a better understanding of human behavior. In sharing this knowledge with others, the behavioral scientist has provided man with a new self-awareness which has also enabled man to become more sensitive to the needs of others. As man assimilates this new understanding of himself and others, he carries it with him as he engages in interpersonal interactions within organizations. With this new understanding, man's values and beliefs are changing. As man begins to understand in a more intelligent way what "makes him tick," he begins to have certain expectations regarding how he should be treated. These expectations carry over into the work situation and have at times been referred to as "psychological contracts." These contracts are not legal in the sense that they are written down and signed by management and the workers. Rather, they are an unwritten set of expectations that exist on the part of management and its subordinates.

The point to be made here is that concomitant with the growth of knowledge of human behavior, the worker's part of the psychological contract has changed. In other words, he has a firmer grasp of what he wants from management and the organization in which he works. Depending upon the level of education of the worker, as well as his level of sophistication in matters relating to human behavior, his attitudes, beliefs, and values with reference to the human aspects of his work will vary. The "Freudian revolution," which greatly changed our thinking about human behavior, has had an impact on a great number of people, even those who are not highly educated or who are college educated but did not major in psychology or some allied discipline. Furthermore, in our brief introduction into the new morality we saw there is greater emphasis than ever before on experience and "feeling." The vast majority of people who work in large organizations have not only "feelings" that management must consider—in other words, the affective aspect of human behavior—but also a sensitivity, an idea, an opinion as to how they would like to be treated by management, as well as to the quality of the interpersonal interactions they experience in the work environment. Here the experiential element returns and brings to the fore considerations of the quality of human interaction.

The worker knows that when he is treated as less than human by management he feels frustrated, angry, resentful, and threatened. He does not enjoy these feelings, and a sense of losing control over one's environment begins to set in. In many such situations anxiety results, and maladaptive behavior takes place. This is in the best interest of neither the individual nor the organization.

As more and more information is disseminated through books, newspapers, television, popular magazines, and movies, the worker's understanding increases to the point where he realizes what is happening to him. Not only do his stomachache and headache tell him, but also a reaffirmation comes from his discussions with fellow workers.

At the higher levels of education and of the organizational structure, the understanding of human behavior becomes greater, and the implications for management are greater in the sense that it is not easy to "psych out" (in the name of motivation) a well-educated college graduate who has more than a passing knowledge of human behavior. The psychological contract takes on different meanings. The backgrounds and experiences of the more sophisticated members of the organization give them a different perception of what organizational life is, and their values may not square with this perception. They understand the concept of self-esteem. They know what alienation is intellectually, and they feel it in an experiential way. They are concerned about their identities as human beings and how the roles they must play in an organizational setting can impede the establishment of a strong sense of identity. How will today's manager and the manager of tomorrow deal with these matters? The interaction between a person's knowledge of the why's of human behavior and his personal values must be understood by management if managers and organizations are to be effective.

Affluence

That we in the United States are living in an affluent society can hardly be questioned. By any number of measures, which will be detailed in Chapter V, the affluence of the United States can be amply demonstrated. An example of such measures are the increased GNP, family income levels, household ownership of automobiles and appliances, and disposable personal income. Once we have established this fact, we must begin to examine what effect this increase in affluence is having on what man values. In other words, is the greater affluence which most Americans enjoy changing their value systems, and if so, what effect is this shift in values having on the business corporation and government agencies?

In the early days of our society, poverty was a pervasive fact of life. Man lived by bread alone; poverty of the flesh was the rule. Man worked to satisfy basic subsistence needs, but in the post-World War II economy of the United States, he has been catapulted to a level of affluence unprecedented in any society of the world. The old values reflected by Calvin and then by Max Weber's Protestant Ethic and David Riesman's "tradition-directed man" have given way to new values precisely because man can now afford to change his values and make new choices. These new choices have very definite implications for the governmental and industrial organizations in which he works because they are affected by his perception of work. His "definition" of work has changed. As the American worker, color of collar notwithstanding, spends less time worrying about survival and security needs, he begins to think more often and more insistently on "what it's all about" as he arises each day to march off to work. He begins to ask questions which to his father and grandfather were unimaginable: What is the meaning of this work I do? In today's technocracy the answer to that question in all too many instances is "I don't know" or "the job is meaningless." When this is the answer, we have moved from a poverty of the flesh to a poverty of the spirit or of the self.

Another aspect of the affluence phenomenon is that many workers who came from lower class backgrounds are now in the middle class and, in the case of highly successful, well-educated executives, in the upper middle class. These organizational members take on the values of their class through interpersonal interactions with new reference groups. New experiences and new relationships shape new attitudes, beliefs, and values, which are then carried into the work organizations. Not as concerned with monetary income (because they have it), they make demands on organizations that have to do with psychic income. Can the work organizations in our society cope with these demands? Unless they can effectively deal with the changing values that rising levels of affluence have spawned, they will ironically find themselves the victims of an affluence for which they were in large measure responsible.

Education

The median level of education of the United States labor force is 13 years. With this nation's commitment to the idea that education is not a privilege but a right for all, this figure can be expected to rise in the future. Business and government organizations increasingly will be recruiting workers who are more articulate, more intelligent, and, depending on the level of educational attainment, more given to thinking for themselves. It is expected that by 1985, one-third of the total labor force will have had some college education. If it is the mark of a good college or university to instill in its students a spirit of free inquiry, a questioning mind, and an analytical approach to problems, then the effect of this type of education on one's values becomes more important. That it is crucial for the business community and its counterpart governmental sector to understand the relationships between education and values can hardly be overemphasized.

In Chapter IV this matter will be dealt with in much more depth; let us sketch, however, some of the dimensions of the problem facing complex governmental and business organizations as they increasingly replace lesser educated with more highly educated workers. To begin with, given an educational system which seeks to inculcate in students a questioning attitude, managers will encounter employees who question the practice of doing something in a given way merely because it is the way it has always been done. Also, the classic management approach to authority which is still very prevalent in today's bureaucracies, both public and private, is increasingly under fire from well-educated, bright young people who do not automatically accept the notion that everything that the boss asks for, says, or commands is either a correct, an ethical, or even a "good business" or intelligent administrative practice, which is unquestionably the best thing for the organization or the subordinate. The effect this has on authority relationships is obvious.

Today's schools, at both the secondary and higher educational levels, are more participative than those of the past. Students educated in a participative environment—one in which they are encouraged to get involved in the learning experience of the classroom, the colloquium, or the seminar through discussions—who move into an organizational environment in which their participation is not solicited or encouraged develop attitudes toward management that are not conducive to organizational effectiveness. Lawrence Appley (1966), for many years the president of the American Management Association, says, "The younger men are not antibusiness but antimanagement; they have a fear of being managed, of being manipulated" (p. 6). Although one could argue that younger people are not anti-business, the point is well taken. What Appley's statement portends for a reconception of the managerial role is interesting.

The values characterized by Whyte's "organization man" now appear to be waning, given our societal realities. If there is a new organization man, his educational experience has armed him with a new set of values which does not place the organization and its methods of operation at the top of the system of values to which he subscribes. He ranks his own satisfaction and fulfillment first, and his professional discipline, e.g., accounting, law, engineering, research chemistry, naturally helps to provide this sense of achievement and fulfillment. He also values his relationships with his peers and other members of the organization more highly than his sense of corporate belonging.

The changing values of educated persons are having far-reaching consequences for the work organizations in our society. Organizational structure, managerial behavior, leadership style, and organizational strategies and policies will have to adapt to meet the challenge presented by an increasingly well-educated pool of human resources.

Technology

Technology has had and will continue to have an impact on man's values, which in turn affect the work organization. Technology offers new possibilities which must be weighed against what man already has. The choice between retaining the old and opting for the new is a value issue because the old values (what man cherishes) become juxtaposed against the new (what man can get as a result of new technology). It might rightfully be assumed that value changes take place through conscious decisions to take advantage of the new conditions made possible through technology. The invention and mass production of the automobile, with the tremendous changes it brought in American life styles and values, is an example. Along these lines, Theodore J. Gordon (1971) notes that changing technology changes the means available to the individual and society for attaining value derived from goals.

There is another facet of this interrelationship that must be examined. It is best expressed by Erich Fromm (1968) as he describes the guiding principles of today's technological system and the repercussions for human beings. He says that there are two principles that dominate the thinking and behavior of those who are caught up in a system which is highly technological in nature. "The first principle is the maxim that something *ought* to be done because it is technically *possible* to do it" (p. 33). For example, if it is possible to put men on the moon or to have sky labs in space, these must be done even if it is at the cost of not providing for many social needs. He suggests that this kind of thinking negates humanistic values. If this principle is accepted, all other values become secondary, and technological development becomes the foundation of ethics. Fromm supports this statement by citing a paper entitled "The Triumph of Technology: 'Can' Implies 'Ought'." This paper, by Hasan Ozbekhan, says that "feasibility, which is a strategic concept, becomes elevated into a normative concept with the result that whatever technological reality indicates we *can* do is taken as implying that we *must* do it" (Fromm, 1968, p. 34).

Fromm's second principle is that of "maximal efficiency and output." The continuous pursuit of maximal efficiency results in minimal individuality. This type of thinking, says Fromm, enhances the belief that society works more efficiently when individuals are dehumanized and made quantifiable; their personalities can be expressed on key-punched cards. Individuals then become "units" which are more easily administered by the bureaucracies in our society. Fromm goes on to say that deindividualization is necessary to keep people in large-scale organizations manageable and less troublesome. They are thus taught to seek their identities in the corporation rather than within themselves.

Technology has created new values which have a feedback effect. The work organization must understand this relationship because our advanced technological development has not been without its costs. For students of organizational behavior and managers of large-scale organizations, the effects of technological change and redefinition of values on institutions in our society are significant. The business corporation and the huge government agencies (especially federal) are among society's most influential and powerful institutions.

THE QUESTION OF VALUES

In this first chapter our discussion has centered around the idea that values are changing and that the changes in values will have implications for work organizations in the public and private sector of our society. The concept of value, however, has not been discussed, and it is appropriate at this point to arrive at some idea of what is meant by the term value. It should be noted that the terminology used in discussions of value is profuse, not terribly precise, and therefore not too helpful in our understanding of the concept. Sociologists have their array of definitions, as do anthropologists. Value theory and welfare economics, two important aspects of the field of economics, have their own definitions of value which differ not only from each other but also from the definitions used by the sociologists, anthropologists, and other social scientists.

It is important that we set some parameters on what we mean by value. In this book we are concerned with the impact values have on the work organization. We can say, therefore, that we are concerned with the survival of the business corporation in our society and with the adaptation of the government organization to the needs of its working members and of society. Each one of these "concerns" has to do with "life processes" inasmuch as we are using words like "survival" and "adaptation." However, as we said earlier, the central factor in society is man, and our primary concern is with the human being at his work. It has also been said that people spend a great part of their lives at work and, depending on the nature of the work and the level in the organizational hierarchy, a great part of their lives working away from their place of business.

It is appropriate, then, that our concept of value relates to life and, to be more specific, the quality or excellence of life. Accordingly we must consider Kurt Baier's (1971, p. 40) important statement that "the value of something . . . is the thing's capacity to confer a benefit on someone, to make a favorable difference to his life." However, as Baier points out, the value that something has is not the same as the values a person holds. He calls the value possessed by things an "evaluative property" and the values held by people "dispositions to behave in certain ways." In other words, we are talking about what Baier calls the "capacities of things to satisfy desiderata" on the one hand, and "tendencies of people to devote their resources (time, energy, money) to the attainment of certain ends" (p. 40) on the other. These are noteworthy ideas, since earlier in this chapter we talked about human values changing, which of course implies that human behavior changes. Baier makes an important point when he quotes Robin M. Williams (1951), who says: "Basic transformations of man and society are now underway, and many vital choices of values must be made" (p. 33). Baier goes on to say that the reason these choices can be described as vital is that in the determination of human behavior a person's values are important factors. He notes that "the values we already have now serve as the rational determinants of our choices. When we choose one course of action in preference to another we do so because we have reason to think that it, rather than the other course, will help us to realize at least some of our values" (p. 33).

The use of the term values includes first, human values (but of necessity institutional or organizational values will be discussed); second, *choices* that human beings make; third, choices being made because the person believes that his choice (as opposed to alternative courses of action) will improve the quality of his life. It must be noted that the quality of life concept as it is used in this book must include sociopsychological, ethical, moral, and emotional facets of life, as well as material ones. Finally, our use of the term values, since it is tied to the concept of choice, takes into account the close relationship between values and concrete human actions and behavior.

Given the above parameters that will serve as our guide to the discussion of values, we must now be prepared to consider the crucial roles that selected forces in society are playing in affecting the quality of workers' lives.

BIBLIOGRAPHY

Appley, L.: *Management News* (AMA). June 1966.

Athos, A. G.: Is the corporation next to fall? *Harvard Business Review*, Vol. 48, Jan.–Feb. 1970, p. 49.

Baier, K.: What is value? An analysis of the concept. *In* Baier, K., and Rescher, N. (Eds.): *Values and the Future.* New York: The Free Press, 1971.

Beckhard, S.: What is wrong with work? National Association of Manufacturers, 1973.

Clapp, V.: *Alcoholism: Trends and Treatment*. New York: Irvington, 1971.

Dempsey, D.: *The New York Times Magazine*, March 28, 1971.

Eisley, L. C.: Alternatives to technology. *In* Warner, A.W., et al. (Eds.): *The Environment and Change*. New York: Columbia University Press, 1969.

Fromm, E.: *The Revolution of Hope: Toward a Humanized Technology*. New York: Bantam Books, 1968.

Gooding, J.: Blue collar blues on the assembly line. *Fortune*, July, 1970, p. 69.

Gooding, J.: The accelerated generation moves into management. *Fortune*, March, 1971, p. 101.

Gordon, T. J.: The feedback between technology and values. *In* Baier, K., and Rescher, N. (Eds.): *Values and the Future*. New York: The Free Press, 1971.

MacIver, J.: American business—its people and their problems. Speech presented at a Conference on the Executive and his People, sponsored by the Lehigh Valley Mental Health Association, October 13, 1971.

Rush, H. M. F., and Brown, J. K.: The drug problem in business. *Conference Board Record*, Vol. 8, March, 1971, pp. 6-15.

Salpukas, A.: Workers increasingly rebel against boredom on assembly line. *The New York Times*, April 12, 1972.

CHAPTER

II

THE NEW MORALITY

THE CONCEPT OF MORALITY

In this chapter we will address ourselves to the issues related to changing concepts of morality and their effect on human values and ultimately the work organization. Any discussion of this kind, however, must begin with a definition of morality. *The Random House Dictionary of the English Language* says that morality is a "doctrine or system of morals." But what are morals? According to the same source, morals are "principles or habits with respect to right or wrong conduct." *The American Heritage Dictionary of the English Language* states that morality is "the evaluation of or means of evaluating human conduct as a set of ideas or customs of a given society, class or social group which regulate relationships and prescribe modes of behavior to enhance the group's survival."

From these definitions we can see that the key to understanding morality is in the idea that we are talking about standards, doctrines, and principles which regulate interpersonal relationships and to which human beings look for a "prescription" regarding right and wrong modes of behavior. The concept that these standards will enhance the survival of the society or group is also a key point. The word "survival," however, cannot be interpreted solely as physical survival.

SOME HISTORICAL DEVELOPMENTS

Catholicism

The standards, doctrines, and principles which served to guide
and regulate the behavior of Western man were primarily of a religious
nature. Historically, it was the Bible which provided the main source
to which man could turn in ascertaining what was right or wrong.
Even after Gutenberg's invention of the printing press, widespread
dissemination of printed matter was not common. Even if it were, very
few people could read during the medieval period. The Catholic
Church became the organization through which the Bible was taught,
and the teachers were the monks, priests, and bishops of the Church.
The development of Church doctrine and a system of religious
thought provided a framework within which man was to carry out his
day to day life.

With the Church as the central life force for man, human behavior
was necessarily oriented around religious teachings. Society in the
Middle Ages was very stratified, but regardless of one's social
status—peasant or prince—the all-important relationship was one's relationship to God. All of man's daily activities were to reflect this in
that this relationship dictated how man was to relate to his fellow
worker, his family, the lord of the manor for whom he worked, and the
church hierarchy. Work was for the glory of God, as was all human
activity irrespective of one's status. There was no thought of rising
above one's state in life if it was a lowly one or changing it if it was a
lofty one. One was born to a certain station in life, and this was to be
accepted as a manifestation of God's will. It was not important that one
was born, for example, into a state of poverty and would remain poor
and illiterate. What was important was day to day behavior which
would, if conducted according to standards prescribed by the Church,
be rewarded by eternal life in the next world. The life after death was
the important one, and all behavior in this life should be conducted so
as to ensure one's eternal salvation. As Thomas Aquinas put it in the
Summa Theologica, "the perfect happiness of man cannot be other
than the vision of the divine essence."

In the medieval period, the Church *was* society and provided the
social system with a framework which guided all human behavior.
Though there were different activities carried out by different strata of
society, there was no separation of activities into religious and social.
The Church encompassed all of life's activities and was the arbiter and
interpreter of how the practical, mundane activities of all persons were
to be geared toward the ultimate goal of life. Thus there was no difference between the life of the spirit and the life of the body. It was a
matter of degree which activities were more conducive to eternal life,
because one of the essential features of the medieval period was that
the Church sought to give to the social order a "new significance by

relating it to the purpose of human life as known by revelation" (Tawney, 1926, p. 26). The purpose of religion was to direct or lead all human activities in this stratified society to the common goal. Each activity had a unique value which was appropriate to its place in the social hierarchy. Thus it was the function of religion to transform man's nature (through grace) to a more perfect state and to make the social institutions of the time a reflection of what Tawney calls "a supreme spiritual reality."

How does this relate to the question of the quality of life? Life in the middle ages was brutish for the vast majority of people. How did the Church look upon this? Certainly not as something alien to religion, for as we have mentioned, religion was the pervasive influence of earthly existence. The Church accepted the realities of class stratification and all the inequalities that went with it. For the Church there was a moral purpose to this, because it viewed the social order much as we view the human organism with its various parts. Each part had a specific function to perform which contributed to the good of the body as a whole when it functioned "according to its nature." Each member of society had a particular function to perform; he was a member of a religious organization, a warrior, a peasant, a trader, or a craftsman. To each would be given the means appropriate to his position, but one was not to expropriate any more. Tawney (1926) puts it very well when he explains that between classes there must be inequality, that peasants, for example, must not encroach on those above them, and craftsmen and merchants must always remain within their callings. The concept of transformation of which we spoke earlier is again highlighted, as we see that the Church attempted to make the material spiritual through a reconciliation that could come about under a divine plan manifesting itself on earth. The quality of one's life was a function of one's place in the social order and, as such, was unchangeable. Moral behavior, then, was that which was expressed through service to one's fellow man, even if in some cases, depending upon one's status, that service meant subservience to those higher in status in the social hierarchy. In short, as the precepts of the Church dictated, doing the work of one's station in life and receiving the just deserts of that station constituted "moral" behavior because it served society through an interlocking system of mutual obligations. In doing so it served God.

Any discussion of morality and human behavior would not be complete if we neglected the position of the Church regarding the conduct of economic activities. The body of thought which so characterized the medieval period and of which St. Thomas Aquinas was the most articulate spokesman was known as *scholasticism*. Since all human activity was evaluated in terms of the contribution it made to an eternity with God, economic activity necessarily was considered to be but one facet of human behavior.

Since all human behavior was to conform to the principles of morality as expounded by the Church, economic activity was also expected to conform to moral principles. Furthermore, if the beatific vision was the be all and end all of existence, economic activity had to serve this end. Earthly possessions, material goods, wealth, and so forth provided sustenance so that one might get on with the real purpose of life. In other words, they were the natural means to a supernatural end. Since accumulation of wealth was the end of economic activities, it was immoral and sinful. Only enough wealth should be accumulated to enable one to earn a living in one's social stratum. Economic activities should be limited to those necessary to satisfy one's needs—no more.

The medieval period, then, took a jaundiced view of economic affairs. They were at best tolerated, but always considered with suspicion. According to Tawney (1926) medieval thinkers assumed that labor was the common lot of mankind—it was necessary and honorable; that trade was necessary but bad for the soul; that finance, if not immoral, was at best sordid and at worst disreputable. The merchant was considered an immoral parasite because he made a profit in his economic activities. Acquisitiveness was condemned as sinful and avaricious.

The morality of economic activity was a matter of whether the person engaged in such activity gained only the wages of his labor. The charging of interest on money that was loaned was considered immoral, as was the practice of selling an article at a higher price than one paid for it. These "immoral" acts were viewed as endangering one's spiritual life and salvation, which, as we have noted, were the *sine qua non* of human existence in the middle ages. Anything which threatened the life of the spirit was condemned. As a result, warnings, restrictions, prohibitions, and sanctions regarding economic activity as a facet of human behavior were the order of the day. In summary, Tawney quotes a passage by Henry of Langenstein, a fourteenth century scholastic:

> He who has enough to satisfy his wants and nevertheless ceaselessly labors to acquire riches, either in order to obtain a higher social position, or that subsequently he may have enough to live without labor, or that his sons may become men of wealth and importance—all such are incited by damnable avarice, sensuality, or pride. (p. 38)

Calvinism

In contrast to Catholicism's idea that all men could be saved if only they remained faithful to God's law as interpreted by the Church, Calvinism introduced the dogma of predestination which, of course, had very definite implications for morality. The concept of predestination held that God had chosen "an elect" who were foreordained to everlasting life in heaven. All others were not of the elect and therefore eternally damned; regardless of how faithful they were or how many good works they engaged in, there was nothing they could do to save their souls; they were "predestined" to spend eternity in hell. This is a very pessimistic doctrine, one which is overladen with a dour gloom because it decreed that man's eternal destiny was decided from his birth. Christ's death and resurrection were not for the redemption of all mankind but only for the benefit of the elect. No one could help an individual achieve eternal salvation, not the Church, not priests or ministers, not even the sacraments; man was utterly alone and could do nothing to assure an eternity with God. The sharp contrast to the teachings of Catholicism is quite apparent. At the beginning of this chapter we said morality was a doctrine or system of principles with respect to right or wrong conduct. It is important, then, that we look at the impact this Calvinistic doctrine had on human activity.

To begin with, this religious doctrine turned man toward individualism. Calvinism put man on his own regarding his spiritual activity. Man was to trust in God alone and not confide in one's fellow man. Calvinism did not reject the notion of Christian brotherly love, but one who held to the tenets of this religious faith perceived brotherly love in a manner different from Catholicism or Lutheranism. To the Calvinists, society existed only for the glory of God, and the "elect" performed their daily activities with this in mind. All social life was organized according to God's will, which meant obedience to his commandments. One's "calling," then, was to labor at one's specialty in a very individualistic way but for the *good of the community or social order*. This is where the concepts of individualism and brotherly love meet. As in other matters of the Calvinistic faith, emotion and feeling had no place in the *rational* organization of society. Utility was the operative word, and "this makes labour in the service of impersonal social usefulness appear to promote the glory of God and hence to be willed by Him" (Weber, 1958, p. 106). We now begin to see the kind of assumptions underlying Calvinism's notion of the human condition and the relationship of these assumptions to moral behavior.

For one who accepts predestination, there is anxiety over whether one is numbered among the elect or the damned. This is an important consideration in relating the doctrine to ethical conduct. All Calvinists were duty-bound to consider themselves among the elect. They were to have no doubts about this, and supreme self-confidence was essential. In order to gain this self-confidence, however, they were to immerse themselves in worldly activity and do so in a most intense manner. This total immersion in day to day work activities not only was related to the concept of one's "calling" but also was the only way of alleviating the believer's anxiety over his eternal salvation. In addition, continuous and purposeful activity in the world should result in something tangible, something objective and far removed from the emotional or mystical. The fruits of one's activities, the results of one's rational behavior, then became a kind of empirical proof of one's "election." Max Weber (1958, p. 115) says that "in practice this means God helps those who help themselves."

An ascetic, disciplined, self-controlled, planned, systematic, rational way of life was the moral norm. The word rational is used in the sense of organizing one's conduct in a systematic manner in order to achieve one's goals in the most efficient way. Here we are talking about an overriding goal—saving one's soul. Thus Calvinism introduced its believers to a systematically planned life based on a coherent and unified framework of continuous activity, not just single or isolated good works engaged in periodically or when one felt the need for repentance. This was clearly a new ethic, the foundation of which was the doctrine of predestination. *Cogito ergo sum* now became a byword of this religious faith because it provided a philosophical foundation for embracing rational thought as the basis for human behavior. By the same token Descartes' classic dictum gave Calvinists their rationale for viewing anything emotional or spontaneous as repugnant. Morality and asceticism thus became one and the same. Puritanism, one of the most prominent expressions of this ethic, sought to inculcate in its followers a constant examination of one's motives. Were they promoting one's salvation? Did one's every act give glory to God? Was one in complete control of himself and not the slave of his passions or his emotions, for the latter were detrimental to achieving eternal salvation? As a matter of fact, in practicing asceticism in one's daily activities in the world, one was to avoid any enjoyment of life. Wasting time in activities that had nothing to do with physical or mental labor was the most grievous of sins.

Puritanism.   This ethic of work found its greatest expression in the religious sect of Puritanism, the major offshoot of Calvinism. The concept of the "calling" was at the heart of the work ethic. One's calling had a spiritual aspect to it which made specialization or division of labor a kind of divine plan. As one developed his special skills at a particular kind of work, it enhanced his own economic interests and therefore the well-being of society. This concept of work was so much a part of the Puritan ethic that it was carried to its extreme inasmuch as irregular work was not looked upon very kindly because it did not reflect the systematic, continuous, and planned nature which was characteristic of the work of the elect. Although hard and constant work was considered efficacious primarily from a religious point of view, its justification as the most moral type of behavior came from the amount of private profit it generated. We have only to contrast the following statement with that quoted previously (see p. 24) to see the change in the relationship between ethical conduct and human values that emerged from the medieval period to the Reformation:

> If God show you a way in which you may lawfully get more than in another way (without wrong to your soul or to any other), if you refuse this and choose the less gainful way, you cross one of the ends of your calling, and you refuse to be God's steward, and to accept his gifts and use them for him when he required it: you may labor to be rich for God, though not for the flesh and sin. (Baxter, 1958)

The importance of this statement for the development of a new ethic and criteria for judging moral and immoral behavior cannot be minimized. The pursuit of wealth is now cloaked with a moral and ethical sanction. Profit making is given spiritual blessing; indeed, it is regarded as one's moral duty.

That these attitudes had a positive effect on the development of a capitalistic ethos is obvious. We can see this developing if we recall that Calvinism strongly promoted rationalism, orderliness, and systematic planning in one's daily life and therefore in one's conduct. It molded a man of stern character—a "no nonsense," disciplined type of person. Since these attitudes found official favor in religion, capitalism began to flourish, and the bourgeois businessman became the symbol of a new breed—the middle class. As long as the members of the new class pursued their riches morally, i.e., for the glory of God, they were free to follow their economic interests wherever they led. But we must remember that set against the blessing given to the pursuit of riches was the concept of asceticism, which meant that there was to be no pleasure, no ostentation, and as a result no spending of the riches on anything "frivolous." Saving was therefore *the* moral and ethical mode of behavior. Following this system of thought, the accumulation of capital became easy, and its investment, therefore, was facilitated. The doctrine of predestination put a stamp of approval on this acquisitive activity because, combined with asceticism, it suggested that the man who worked continuously made money and in saving it was visibly blessed by God, which was proof that he was numbered among the elect. God's grace was his.

Into this eminently logical system entered an idea which would make the ethical foundations of capitalism even more solid. This was the notion that one's "calling" may offer little opportunity for gaining riches. If this is so, the good and faithful laborer is still pleasing in the sight of God because he is discharging his obligation to work hard. The attitude toward labor that developed was that it, too, was a calling, just as was the pursuit of riches by the businessman. If the laborer could do nothing else and must work to justify and give proof of his "election," then it was as morally and ethically correct for the laborer to be paid low wages as it was for the middle class businessman to accumulate wealth. The concept of the "calling" and its manifestation in hard and continuous work were used to the utmost advantage in the promotion of beliefs and values regarding the businessman and the worker. Two standards were developing, but within one system of thought; the spirit of capitalism began to flourish.

We have defined values as choices made because they are perceived by the individual to enhance or improve the quality of his life. The values of Calvinism and the social order it established are quite clear. The believer was taught to value hard work, consistently pursued over his entire life. Sobriety, repudiation of pleasure, and austerity were also valued. The accumulation of wealth was morally good; it was one's means of giving glory to God. Poverty was never seen as a value, and begging, which was acceptable by Catholicism in the medieval period, was repugnant to Calvinism. It was indicative of the fall from God's grace—a sign of eternal damnation. There was to be explicit conformity to these beliefs, because in practicing them man was making a choice which had ultimate value—the glory of God and relief from the anxiety of thinking about where predestination had placed him in eternity. In outlining the implications of Calvinistic values, we must remember the point made regarding our definition of values in the first chapter. When we include the concept of "improving the quality of one's life" in the definition, it must be remembered that the quality of life was not to be considered solely from a materialistic point of view. Though Calvinism and Puritanism did sanctify wealth and material gains, the glory of God, freedom from anxiety over one's destination in the next life, and, last but not least, the leading of an ascetic existence in this life were very positive and important paths that believers were to choose or value.

Scientific Management Movement

The Industrial Revolution further reflected many of these values, most especially those which had to do with economic activities and continuous work. Adam Smith's discussion of the specialization of labor is not far removed from the Calvinistic interpretation of the "calling." But to move ahead, let us consider the United States in the early twentieth century and some of the forces which had an impact on the concept of work and how it should be carried out within an organizational setting. The first ideas that come to mind are those of the "scientific management" movement, the father of which was Frederick W. Taylor. He decried the great loss or waste that was occurring in our

industrial plants and factories. Taylor observed that there was too
much goldbricking or "soldiering," as he put it. This coupled with
what Taylor perceived to be a tremendous inefficiency in the way work
was done resulted in a great loss to our corporations and the nation.

He set out to solve this problem by taking the concept of work and
subjecting it to rational observation and analysis, much the same as a
scientist in another field would study a problem in his discipline.
Taylor's use of the scientific method in attacking the problems of inefficient work methods was a pioneering step for the industrial world.
By breaking a job down into its smallest components, he could determine what the most efficient movements should be in carrying out a
given task. He would time these movements with a stopwatch and
come up with the "one best way" to do that particular job—best in
terms of time and bodily motions. This would then be set as a standard, and anyone doing this, job had his performance appraised in
terms of how closely he conformed to the standards established "scientifically" for that task.

Other disciples followed—Gilbreath, Gantt, and Emerson, to
name a few. They brought to the scientific management movement a
religious type of zeal, but they were preaching a different gospel—the
gospel of efficiency. This was the common theme of these men and all
the other great pioneers of the movement. That they made great contributions to the field of industrial management cannot be denied.
They not only sought to reorient the nature of work on the shop floor
but also attacked the problems of organization and administration.
What is the best way to structure an organization? The span of control
principle was a key concept. It suggested that there was an optimum
number of subordinates who should report to any one supervisor. The
number was approximately six or seven. Other principles were
developed to bring rationality and order to the field of work and the
organization and management of this work. Unity of command, the
scalar principle, division of labor (of which we have already spoken),
parity between authority and responsibility, and functional authority
were but a few of the excellent ideas advanced by these and other
great men.

Lacking space, we can only sketch the scientific management
movement in its most rudimentary form. What we want to do, however, is examine some of the assumptions underlying these new attitudes toward work, organization, and administration and to ascertain
the relationship between the evolving attitudes in the corporations
and the classic concepts of morality as expressed in Calvinism and its
major offshoot, Puritanism. These two religious movements, as well as
the other religious movements which were philosophically compatible with them, i.e., Methodism and the Baptist sects, gave the United
States in the early twentieth century a religiocultural ethos which

provided a very strong foundation for American business. Though it was to be another generation before Calvin Coolidge (note his first name) would say, "America's business is business," this was already the case in the early years of this century. The major form American business was taking was the corporation. The influence of the concept of private property, which was so eloquently articulated in the eighteenth century English Enlightenment, was great. The role of scientific management, however, in developing organizational concepts and new ideas in administration cannot be minimized either. The American business corporation not only was built on the solid foundation of the Protestant ethic but also played a large part in promoting the ethic's concepts of morality. In other words, the corporation reflected the values of the United States in the early twentieth century. There was an interrelationship between the corporation and society which was eminently harmonious, most especially in the area of societal values.

Frederick W. Taylor deplored the waste and inefficiency that was rampant in the industry of his time. This reflects Calvinism's notion that not assiduously pursuing one's "calling" was sinful. Taylor, as we said earlier, deplored what he called soldiering or goldbricking. Is this not related to Puritanism's view that sloth and idleness were signs that one was not a member of the elect? Taylor's pioneering wage incentive plans had as their underlying assumption that if a man were paid more, he would automatically be motivated to work more. For didn't every man want to make more money? Wasn't material gain a positive and unquestioned good? If this does not reflect in an accurate enough way some of the tenets of Calvinism and Puritanism, perhaps we can turn to the capitalists of that era to find a closer relationship between values and morality. Some of the great industrialists such as John D. Rockefeller, Andrew Carnegie, and Henry Clay Frick were the very personification of the Protestant ethic. Rockefeller taught Sunday school. There was nothing incompatible with amassing great wealth and being ethical and moral in the religious sense. In fact, as we saw earlier, it was one's moral duty to do so because it was a sign of God's grace to have material riches. The justification for amassing tremendous fortunes was there. The justification for paying low wages was also based upon the Calvinist notion that one must be faithful to his labor even if it does not pay well, because if the worker can do nothing else in terms of other jobs or has no other abilities or opportunities to "improve himself," he is following his calling and is therefore blessed by God.

With reference to concepts of authority, scientific management propounded the *scalar principle*. There was a chain of command in the work organization, to which one strictly adhered. Short-circuiting this chain of command was not to be tolerated; it was not good "organizational behavior." Every employee in the corporation knew his place and was to act accordingly—the concept of the calling again. To ensure that the manager could exercise his authority to the utmost, he should have only 5, 6, or 7 people reporting to him. In this way he could see to it that they discharged their moral duty to work continuously and not engage in any idle talk or other frivolous activity. For wasn't it easier to control 5 or 6 subordinates than 50 or 60? The span of control principle, as well as some of the others, were organizational manifestations of beliefs about man. McGregor's Theory X consists of those assumptions about human nature which were prevalent in the early years of this century. Among the assumptions were those which believed man to be lazy, irresponsible, and not very intelligent. If a manager subscribed to these assumptions, then what better system of religious belief than Calvinism and Puritanism was there to deal with "sinful" man? And what better way to organize the corporation, structure the work organization, and design the work if not on the basis of clearly established lines of authority, division of labor, and narrow spans of control? There was a dual justification for scientific management; its principles were rational, and they were "moral" inasmuch as they reflected and promoted the contemporary ideas of morality in the United States.

CONTEMPORARY CURRENTS OF THOUGHT

There is a new understanding of morality in the United States today. One hesitates to call this a "new morality" because the phrase is becoming not only shopworn but also meaningless, inasmuch as it has been used to signify so many different things to different people as to be rendered obsolete. What is this new understanding? How and why did it evolve? What are the value changes that this new understanding precipitated?

In the first chapter we said that morality was a doctrine or system of principles which defines right and wrong conduct. Though the term "new morality" may be used in the remainder of this chapter, it should be emphasized that what is new is not so much "morality" but rather an *understanding* of what it means to be moral. In other words, man is still moral, but his understanding with respect to right or wrong conduct has changed. Modern man's understanding of moral behavior differs from that of those who lived in previous times.

The changes in morality began to evolve in the early years of the past decade as formal religious, political, and economic institutions were losing their credibility because of their inaction in promoting human rights. The "clients" of these institutions expressed an ever deeper dissatisfaction with customary modes of religious expression and questioned the long-accepted views of the church, the university, the state, and the corporation. Ludwig von Bertalanffy (1972) suggests that the ills of society are related to a loss of human values. He says that the emptiness and meaninglessness of life results from a "mass civilization which does not recognize the value of the individual" (p. 10). The institutions referred to above reflect the society in which we live. They are, depending on their function, overorganized, highly structured, impersonal, mechanistic, and technological to a very large degree. Not every institution is all these things, but what they all seem to have in common is the reduction of the human being to an expendable and interchangeable part. The system is valued, not the individual.

Though there was a dramatic turning point in American society after World War II, the social forces which were building up after the war culminated in the 1960s. Many of the long-term trends and conditions which were set in motion at that time were swelling into a critical stage through great economic expansion, the terrific pace of technological developments, and very rapid social changes. Some of the more important trends reflecting these changes were:

1. The decay and deterioration of the environment, most especially the great urban centers. Ahlstram (1970) described it well:

> The long developing problems of rampant, unregulated urban growth began to create environmental problems with which American political and fiscal practices could not cope. Problems of management, crime, medical care, education, sanitation, communication, housing, pollution, and transportation made American cities barely capable of sustaining the levels of existence and popular acceptance that are necessary to their viability. This situation had a timetable of its own, moreover, and crises were developing even in cities where race conflict was almost nonexistent. (p. 6)

2. Pluralism. The election of a Roman Catholic to the presidency, the supreme court's reapportionment of legislative districts on the principle of "one man, one vote," and the civil rights movement are but a few examples. The assassinations of the 1960s brought home clearly to the American people that militancy, radical discontent, and violence were part and parcel of this social turbulence.

3. Sensational scientific achievements, such as the exploration of the moon, heart transplants, and the breaking of the genetic code. These and other such developments gave the impression that the scientific potential of the United States was unlimited. Belief in the omnipotence of science was growing more rapidly than ever, contributing to the secularization of men's minds.

4. An increased capability for destruction. The wonders of technology were not an unmixed blessing. The Cuban missile crisis,

continued testing of nuclear military devices, the arms race, and the inability to achieve international control of nuclear armaments provided Americans with a grim reminder that though scientific developments seemed unlimited, so did man's potential for self-destruction.

   5. Escalation of the Vietnam War at the very time when the nation's political leadership was preaching peace. The gap between the expectations of society, as represented by the reverence for human values, and the nation's actions was reaching a critical point. Ahlstram (1970) said that the escalation of the war

> . . . not only prevented an effective assault on the nation's problems of poverty and urban dislocation, but also exposed the terrible inequities of the United States system of military conscription. When coupled with other signs that military considerations were determining American priorities, these policies activated the student movement of dissent and led to an unprecedented loss of confidence in American institutions. With practice so far removed from principle, the entire "system" became suspect. (p. 7)

   The impact of these converging events upon the traditional concepts of morality as espoused by the dominant religious institutions was dramatic. Traditional religion was perceived by many to be irrelevant and unable to cope with the social problems of the times. Churches in the United States in the 1960s were not in the vanguard of social and political reform. Moral confusion, nagging doubts, and even despair seemed to be the culmination of the developments outlined above. But these feelings were not merely those of the radical left, Students for a Democratic Society (SDS), or college students in general. Many Americans of a more conservative bent were suffering, albeit silently, the same pangs of helplessness and alienation from society's religious, economic, political, and academic institutions to which they had looked for a leadership which proved to be nonexistent. What kind of leadership were people yearning for? One that is essentially moral. But the problem facing society was one of the credibility of leaders who spoke in moral terms. The problem was also one of whether classic concepts of morality were still adequate in reconciling man to his fellow man and to the institutions to which he had to belong. The mood of the nation was conducive to an exploration, a searching for something that could help answer the question, "what's it all about?" Much of the searching and exploring led to greater involvement in sensitivity or "T" groups, encounter groups, communal living, drug experiences, increased sexual activity, transcendental experiences, and the like. These are merely coping mechanisms for deeply rooted problems people have in our complex society. But the forms the searching took cannot be considered a "new morality." This is why the term can be misleading. The popular communications media have in many instances given the term a connotation of moral laxity. This is unfortunate, because a relaxation of ethical or moral conduct suggests the removal of ethical and moral aspects from behavior, and this *a priori* cannot be done if we are talking about principles of right or wrong conduct. We would be talking about no principles, no guidelines, and no rules. We would be talking about the law of the jungle.

Situationism

What, then, are we talking about when we suggest that, as a result of many of the above developments, there is evolving a "new definition" of morality or a new formulation of principles which can guide human behavior? We are talking about situationism, an approach to behavior which has an increasingly powerful appeal and utility for the making of moral decisions. Situationism is by no means divorced from Christianity, only from conventional wisdom. Fletcher (1966), the most articulate spokesman for this approach to morality, says:

> The situationist enters into every decision-making situation fully armed with the ethical maxims of his community and its heritage, and he treats them with respect as illuminators of his problems. Just the same he is prepared in any situation to compromise them or *set them aside in the situation* if love seems better served by doing so. (p. 36)

Scripture can be quoted here to illustrate the biblical roots of situationism and to emphasize that moral laxity is not the goal of this approach to morality. St. Paul said, "The written code kills, but the Spirit gives life" (II Cor. 3:6), and "For the whole law is fulfilled in one word 'You shall love your neighbor as yourself'" (Gal. 5:14).

The operative word, then, in the new morality is love. This word has many connotations—erotic, materialistic, divine, and esthetic, to name a few. Fletcher is more specific because he uses the word "agape." Webster's defines agape as "the love of God for man"; it is "Christian brotherly love in its highest manifestation." It connotes an unselfish type of love which does not consider the benefits accruing to the giver or the cost to him. In addition, the concept of agapeic love is not calculating in its consideration of whether the recipient deserves tne love. We can readily see that there is nothing morally or ethically lax about this concept; rather, it is one that is quite challenging. Agapeic love is the only absolute. The legalisms of the medieval period and the rules and absolutes of Calvinism and Puritanism were the bases for human conduct, and this conduct was judged to be moral or immoral according to how well it conformed to the law, the absolutes, or the rules. With agapeic love as the only absolute, there is a

new definition of what is moral or ethical. Is this love put into action
and practiced? Is it the criterion for one's decision making? The decision must, of course, be made in a specific situation or context. Since
each situation is unique, one's conduct must be judged in light of the
situation in which it occurred, and there can be no prejudging or condemnation of the decision-maker so long as the only absolute, i.e.,
agapeic love, was obeyed.

It would be helpful in our understanding of the "new morality" to
explore some of the key concepts of situation ethics. Fletcher (1966)
suggests that four factors are at work: (1) pragmatism, (2) relativism, (3)
positivism, and (4) personalism.

Pragmatism is a particularly American way of looking at things
and is no stranger to the businessman. The pragmatist says that whatever works is good. Applied to ethical or moral behavior, pragmatism
must consider ends. If pragmatism holds that what is good is that
which works, then the question must be asked, "works for what?" In
considering the morality of a given act, one must define for himself
what he seeks, chooses, or prefers. This, then, is a matter of values.
Once an individual understands what it is he wants, he can act prag-
matically. He can take action based on facts and knowledge.

Situation ethics is *relativistic* inasmuch as it recognizes that
legalistic bases for behavior do not necessarily result in ethical or
moral conduct. It recognizes that laws are not free of ambiguities just
because they are laws. Paul Tillich (1963), one of the greatest Protestant theologians, says: "Every moral law is abstract in relation to the
unique and totally concrete situation" (p. 47). This concept takes on a
particularly important meaning in today's society. One has only to look
at the many problems created in the United States by staunch adherents of a law and order mentality both in government and business to
see that legalism and "code ethics" do not necessarily lead to truly
moral conduct. However, the concept of relativism, taken to its extreme, can lead to a behavior that is amoral. Fletcher (1966) makes this
point: "To be relative means to be relative *to* something. There must
be an absolute or norm of some kind if there is to be any true relativ-
ity" (p. 44). This absolute in situation ethics is love.

Positivism in the theological sense refers to the concept that faith
in a divine being is not a completely rational process. Positivism faces
squarely and honestly the idea that logic has its limits and that matters
of faith and morals are not decided through deductive reasoning.
Moral behavior, then, is a function of conscious choice. Since values
are choices, moral values are decisions which can be justified but not
verified. Value preferences cannot be statistically validated. This is
something that "rational" managers and executives who are tough-
minded, and too often overly enamored with measurement, must understand. Moral values can be justified by the situation. Situationists

realize that values, since they are choices, are not based upon water-tight logic but, like faith, are a matter of affirmation or commitment. Managers who believe that an employee who "has all the facts" and is kept well informed will logically come to the same conclusions they do are seriously in error in their perception of human behavior and therefore of morality.

The concept of *personalism* holds that the human being is the central actor in society. The new morality is person-centered and not oriented around laws or codified rules and regulations, or around objects. To paraphrase John Donne's "no man is an island unto himself," one's humanity is only found through interpersonal relationships. Martin Buber (see Friedman, 1964), the great Judaic theologian, conveyed the same idea when he talked of the I-Thou relationship. It is only when the personal I meets the personal Thou that man becomes truly human and therefore meets himself. When an individual "meets" himself, he knows himself, he is true to himself, and therefore he is in possession of himself. In this sense he is free. He can be truly responsible. In this way he makes decisions which are people-centered, because if he knows himself, he knows his fellow man, understands him, and behaves in a moral way that recognizes obligations to others.

This personalistic individual does not use people, because he considers them not as means but as ends. Using people is the epitome of immorality, and much of the knowledge of human behavior attained by managers has been put to illicit use through the manipulation of people in work organizations. This would not so readily happen if managers made decisions which were personalistic, i.e., person-centered. Decision making is one of the manager's most crucial functions. In today's complex organizations, managers must integrate marketing, financial, economic, production, and engineering data in deciding upon a course of action. The ultimate level of integration in decision making, however, should be at the human level, where the person emerges as the unique, all-encompassing gestalt. Human values must therefore be considered by the manager in the situation ethics aspect of decision making. The manager must understand that *his* values affect his decisions. If he believes his decisions are value-free, he is at best naive and at worst ignorant of the behavioral facts of life.

We can sum up the new understanding of morality by citing six propositions made by Fletcher:

1. Only one "thing" is intrinsically good—namely, love—nothing else at all.

2. The ruling norm of Christian decision is love—nothing else.

3. Love and justice are the same, for justice is love distributed—nothing else.

4. Love wills the neighbor's good, whether we like him or not.
5. Only the end justifies the means—nothing else.
6. Love's decisions are made situationally, not prescriptively.

The first proposition ties in with personalism in that it is the human being who *gives* value to a thing, and it has value for him but not independent of him. Situation ethics suggests that if something helps a person it is good, and if it hurts a person it is bad. The end or goal of values is the person, and it is for a human being's benefit that love is good. This understanding of love differs somewhat from the medieval and Calvinistic-Puritanical concept in which love is considered a property, i.e., something that can be measured or weighed like the physical quantity of an item. Calvinism and Puritanism *measured* God's love for a person by the wealth he possessed or the capital he accumulated. Furthermore, the notion of a *state* of grace was measurable, e.g., how long and hard one worked at his calling. The word "state" connotes the same notion of love being a property.

Situationists hold that it is not a property but an action-oriented concept. This is a new understanding of the word and of morality. The new morality speaks of *doing* the loving thing. Fletcher says that love may only be "predicated" on human actions and relationships according to how they take shape in the situation. The contextual or situational consideration means that there are no intrinsically right or wrong actions based on absolute moral laws. The only law is love, and we must remind ourselves that we are talking about agape, not saccharine, sentimental, or emotional love. This love takes place in the existential setting—in what *is*, not in what we would like things to be. Existential ethics or situation ethics are interpersonal; the framework of the situation involves another human being.

Fletcher's second proposition suggests that the new morality replaces the ethic of law with the ethic of love. The major Western religions identified law with love much in the same way as the Pharisees did. The result is a plethora of rules, regulations, and codes which result in the casuistry necessary to attempt a "way out" of conflicting laws. One had only to watch the Watergate scenario being played out to see the tragedy of how legalistic hair splitting, the use of legal loop holes, and "playing with words" seemed more important than questions of justice and morality. If this is what the "legal mind" can do in the framework of law and order and classic concepts of morality, then should it be surprising that there is a new morality gaining ground in our society? During the height of the energy crisis in late 1973 and early 1974, many oil companies who were conducting themselves in a perfectly legal manner and always acting well within the law could be looked upon as acting in less than a moral manner. However, they were behaving in a legitimately legal way and in the best spirit of the Protestant ethic with respect to their obligation to

accumulate as much money as possible, regardless of its consequences
for the American consumer. The new morality does not see any "saving grace" in playing out the values of the classic morality when so
many sacrificed for the benefit of so few. Morality obviously cannot be
legislated.

So, then, love for one's fellow man is the principal law. Lest the
reader think this "soft," let him understand the full import of the new
morality's aversion to dependence on law for ethical behavior. Relying
on codes, laws, rules, and regulations makes us slaves to them and
allows us to hide behind them or take shelter in them. Witness the
abuses of people engaging in income tax evasion. They are following
the law. A slavish reliance on law erodes our ability to examine our
own personal values. As long as we "obey the law" or "go by the
book," we do not have to be concerned with human values. This is as
much a problem of the bureaucratic mind as it is of the legal mind. The
bureaucrat can be irresponsible, and in so doing he is no longer a free
man. How many truly free men can be found in our large and complex
organizations? Managers must learn that freedom becomes responsibility when a person is confronted with the meaning of a situation.
Man becomes responsible for finding his own specific meaning, because each individual is unique *as is every situation*. This new understanding of morality is not promoting license but rather personal responsibility for making one's own decisions—certainly within a
framework of decision parameters. But the new morality calls these
decision parameters by a new name—agapeic love. This is the new
"law."

The third proposition—that love and justice are the same—finally
dispels all doubts that the agapeic love of the new morality is nothing
but sentimentality. The concept of prudence is introduced here, a
factor frequently ignored by so many of our managers (note the word
"leaders" is not used) at the highest governmental and corporate
levels. Prudence is calculating, not irrational; it is intellectual, not
emotional.

The new morality holds that justice is not merely giving each man
his due but rather having an *attitude* that since we live in a corporate
society, all men are our neighbors. Therefore, in situationism we use
prudence to unite justice and love. This is not easy, because in our
complex organizations managers are dealing with many people in a
pluralistic environment. Looking at the work organization as a system
made up of interrelated and interdependent subsystems makes the
manager's consideration of "justice" a difficult task if he does not
equate justice and love. Making them equal as the new morality does,
however, is not enough. The manager has to humanize justice and take
the sugary-sweet connotation out of agapeic love, for it has no place in
its true meaning. Institutional management can use situation ethics in

the social framework of complex organizations, but what is required of management is an approach that considers *all* organizational members as worthy of the agapeic love, not just the "yes" man or the organization man. Managers who engage in managerial vanity by promoting only mirror images of themselves not only are being less than moral, inasmuch as their justice does not go out to all promotable possibilities, but also are poor managers in the strictest "business" sense of the term.

Fletcher said that "love is using its head." What he meant, of course, is that love must be the motor force for rational decision making. Managers are not unfamiliar with the decision-making process. The new morality is no less interested in calculating the consequences of one course of action over another. The new morality, however, says that love must do the calculating through the use of prudence as managers try to cope with the complex problems of business and government. If justice for all the organization's members is recognized as a goal and justice is the same as love, the purposeful, calculating, and rational love will ensure a moral decision. These decisions are inevitably of a high quality.

"Love wills the neighbor's good whether we like him or not" is Fletcher's fourth proposition. Our concern for our fellow man should not depend on whether we like him or dislike him. Once again we see that this new understanding of morality is not soft or sentimental; it is not a simple matter to get along with those we do not care for. We can "reach out," however, to those whom we like, to those who believe the same things we do, and to those who share our values. We ought to consider how great a part this plays in organizational relationships. Managers like "team players." They like employees who are unswervingly loyal to the organization. They do not like the "loner," the maverick, or the outspoken person. It is curious that so great an amount of lip service is given to words like "creativity," "innovation," "self-starter," and "initiative." These are fashionable buzz-words in the managerial vocabulary, but when they are practiced by an individual, he is not too well liked and he may even be written off as "flaky."

Contrary to what many critics of the new morality believe, it is not an egoistic ethic in which the cardinal principle is "do your own thing." In a rather ironic way, the egoistic ethic may be that held by management insofar as the aggressive, upwardly bound executive says, "I look out for number one," or "I'll take care of you if you take care of me." This is not the essence of agapeic love and, as we are too slowly learning, not the essence of effective management in a society in which values are changing. The new morality, toward which our society is moving, is not proposing that we enter into a deep, emotional, and "loving" relationship with every person we know or work with in an organization. What it is proposing, and this is vital for the management of the future, is that we engage in dialogue with the other person. Liking the person has nothing whatsoever to do with it. The new morality calls for an *unconditional* acceptance of the other person. Carl Rogers (1961) calls this "positive regard." This acceptance involves understanding the feelings of others—a "sensitive empathy." This can only come about through dialogue, discussion, and listening. Dialogue implies two-way communication, and this in turn means listening for the feedback so necessary in understanding the other person.

Contrast the above with classic management principles which hold that relationships in the organizational hierarchy are between positions, not people. How can one have a relationship with a position? It is the person in the position with whom we must interrelate in our work organizations. A job has no meaning without a human being filling the position and interacting with other people as he carries out his job duties. It is the human being who gives the job vitality. Contrast, once again, the concepts of the new morality with those of the classic morality in regard to relationships between individuals. Calvinism stood staunchly for an individualism so intense that the concept of "sensitive empathy," to which we have alluded, would be sheer nonsense. In the name of morality, many of the dominant institutions of the sixteenth, seventeenth, and eighteenth centuries had no sympathy for the poor or the idle. They were obviously damned and not among the elect. That this provided a basis, albeit tenuous, for what we have come to consider moral or immoral is not difficult to see. Because the ethos of those dominant religious institutions provided a support for much of our organizational notions and the conventional wisdom they precipitated, we have an organizational ethic which is not particularly disposed to a concern for others.

The concern centers around what Erich Fromm (1947) calls the "marketing orientation." In this view, which is a realistic one in today's impersonal, complex private and public organizations, a person is not looked at for what he is but rather for what he can do for the organization. The individual is not looked at in his total humanness but only as a commodity which management buys. The individual's value lies not in his humanity but in his salability—in what he "has to offer" in the way of skills, expertise, or ability in comparison with another competitive commodity. The individual is not hired, he is bought. He is paid a fee in return for his services. The effect in human terms is not very uplifting. The individual seeking to become a member of a work organization must set his mind to "selling himself." He must perform at the employment interview (and continuously if he gets the job and wants to advance) in such a manner that he is always doing what the organization wants—dressing the way it wants, saying what it wants him to say, and behaving according to company rules and regulations both written and unwritten. In effect, he has given up his identity and clothed himself in the organizational mantle because he wants to be liked. The irony, however, is that he may not be liked, and the new morality is suggesting that he does not *have* to be liked. It is suggesting that he is a "claimant" to agapeic love, as are all persons. Thus the new morality is nondiscriminating, impartial, and unemotional.

"Only the end justifies the means—nothing else." This is Fletcher's fifth proposition of situation ethics. It is the one that probably arouses most antagonism and disagreement among classic moralists. This statement very simply proposes that if the end does not justify the means, then nothing does. For the situationist, the ends that are chosen are of utmost importance. Pragmatism, one of the four suppositions noted earlier, comes into play here. The situationist must know what the costs of the ends are, what the consequences of choosing the ends will be. There must be careful calculation as in any good decision-making process. We see, then, that there is an interaction between ends and means which no classic moralist could argue with. Though the situationist and classic moralist agree on this, the new understanding of morality holds that the end that must be sought is agapeic love. If this type of love is served through a decision, then the end is good—not intrinsically good, but good in the context of the specific situation. Similarly, means are neither good nor bad outside of the situational framework.

According to Fletcher, there are four factors that must be considered when one is analyzing a situation in order to make a decision. Managers are constantly making decisions, and these decisions must be moral ones. As our society's values continue to shift, employees will expect managers to ask themselves some hard questions when making moral judgments. In asking himself these questions, the manager must balance one against the other. The first question concerns what it is that the person is seeking. In other words, what is the intended goal? Secondly, the decision-maker must ask himself how he will go about achieving his goal. This involves which means will be used. A third consideration, one that decision-makers all too often ignore, is their motivation. In organizational behavior we are always discussing the concept of motivation from the standpoint of how we can help managers employ motivational strategies which will result in a high level of employee performance. Now we are asking managers *to question their own motives* when making decisions. Does a manager fully understand the driving force behind his action? Does he know himself well enough to understand his needs and wants? This is a matter of introspection—something most people would rather not engage in. Finally, no decision of a high moral quality can be made without the decision-maker asking himself what the consequences of that decision will be. Any experienced manager knows that many un-intended results occur when a decision is taken. This is why a con-scious, well thought-out, and analytical examination of the probable consequences of an act is necessary. The prudent manager under-stands this, and as Fletcher says, " an action is imperative *only if* the situation demands it for love's sake" (p. 129).

The last proposition, that love's decisions are made situationally, not prescriptively, is a further extension of the previous five and can be said to sum up our new understanding of morality. This proposition is appropriate and relevant to the technologically complex society in which we are living. This society of ours is dominated by large, com-plex organizations which employ a majority of our labor force. These organizations are cumbersome and bureaucratic. They are adminis-tered through the use of classic management principles developed at a time when our society was much more simplistic. These principles of scientific management and the dominant ethos from which they were formulated may not be appropriate in dealing with the complexities of modern organizations in a technologically sophisticated society. If we look at the total organization as a system made up of interrelated and interdependent subsystems, we begin to see the innocence or naivete of earlier managerial principles. When we talk about approaching the organization from a systems point of view, we have automatically in-troduced multidisciplinary complications. The series of interactions which must take place among organizational members with different technical specialties, different ethnic backgrounds, and different amounts of expertise, knowledge, and education makes prescriptions based on simple management and moral codes unequal to the task of moral decision making.

Comparison with Classic Management Principles. We need a new approach to decision making based on a new morality. This will make more than a few managers uneasy. They long for the "good old days" when the data needed for making a decision may have been more difficult to get, but were simplistic when the manager did get them. Moreover, his decisions were rather easy to make because his organi-zation, be it a governmental agency or a private profit-making corpora-tion, was "hooked in" to the morality of the society. The dominant organizational morality as expressed by scientific management was the same as the dominant societal morality as expressed by the Protestant ethic. The manager was secure in knowing that his practices or methods in dealing with subordinates, customers, clients, other man-agers, churches, schools, and other societal institutions were "right" because almost everyone shared the same values. That which consti-tuted moral behavior was widely agreed upon, because if one consid-ers morality a system of principles with respect to right or wrong conduct and if the system is fixed, i.e., unchanging, the "rules of the game" are known and accepted by the great majority of society. The decision-maker "goes by the book"; he has a code of ethics all laid out for him. How can he make the wrong moral decisions when everyone accepts the code? Acceptance of the code is rapidly diminishing, however. Moral decisions must be made on an *ad hoc* basis. The manager can no longer wrap himself in the security blanket of classic morality based on a long list of rules, regulations, and codes providing him with ready answers for any problem in any situation. There is only one principle: "Always be moral." But what is moral? When making decisions the manager in today's society is forced to be responsible. He is free, and this freedom is not to be taken lightly, although it is this very freedom which makes his task of managing so difficult and challenging. His choices of alternative courses of action must be guided by one principle only—agapeic concern for one's fellow man in the context of a specific situation.

The new morality evolved as a result of some critical dislocations that took place in our society in the post–World War II era and particularly in the 1960s. Implicit in this evolution are different assumptions about the human being. Man is at center stage in the drama of life; he is the protagonist, the central actor in society. This means that society's institutions exist to serve man. The church, the law, the government, the university, and the business corporation all have specific functions to perform in the cause of a civilized society. But how can there be civility when society's institutions do not contribute to it? What are society's institutions doing to improve the quality of human existence? This is the question of greatest concern for work organizations like government bureaucracies and business corporations. The new morality is existential in its approach and has much in common with existentialism as a movement. The basis of this movement is the concept of human existence. Existentialism rejects the reduction of uniquely human qualities to frames of reference which appropriately depict animal behavior but represent a less than total conceptualization of man because they only capture that part of man which is not specifically human. Reference is made here to "rat psychology," which tends to take a reductionistic view of man—one that can result in treating human beings as though they were animals that can be conditioned if the "fundamentals" of operant conditioning are applied. This is not a moral approach to human relationships, especially if it leads to manipulation. Since existentialism is implanted in experience, it is not given to wishful thinking, subjective imagination, or theoretical prejudices about man. This is what is meant by the phenomenologic approach to human behavior. Phenomena are described as they are, without cultural or personal prejudice. Theoretical constructs of existentialism are person-oriented, not function-oriented. The new morality places human values above all others.

If human values are to assume their predominant position, we must consider whether we have been making very realistic assumptions about man. A new understanding of morality requires that in our interpersonal relationships we deal with a person in his unity and wholeness, which is the way he participates in life. The new conception of morality does not hold that one's behavior is moral when one deals with people as instrumentalities or as means to one's selfish ends. Scientific management has been called the "man-machine theory" of organization because man is viewed as an adjunct or appendage to the machine. He is not viewed as a human being with a unique personality. Rather, he is to be synchronized with his machine so that man and machine can "interact" harmoniously, working together as one, in the most efficient manner possible.

With reference to the organization structure, man is to be molded, shaped, or bent to fit into it. The classic principles of management we have referred to earlier are to guide the manager in structuring and administering his organization. The human being is pressed into the service of the organization, and an elegant organization structure conforming to the classic principles is more important than the human beings who comprise the organization. Was there an "ethic" supporting these ideas of how organizations should be administered? The organizational ethic was based upon the Protestant ethic, which in turn had its basis in Calvinistic thought. We saw, in examining this system of religious thought, that the concept of the "calling" was central to it. This concept contributed greatly to a division of society into clearly defined classes. As a result the hierarchy of the work organization coincided with the hierarchy of society. Just as Calvinism had its "elect" and its "damned," so society had its "good" and its "bad," its "elite" and its "masses." With respect to authority, it was obvious who should obey whom in the organizational structure. The tradition of religion had ordained it so, and influence by tradition found its way into the management of organizations. As a social philosophy, Social Darwinism found fertile ground in the American society of the early twentieth century. It was well nurtured in the contemporary business corporation and flourished in the receptive climate of this social institution.

We also saw earlier in this chapter that Calvinism engendered individualism inasmuch as it put the person on his own with respect to his salvation. Man was utterly alone and without help from ministers, priests, sacraments, or even God. The individual had to work day and night to relieve himself of the anxiety of whether he was among the predestined elect or damned. The individual alone must "prove" himself in the world, and the stage was set for a spiritual aristocracy which was composed of the predestined elect. The effect on human relations in society was not particularly salutary. Where is the agape in this religious system? It is not there and as a result is not the focal point around which all human behavior should turn. The new morality, on the contrary, places concern for one's fellow man at the very center of its methodology concerning right or wrong conduct.

Frederick W. Taylor called for a "mental revolution" as he formulated his principles of scientific management. It is appropriate once again to call for a mental revolution in management and administration. New managerial attitudes are needed to correspond to shifting values in society. The old attitudes and beliefs which provided a foundation for organizational action are not accepted by those who are simultaneously members of society and complex work organizations. The foundations are crumbling. A new organizational ethic is needed. This ethic places man at the center of all action. What is good for man is good for the organization.

Existentialism

Man is now being called upon to be himself or, as Soren Kierkegaard put it, "to be that self which one truly is." This means that man's potential to be fully human, to be self-actualizing, does not lie outside himself in objective rules but rather within himself and therefore in his freedom. Freedom to do what? Freedom to be all that he is capable of, freedom to achieve his potential. This inner freedom does not mean irresponsibility or license but rather freedom to further the aims of agapeic love.

Existentialism is not a philosophy but rather an approach, an attitude, a movement toward understanding human existence and its relationship to morality. Friedman (1964) suggests it is a "mood" that takes in widely divergent philosophies. He describes the commonality "as a reaction against the static, the abstract, the purely rational, the merely irrational, in favor of the dynamic and the concrete, personal involvement and 'engagement,' action, choice, and commitment, the distinction between 'authentic' and 'inauthentic' existence, and the actual situation of the existential subject as the starting point of thought" (pp. 3, 4).

Classic morality embraced Descartes' *cogito ergo sum* (I think, therefore I am), but existentialism suggests that equating the "I" with the thinking is not adequate in describing what makes man or what constitutes the greatness of man. The criticism is that Descartes' view is impoverished. It does not deal with the whole person, seen from within. Existentialism stresses the importance of man in his wholeness and concreteness. We are living in an age of logical positivism and empiricism in which a great deal of importance is placed upon "proof," "facts," and statistical data. Man is considered an instrument, an object to be viewed in a detached manner, much in the same way a scientist looks at a microbe under a microscope—uninvolved and very objectively. Existentialism holds that man must be viewed from within, from the vantage point of the life he is living. The logical positivists and the empiricists who dominate and influence the policies in our government and private bureaucracies do not believe as Nietzsche did that "man is the valuing one," or that "without valuing the nut of existence is hollow."

To the existentialist life has to be lived from within, from the point of view of the person or the self. There is a difference between authentic and inauthentic existence. What is the new vision of man inasmuch as this vision helps us to understand man and what the German existentialists call *Dasein* or being in the world? Friedman says:

> Man's task in life is to authenticate his existence, and to the existentialist this can never mean the mere adherence to external moral codes, on the one hand, or the romantic's deification of passion and feeling, on the other, nor even the vitalist's emphasis on the organic flow of life. Instead it means personal choice, decision, commitment, and ever again that act of valuing in the concrete situation that verifies one's truth by making it real in one's own life—in one's life with man and the world. (p. 9)

The existential subject, the person, the human being, is at center stage in society, where all organizations operate. For Kierkegaard, the achievement of authentic existence is within every person's power unless that person chooses to become just another face in the crowd, in which case he forfeits his individuality.

How is one to be an individual in a mass society? Kierkegaard suggests that the *cogito* of Descartes has got us too "hung up" on objective thought. Descartes suggested that it was objective, rational, abstract thought that "proved" one's existence as a person. Kierkegaard and other existentialists contend that this only leads to an indifference or neglect of the person and his existence. The person who thinks subjectively (as an existing individual) is inwardly reflective, and his thoughts are therefore his own and do not belong to the group or the organization. We are all familiar with the spate of management books and articles which use the word "results" endlessly. After all, is not management by objectives results-oriented? This, of course, is not necessarily invalid or useless. What can be negative is the obsession with results that can occur with so-called "objective" thought. If a manager permits himself to be constantly identified with results and with the abstract and the "rational," he begins to operate by rote. On the other hand, subjective thought does not make results ends in themselves but "puts everything in process," as Kierkegaard has said. This forces us to alter our vision of man from one in which being human is finally and solely a matter of abstract thinking to one in which being human is a continuous process of coming to be. An individual is always reproducing his existential situation in his thoughts. His thinking thus becomes translated into process—the process of becoming. Morality is realized by the existential subject, who is always in the process of becoming a person and who is the only one who has a grasp of reality for him. Ethical conduct cannot be judged by an outsider.

In our discussion of the classic morality we saw that it was based upon a static concept of the nature of man. Evil was defined as that which was contrary to man's nature, and good was that which was consonant with man's nature. Existentialism, on the other hand, says that man's nature is in a constant state of flux. What is contrary to his nature is also constantly changing. Jean-Paul Sartre states that man determines by choice his nature or what it means to be a man. How can anything be contrary to what man himself has chosen to be? By his existence in the world an individual comes to a decision of what his true self is or, in the old terminology, what his "nature" is. How, then, can anybody say "this is contrary to man's nature" when there is no such thing as abstract human nature? There is only man and what he decides to be—his own reality. Therefore, the manager and other executives in our complex organizations cannot arbitrarily decide what is right or wrong for employees—something that the Puritan ethic and scientific management said they had every right to do.

The attitude of existentialism is to develop in the individual an awareness of what his existence means to him and to get him to take complete responsibility for his existence. There is no determinism and no predestination which leave man powerless and helpless. Man is free to make choices. There is no fatalism as in Calvinism; there is responsibility for one's own actions; man makes himself what he is. How strongly man is responsible is a matter of the quality of his consciousness.

Carl Rogers talks about owning one's feelings, i.e., being completely aware of or conscious of what one feels. Many people go through life not being aware of what they truly feel, and in this respect they are not fully human, inauthentic, and not truly free. The current societal trend toward placing a greater value on understanding ourselves is important because it puts us in a better position to understand the next person. The importance of this for the management of work organizations is self-evident. Self-knowledge is more than just egotistic awareness. It is a subjectivity which is not self-serving, because man is more than just a body or a machine. He has a spiritual existence which creates an interdependence between him and his fellow man. The congruent person, for Carl Rogers, is the one who, after being *truly* aware of his feelings, takes conscious possession of them, i.e., accepts them and communicates them honestly to the other person. It is a goal which many persons are seeking in today's society and will continue to seek in ever increasing numbers in the future.

How does man find his authentic self? How does he discover who he is so that he may get on with possessing his self? Martin Buber (see Friedman, 1964) says that all real living is meeting, the meeting of the personal *I* with the personal *Thou*. In other words, it is only through man's relationship to another that he becomes an authentic person. This means that reality exists only in what he calls "actual present-ness." The present comes about only when the *Thou* becomes present. Buber speaks of *I-It*, which is a relationship between man and things he uses, objects he owns, and other such "contents." If this is all that man relates to, he is not fully human or truly authentic because he is not existing in the present but always in the past. The world of the past is the world of *It*. Man is not bound by that world and can leave it for the world of relation, i.e., with one's fellow man. In the *I-Thou* meeting, *I* becomes a person conscious of himself as a unique individual differentiated from other individuals and shares in a reality. Buber says that no sharing means no reality, and it is only inasmuch as the *I* shares in reality that it is an authentic being.

How does one "share" with another human being? What is the activity we must engage in, and how is this activity reality? An impor-tant way in which these questions can be answered is through Martin Buber's concept of dialogue. He distinguishes three types—genuine, technical, and monologue. The first is either verbal or nonverbal, but its essential feature is that both persons keep each other in mind from the standpoint of their particularity of being. The object of genuine dialogue is to establish a vital and dynamic relationship between the two persons. Obviously it is only through genuine dialogue that shar-ing takes place. Technical dialogue is necessitated by having to under-stand some objective facts. In monologue there can be two persons engaged in a conversation which is only a superficial and artificial dialogue. It is not true dialogue in the sense that each person speaks only to himself, does not really listen to the other, and has no intention of establishing a reality-centered relationship with the other. The per-son whose entire life consists of monologues is not living in reality and therefore can never become an authentic person. The monologic per-son cannot share in reality-activity because he cannot see the other person for what he is, accept the other as a person in his own right, and perceive the other person in a nonjudgmental, nonprejudicial way. The other person is viewed as "just like me," or "just like all the rest of them." There is little hope for morality in monologic encounters be-cause the other person is never "allowed to be." The question of rele-vance here is to what extent are relationships, communications, and encounters in complex work organizations and government bureaucracies monologic rather than dialogic? To the extent that there are more of the former, we have work organizations that are highly populated by inauthentic, underdeveloped persons.

Buber suggests that every man wants to be confirmed as to what he is and even as to what he can become. Man also has the innate capacity to confirm his fellow man. In the impersonal and technocratic age in which we live, this innate capacity in man is latent. This perhaps explains man's insensitivity to man, especially in the work environment. We are not "confirming" one another in complex organizations. The ethos of the bureaucratic organization is "get ahead," "get to the top," "be aggressive," "look out for number one." This is monologic, man relating only to himself, and it is suggested here that the corporation of the future will foster a continuation of this ethos only at its own peril.

Carl Rogers (1961) says that "a drive toward self-actualization, or a forward moving directional tendency . . . is the mainspring of life" (p. 35). Based on his many years of experience as a psychotherapist dealing with emotionally troubled people, he suggests that what really motivates a patient is to strive to become a fully functioning person. In other words, the goal is to become himself. Rogers goes on to say:

> It is the urge which is evident in all organic and human life—to expand, extend, become autonomous, develop, mature—the tendency to express and activate all the capacities of the organism, to the extent that such activation enhances the organism or the self. (p. 35)

What must be stressed here, however, is Rogers' belief that a relationship must develop between the counselor and the person he is counseling in which that person feels safe and free. There must be this atmosphere of freedom before the individual can get in a "forward-moving direction." This is also the importance of freedom in our organizations. It is what Buber means when he talks of allowing the other person to be. When the organizational climate encourages freedom, individuals begin dropping their masks and facades. Behavior becomes more reliable in that we can be more certain that people are true to themselves and trustworthy. Behavior becomes less defensive and less maladaptive.

Management must look to the future—to a new organizational ethic—and not feel threatened in doing so. In striving to discover his true self, the individual is discovering reality—a key word in the language of existentialism. Does the individual exist only as an object to be manipulated by management? Is his existence a question of what he wants to be or what others demand he be? What motivates his life—discovery of his true self or having a self that others think he should have? Organizations not only should encourage "freedom to be" but also should embrace the idea of personal responsibility because man's values are moving in this direction.

In his desire for the confirmation of others, man may lose his sense of self in the continuous role-playing he engages in as he pursues his career in the organization. In seeking social approval, which the organization desires and rewards, man loses his sense of self, his identity, and his personal integrity. However, man's values are shifting as he begins to ask himself, "What am I doing playing this role (game)?" He can no longer identify himself and lives in an existential vacuum which is a major problem of this age of anxiety in which we live. Man is beginning to fight for his freedom and autonomy, however, because he knows that the quality of his life, regardless of how much money or material possessions he acquires, is impoverished without the freedom to be. It is a struggle, and though man has not completely won it, there is a new awareness that the quest for self-understanding and the identification of self are important. Man is increasingly realizing the importance of this, and in so doing he is questioning the fabric of society's constituent institutions. Work organizations will have to adapt to this new understanding of morality inasmuch as their structure, leadership, and tasks are consonant with the worker's growth and development as a person.

BIBLIOGRAPHY

Ahlstram, S. E.: The radical turn in theology and ethics: Why it occurred in the 1960's. *Annals of the American Academy of Political and Social Sciences*, Vol. 387, 1970, p. 6.

Baxter, R.: Christian directory. In Weber, M.: *The Protestant Ethic and the Spirit of Capitalism*. New York: Charles Scribner's Sons, 1958.

Bertalanffy, L. von: The world of science and the world of values. In Luthans, F. (Ed.): *Contemporary Readings in Organizational Behavior*. New York: McGraw-Hill, 1972.

Fletcher, J.: *Situation Ethics*. Philadelphia: The Westminster Press, 1966.

Friedman, M.: *The Worlds of Existentialism*. New York: Random House, 1964.

Fromm, E.: *Man For Himself: An Inquiry Into the Psychology of Ethics*. New York: Holt, Rinehart & Winston, 1947.

Rogers, C. R.: *On Becoming A Person*. Boston: Houghton Mifflin Co., 1961.

Tawney, R. H.: *Religion and the Rise of Capitalism, a Historical Study*. New York: Harcourt, Brace, 1926.

Tillich, P.: *Systematic Theology*. Vol. III. Chicago, University of Chicago Press, 1963.

Weber, M.: *The Protestant Ethic and the Spirit of Capitalism*. New York: Charles Scribner's Sons, 1958.

CHAPTER

III

MAN'S INCREASED UNDERSTANDING OF HUMAN BEHAVIOR

INTRODUCTION

Behavioral science entails more than just the study of human behavior; it also involves the control of human responses. To understand behavioral responses, one must study their causes. These cause-effect relationships are cyclic in that a particular thought or action may be both cause and effect simultaneously, thus forming a causal chain. The observation of these chains is in itself an input to various causal chains. Any science (e.g., behavioral science) is a response to reality (i.e., observational inputs) due to mankind's mental predilections. It is dynamically responsive to changing observational stimuli and utilizes its resultant findings to change the nature of life. These responses, however, also serve as stimuli to "reality," thus forming a cyclic relationship. Science builds upon its own past findings.

Individual humans are in this respect quite similar to a branch of science. What one is today is based upon what one was yesterday. People build upon the foundations of their past—their characters and personalities. Thus mankind changes and builds upon new stimuli such as those provided by expanding scientific findings. This is especially true in the field of science, since one of its primal functions is the expansion of man's control over his life and environment. This enables man to live his life in accordance with logic derived from mental processes rather than through random responses to nature. While science in general changes man's thinking (and thus his responses), behavioral science in particular has the potential for directly affecting man's thinking. By understanding himself, man can achieve control over his stimulus-response cycle. Understanding is the key to improving the decision-making process. The control gained through knowing *why* is far superior to that gained by merely knowing *how*.

By understanding his own behavior, man can gain control over himself and ultimately the environment of which he is a part. It has become evident through much research that the mechanism through which one's responses are filtered is his value structure, which is based on past situations and judgments (not precluding other factors). One may define a human being as the algebraic sum of his interrelating values, cultural and otherwise. Man's learning cycle can then be depicted as a directional (arrowed) circle with "personal values" for the first half cycle and "personal experiences" for the second half cycle. Behavioral science can provide an individual with the knowledge needed to change his responses to given experiential stimuli and improve his value system stimuli to his environment (i.e., his behavior). An individual will then be better able to formulate his goals logically and consistently and to improve his chances for achievement. Thus he will be better able to establish an appropriate "psychological contract" on the job, as well as in his other relationships.

THE FREUDIAN REVOLUTION: PSYCHOANALYSIS

Sigmund Freud initiated and developed the most widely publicized psychological system, which had special impact on the nonpsychologist. To a great extent, modern behavioral science has its roots in Freud's concepts or in its reactions to these concepts. Freud's theories concern the unconscious determinants of behavior. After using hypnosis on hysteria patients, Freud developed the method of psychotherapy termed psychoanalysis, which used the free association technique and alleviated unconscious resistance. He later added dream interpretation to the regimen in his treatment of neuroses. He explained human behavior in terms of unconscious motivations. These included various defense mechanisms used by the psyche to obscure unacceptable drives and emotions. The terms repression, regression, reaction formation, rationalization, projection, identification, sublimation, conversion, and fantasy may be found in basic college texts and are familiar to many nonpsychologists. Freud hypothesized that by reliving the incident causing the neurosis, the patient could be permanently cured. These incidents were often sexual in nature and occurred in early childhood. Upon the two great Freudian forces, sex and aggression, was built the familiar trio of id, ego, and superego. The id is based upon sexual libido and the "pleasure principle," the ego upon the "reality principle," and the superego upon moral dictates. In addition, Freud postulated dual universal drives toward life-sex (eros) and death-aggression (thanatos). While Freud's model depicting the rational ego torn between desire (id) and autocratic norms (superego) is readily accepted by many, extensions and related theories are not so easily favored.

Freud's theories met with great opposition initially because of his emphasis on the sexual aspects of motivation, especially in children. Theories such as the Oedipus and Electra complexes were frequently frowned upon. Freud's critics claimed that his model was merely a reflection of his own emotional problem and they were prepared to discard his theory altogether. They also considered his methodologic procedures biased, since patients' statements were accepted uncritically, and the whole approach used was too instinct-oriented. The lack of control and repeatability of his clinical studies came under suspicion, and he was criticized for being cultish, dogmatic, narrow in his views, and insensitive to different points of view. Despite all this, his influence remains unquestionable.

Freud's goal was not merely to cure neurosis in the individual but to understand humanity as a whole. He extended the study of psychology into religion, sociology, anthropology, and civil problems. He stimulated thinking in many neglected areas. Dream interpretation is now widely used in psychotherapy. He also added insights into homosexuality, narcissism, pychosomatic medicine, humor, and child psychology. His scientific attitudes toward religion are paralleled today by the revelations of General Semantics. He advocated sex education and the use of nonmedical practitioners of psychoanalysis, both forerunners of current developments. He not only popularized psychology but also advanced psychology into the realm of science and provided a colorful language usable by both disciplines. Freud developed the world's most widely influential theory of personality.

Extensions and Variations of Freudian Psychology

Alfred Adler: Individual Psychology.   It has been said that it is necessary for students to back away from their teachers and form their own schools and theories in order to have scientific progress. The first person to break with Freud and psychoanalysis was Alfred Adler. At first he merely expanded the Freudian concept of compensation, in which an individual with a real or imagined deficiency attempts to overcome it. Sometimes through overcompensation an individual can achieve greatness, e.g., Demosthenes, Alexander the Great, Julius Caesar, Theodore Roosevelt. Freud applauded Adler's extension of the concept of compensation into the area of sexual, biological defects. However, Adler soon extended his theories further, promoting a dual system of compensation involving the feelings of inferiority and power, which took precedence over Freud's sexual basis. Eventually Adler changed his emphasis from past experiences to present experiences and from sexual factors to social factors. In the end, Adler's views came to be diametrically opposed to those of Freud.

To Adler personality was an individual's method of responding to frustration. He agreed with Freud that the child's early, formative years are of utmost importance psychologically, since these years are instrumental in the development of the individual's style of life. He differed from Freud in that he felt the sexual aspects become important much later. The child, an utterly dependent and physically insignificant entity, quickly develops a sense of inferiority within the world around him and soon learns to use social power in his dealings with his parents. The weak, inadequate, and frustrated child soon wishes not to be dominated by the large, strong, and overpowering entities surrounding him. His means of compensation depends on the nature of his family and could develop accordingly into hyperintellectuality or hypermaturity, which may extend into the school as well as the home. The order of birth is also quite important. The firstborn child can attain a certain degree of domination over his parents, resulting in a typical conservative style of life. The next child's arrival generally marks the emergence of sibling rivalry, and this too may have compensatory connotations expressed in the acquisition of a more radical style of life for the sake of getting attention.

The parent-child relationship, rather than being based on infantile sexual factors, involves an interplay between the child's native friendliness and his need for power or dominance. The Oedipal conflict, then, involves the conquest of the mother in a noncarnal sense. The sex act itself becomes, to Adler, assertion of dominance by the male over the female. Indeed, men and women have both masculine and feminine segments, and both sexes try to overcome the feminine segment through "masculine protest." Thus masculinity becomes a social rather than a biological concept, and feminism can be considered symptomatic of the response to frustration (inferiority). Similarly a pampered or a rejected child may eventually show hostility toward competitors, as well as antisocial attitudes, neurosis, or psychosis. The child seeking security and superiority can become egocentric, and his style of life and goals, adopted in childhood, may be destructive and neurotic in later years.

Adler's methods of treatment for people with these unacceptable styles of life were quite different from Freud's. Rather than employing the typical psychoanalytic couch, Adler instituted face-to-face interviews with the patient within an atmosphere of openness and equality.

While dreams were studied, they were seen as representative of current attitudes rather than mere wish-fulfillments. He regarded the patient as an integrated, striving individual rather than a conglomeration of warring segments, so that conflict occurred between an individual and the environment, often to the detriment of the individual. Although the patient's past was important (Adler researched one's childhood), he put more emphasis on current situations. His theories proved helpful in solving many educational and social problems. In spite of the great contribution he has made, Adler has been severely criticized for his superficial treatment of dominance and power and of femininity, as well as his inadequate explanation of submissive individuals. His methodology and treatment process also came under scrutiny, and he was alleged to be closer to Freud than he dared to admit.

Despite the shortcomings of his "Individual Psychology," Alfred Adler made great contributions to his field. His shifting of emphasis from libido to ego resulted in an awakening of optimism. Man became a positive, creative entity rather than a biological puppet. Improvements in his self-image and understanding could aid him in improving his social situation. This view gave impetus to the study of motivation, personality, and perception. Psychological emphasis was placed on the marital, vocational, and social aspects of life styles. Freud's distorted picture of personality, wherein few could live a life of reason, was rectified. Adler added to the vocabulary of the masses such terms as sibling rivalry, inferiority complex, and life style. He profoundly influenced later behaviorists, became the Godfather of the Neo-Freudians, and was a forerunner of the existential psychologists.

Carl Jung: Analytical Psychology. Carl Jung was the second great disciple to break with Freud. Although the basis for this separation was essentially the same as Adler's (opposition to the emphasis on sex in Freudian psychology), Jung's system evolved in quite a different direction. Strangely, however, the two systems had many similar results. Though in many ways Jung remained closer to Freud than Adler did, he also rejected Freud's theories as being too mechanistic. While Adler replaced sex with power (or dominance) as the ruling function in human psychic development, Jung adopted a less restrictive view. To Jung, the libido represented a general life urge. Freud's stages of infantile sexual development—oral, anal, phallic, latency, genital— were transformed by Jung into a progression of more varying and material influences. It took a nutritive form in infancy, a playful form in childhood, and a heterosexual form only after puberty. In each stage of development, the life energy became manifest in an appropriate form—eating, elimination, sex, and so forth. Jung did not believe all pleasurable sensations were sexual in nature. Thus the Oedipal relationship involved the nutritive dependence of the child on the mother and only later become overlaid and combined with the child's developing sexual feelings. To Jung, psychic energy took on an almost physical reality, being described as adhering to the known laws of energy physics. Thus Jung predated Freud's eros theory and tended to encompass both Freud's and Adler's more elaborate yet more pragmatic structure.

Furthermore, Jung tempered the effects of childhood trauma by asserting that it represented only a "predisposing cause" which required an "exciting cause" in the present in order to develop a neurosis later. A blocked problem in adult life could demand an excess of psychic energy, causing a regression to previous behavior patterns and thereby unlocking an unadjusted complex. Thus free association and dream analysis (using personalized symbology) were useful in uncovering present difficulties. Indeed, these techniques were even useful in crime detection, and experimental comparisons with devices similar to the current polygraph substantiated the value of systematic free association tests. Jung synthesized both past and present causal determinants of behavior. Indeed, Jung's view of a united and creative self went beyond Adler's optimism to encompass individual goals and intentions as motivations, shifting emphasis much into the future. While Jung accepted the doctrine of universal masculine-feminine character elements, he believed that they must be understood by an individual, appreciated, and utilized in balance. He did not share Adler's negative sentiments toward femininity.

Like Freud, Jung tended toward a series of dualistic polarities and proposed a system of conflicting tendencies. While Jung rejected Freud's thanatos, he hypothesized a duality of consciousness, establishing the concept of the collective unconscious which consisted of ancient social-genetic imprints shared by all. In addition, he proposed the existence of a personal unconscious filled with latent tendencies repressed by the dominant trait of each of a number of specified polarities. Thus if an individual is consciously masculine-dominant, he is unconsciously feminine-dominant. The most important of these polarities is the introvert/extrovert duality. This theory involving an individual's relating inward to himself or outward to society gained immediate and enthusiastic acceptance from both professionals and laymen. Furthermore, mental activity was said to take four dominant forms—sensation, intuition, thinking, and feeling—sensation and intuition being polar opposites, as well as thinking and feeling. While all are simultaneously present, one of each pair becomes dominant in an individual. In addition, archetypes are formed as a result of the universal experiences of man in his evolution. These include the anima (feminine), animus (masculine), persona (inner self), socius (social mask), shadow (animal instincts), and most important of all, self (man's striving for unity and an integrated personality). Various types of individuals emerge by combining the dominant attributes of these systems. Hence, a feeling-intuiting introvert might become a prophet or a monk. The self archetype holds together this multiplicity of systems. It strives for oneness of the individual with the world via mystical experiences and for oneness within via integration of the various psychic systems.

The self, however, appears only when, in middle age, separation of the other systems requires integration. After this "breaking point," sex becomes subsidiary. With so many diverse and conflicting tendencies and society's call for specialization, balance is easily lost, leading to feelings of emptiness, futility, and confusion in middle age. Thus the Jungian therapist explores the patient's personal and collective unconscious in order to develop balance and a oneness with humanity and the universe within the patient. While perhaps becoming rather mystical, the patient should emerge to find life more meaningful and worthwhile. In doing so, the patient realizes potentials latent in his unconscious. Utilizing art, mythology, mysticism, symbology, and studies of primitive peoples, Jung attempted to aid the individual in a search for his soul. Interestingly, personality tests based on Jung's types (the Minnesota Multiphasic Personality Inventory, the California Psychological Inventory, and the Type Inventory) consistently show that creative people are more psychopathologic. It is asserted, however, that they also possess greater ego strength and self-control. They often have both the need and the ability to create, and a strong self archetype could possibly be expected.

Of course, such mystical doctrines infuriated the naturalistic, monistic Freudians. Freud asserted that Jung desired to be a prophet. Jung responded that Freud's theories reflected his own aspirations. While the description of Jung's theories as being encumbered with psycho-anthropologic-pseudo-genetic speculations may be valid, the mystical direction of his viewpoints not only may be beneficial but also may form the foundation for the reconciliation of science and religion to the betterment of both. Jung's desire for balance is indubitably applicable to both. It must be admitted, however, that Jung's theories and writings are quite difficult to comprehend and that they comprise an extremely complicated body of views, often inconsistent in content. Although the specifics of Jung's system are open to criticism, the general trends which he established are far-reaching and eminently productive. His Analytical Psychology stressed personality typing and treated the patient more as an individual. Dream analysts today will generally agree that one's personal associations do affect one's meanings for dream symbols. Jung utilized free association to determine these meanings, and his views were novel and provocative. He helped to popularize psychology through his interesting terminology and concepts such as complexes, introversion, and extroversion. He also developed the concept of synchronicity, the simultaneous occurrence of noncausal events. Jung's greatest contribution, however, was his refreshing view of man, a view which implied that each individual should through balance attempt to develop fully his personal potential, leading to oneness with humanity. By adopting this mystical viewpoint, Jung went beyond Adler, shifting emphasis toward the future, incorporating man's thirst for the divine (religion) into psychological realms, and predating Maslow's self-actualization in a grand manner.

BEHAVIORISM

B. F. Skinner: Operant Conditioning. In opposition to the psychoanalysis group is a more scientifically oriented group called the Behaviorists. Their work is derived from Pavlov's earlier work with conditioned reflexes. Burrhus Frederic Skinner (1971) is probably the most extreme and best-known stimulus-response (S-R) proponent. Pavlov observed that if a dog were given a stimulus (e.g., ringing of a bell) before food was presented, the dog would soon associate the stimulus with the food. Thus, the dog would salivate on hearing the bell before food was presented. This classic conditioning situation occurs when reinforcement (reward or punishment) is contiguous with the learned response but independent of performance. Also referred to as respondent conditioning, it is automatic in nature, involving an involuntary, autonomic response to a given stimulus. Thus this smooth muscle type of action can be represented as $R = f (S,A)$, in which R = the response, f = the relating function, S = the stimulus, and A = the antecedents, state variables, or surrounding environmental conditions. Skinner refers to this associative type of conditioning as Type S. Alternatively, Skinner's system, called Type R, involves no known stimulus. Thus the equation becomes $R = f (A)$. Type R, or operant conditioning, involves a voluntary, learned response, thus utilizing the striped or striated muscles.

Skinner's technique for eliciting Type R responses involved the construction of the famous Skinner Box. In it, the subject (rat, pigeon, or child) would unintentionally or randomly strike a control which would release food. The subject would soon associate the two events and appease his hunger via the control mechanism. An automatic recording device would record the responses over time. Thus evolved Skinner's Law of Acquisition: if the occurrence of an operant is followed by presentation of a reinforcing stimulus, the strength is increased. Thus operant behavior (for which there is no known eliciting stimulus) resulted in instrumental conditioning, in which the stimulus is contingent upon a prior learned response. This entire procedure is usually referred to as operant conditioning. Results from these experiments were analyzed with regard to rates of response and extinction (length of time the learned response is emitted after the stimulus is no longer given or contingent). The most important findings derived from these experiments were the effects of various reinforcement schedules upon performance. Reinforcement need not be complete; indeed, partial or intermittent reinforcement produced higher rates of response and longer extinction times. Such schedules could depend upon fixed intervals, fixed ratios, variable intervals, or variable ratios. With a fixed interval, the subject would be reinforced only if he responded *after* a given interval of time. With the fixed ratio, reinforcement would be permitted after various time intervals whose *average* would be fixed. The improved performance with variable ratio reinforcement schedules has many applications in the real-life situation as described below.

Skinner elaborated his procedures by instituting secondary stimuli which the subject would soon associate with the primary. The association would persist even when the primary was deleted, leading to a possible explanation for phobias. Likewise, reinforcers similar to the primary would be recognized by the subject. These generalized reinforcers could be inhibited through extinction or punishment, or they could be selectively reinforced. The experimenter could at will achieve a specific set of reinforcers; money may be such a generalized reinforcer in society today. Selective reinforcement could be employed in shaping behavior whereby a complicated series of activities could be learned sequentially. This is especially important, since Skinner extrapolated his findings to human action, stating that behavior consists mostly of operants and that simpler laws could be combined into higher ones. Thus superstition may exist in certain subjects whose noncausal, random actions become associated (to them) with reinforcement because of accidental simultaneity with the first few reinforcements. Subsequently, the particular action would be repeated, improving the chance of accidental reinforcement, and such fixated responses would be perpetuated indefinitely.

Inhibition through extinction and punishment (negative reinforcement) was also given great attention. Punishment did not destroy conditioning; it merely inhibited it, only to return when punishment stopped. Indeed, the total number of responses necessary for extinction was not reduced by punishment. Many other interesting experiments were made using delayed responses, deprivation time, different subjects, different reinforcers, and so forth. Indeed, it was discovered that monkeys would perform in order to view other monkeys.

Skinner's contribution to behavioral science consists mainly of his ingenious research methods and their results. While his findings are provocative and stimulating, Skinner has been criticized on several grounds. To begin with, Skinner concentrated on fine controls for his experiments, but refused to use statistical analysis, which requires great numbers of experimental samples. He utilized cumulative curves to represent his data, with resultant averaging out of findings. Furthermore, he refrained from making any summarizing comment on his data, preferring to let it speak for itself. This is characteristic of his atheoretical, neobehavioristic approach. While his antipathy toward personal involvement in theory is understandable, the need for theory to at least direct experimental approaches is obvious. Though, as Skinner asserts, the state-of-the-art of psychology may be poor, even incorrect theories serve to motivate and organize research. They may also include a small contribution of truth which Skinner's noneclectic attitude would overlook. In addition, he concentrated exclusively on learning, even wishing to eliminate the terms emotion, motivation, and perception (since they were abused and variable), and was thus accused of peripheralism. Even within the field of learning he studied responses only, declaring stimulus analysis to be unnecessary and undesirable. Yet he was not loathe to declare that all learning was simply conditioning (mostly operant conditioning) and to extrapolate beyond his data. Obviously, Skinner's view of man as totally shaped by his environment is extremely unattractive.

Many psychologists are antagonized by Skinner's deterministic point of view, as they were with that of Freud. Indeed, Skinner acclaimed Freud's emphasis on the causal importance of events in an individual's life. Skinner even refers to learned behavior as reflex. While his scientific methods are, in general, applauded, his failure to discuss the internal mechanisms of his Descriptive Behaviorism is not. Nevertheless, Skinner's contributions are quite substantial. He taught pigeons to inspect paint jobs and to pilot missiles. He invented a baby-tending device, a speech machine, and a teaching machine. His findings have found great and varied application, especially in the area of motivation and control. Proper reinforcement scheduling has improved remuneration procedures and absentee rates in business. The inefficiency of punishment as a motivator and the necessity for immediate feedback are important to both managers and parents. Experimental studies among mental patients, school children, and workers have proved extremely successful, revealing that under proper conditions reading, stimulation, and achievement can act as their own rewards. Since behavior is a function of its consequences, desired behavior will be emitted if rewarded. Rewards should then be structured by business so as to achieve the desired behavior. Skinnerians thereby describe the characteristics of pay contingency, leisure, information, job enlargement, conformity, informal groups, fringe benefits, and welfare as motivators or nonmotivators. They even apply Skinnerian findings to the theories of McGregor and to social systems design. The mutuality of control in Skinner's methodology, whereby the animal actually controls the scientists (they must reinforce him to achieve their aim), is interesting in regard to McGregor's Theory Y and represents an apparent retreat from Skinner's biological determinism.

THE THIRD FORCE IN PSYCHOLOGY

Behavioral science has recently turned more humanistic and less biological in both theory and treatment. Humanistic theories are to a great extent dependent upon previous findings but tend to be more concerned with explaining behavior in terms of man's existence as a *complete* human being. The psychology of what it means to be human is where the emphasis lies. These theories place little emphasis upon learning (Skinner's research) and reject the extremity of Freud's sexual emphasis and therapeutic techniques. Some expand in Adler's direction, emphasizing the division between man and society. While ignoring or deemphasizing Jung's elaborate personality system, they do accept Jung's mystical views of the positive nature of man and his emphasis on the future. These psychologists are, perhaps, at the forefront of a movement to return to the philosophical origins of psychology. Indeed, they are sometimes referred to as existential psychologists because they stress self-understanding. Unlike Skinner, their view of man is nondeterministic; they believe that man can control his actions through understanding. They are not pessimistic, however, as existentialists are said to be, but rather believe in positive human development. Indeed, like Jung, they at least border on the mystical in aiming for an ideal balance in their patients. They do not treat a particular disease; they treat a particular patient, attempting to aid him in developing to his greatest potential. They adopt a positive attitude toward therapy and humanity, expanding a psychology to meet the needs of all men.

The Neo-Freudians

Erich Fromm. Often referred to as a Neo-Freudian, Erich Fromm (1963) synthesizes existential philosophy and Adlerian psychology and applies it to modern sociology. Fromm is a humanist; he contends that self-perception and lifetime goals are necessary for psychological development and environmental adjustment. Like Adler and Rogers, he asserts that proper adjustment implies openness to new experiences and to opportunities to express creativity. His self-image thesis is quite similar to Adler's "guiding fiction," which is adopted by many humanists. In addition, he considers insecurity a focus in personality theory, accepting an "authority and the family" view of the Oedipal relationship. Taking the sociologic point of view, Fromm asserts that cultural influences determine the nature and extent of repression, projection, rationalization, and so forth. To Fromm, man is a social creature, and neuroses develop as a result of social pressures. According to Fromm, man's reason, imagination, and self-awareness have disrupted the harmony of his existence, alienating man from himself, his fellow man, and nature. The resulting separateness leads to anxiety and a need to escape the feelings of helplessness and aloneness. Man, the "freak of the Universe," is the only animal that can be bored. Man alone must face insolvable contradictions: inevitable death vs. man's life wish, the shortness of life vs. the desire to reach goals, and reason's requirement of independence vs. man's unbearable loneliness.

The answer to the problems stemming from man's basic estrangement lies in productiveness, reason, and love. Fromm applies certain ideas from Eastern mysticism (Zen Buddhism, in particular) to sociologic/psychological problems. In their paradoxical combination reason and love become merely different ways of comprehending reality. Since only love is interpersonal, love is the answer to the problem of human existence. Through love man can reunite himself with nature, others, and himself. Indeed, man must express caring and responsibility for others in order to retain his own personal dignity. Actualizing one's self-potential and developing one's sense of belonging are concurrent and causal occurrences. True individualism is achieved not through independence but through love. Fromm's use of the word "love," however, differs from that of the layman today; love, in the pure ethical sense, is unconditional and without reference to values or arguments. Love is a demonstration of the giver's potency, and it is man's deepest longing. Unfortunately, spiritual concerns have been grossly neglected in modern society.

In *Escape from Freedom*, Fromm states that the evolution from a medieval to a capitalistic state created a further lack of structure and security. Increased freedom produces an "anonymous authority," e.g., public opinion, which causes people to be indirectly afraid of themselves. Indeed, Fromm battles against capitalism, asserting that it destroys man's spirit since man becomes a mere commodity, materialistically oriented and alienated from the product of his labor. Further, competition creates a devastating psychological problem, pitting individuals against each other. Rather than satisfying people's psychological needs (love, relatedness, and personal identity), society warps individuals to fit its needs, eliminating the opportunity for self-development. Thus, according to Fromm's Neo-analytical approach to personality, people develop different relatedness orientations. *Receptive* individuals identify with a group or leader in power, and their assumption of superiority leads to intolerance of any questioning of their authority. The *exploitative* type of person attempts to obtain objects of value to others, and by doing so, he accepts their values as his own. The *hoarding* type of person is remote and miserly, equating tangible, physical wealth with security. The *marketing* type of individual follows fashion, emulating the social system. None of the above types establishes his own set of values but rather depends on others to do so. The *productive* type of person, however, is creative, mature, and loving. Fromm points out that selfishness and self-love are actually antithetical. Self-hatred or a sense of inner worthlessness leads to outward selfishness, whereas self-love or a sense of inner worth leads to outward generosity. He equates insecurity with the former and security with the latter. The types never appear in pure form but blend with each other, being dominant in some individuals and diminished in others.

Since love and capitalism are inimical (the productive, loving type being a rarity), Fromm proposed Humanistic Communitarian Socialism. This would eliminate consumer's brainwashing via advertising and "need to consume" conditioning. Instead, minimum subsistence and decentralization of ownership should be instituted, leading ultimately to a sense of human brotherhood and relatedness. Increased stability and tranquility would then prevail. Fromm asserts that people can escape the insecurity of increased freedom through either authoritarianism or humanism. The first four types outlined by him choose authoritarianism, while the last type, the "productive" selects love and cooperation.

Fromm's socialistic views aroused the ire of staunch capitalists, who attempted to refute all of his theories. Despite their criticism, his condemnation of the misuse of the term "love" and his definition of it cannot be ignored. His ideas about love are readily accepted by most mystics, initiators of religions, and the youth of today. The latter also show a deep interest in mysticism, an interest shared by some highly respected behavioral scientists. This is perhaps indicative of a new and fortunate trend, a metamorphosis in academic conservatism. Despite severe criticism coming from many directions, Fromm and his young disciples in spirit have rediscovered mankind's vital need for closer ties to one another and to nature.

Existential Psychology

Carl Rogers: Client-centered Therapy. Carl Rogers (1965) is representative of the new group of existential psychologists. His views are optimistic, humanistic, and future-oriented. His entire theory and the therapy from which it originated center on his ideal man, the "fully functioning person." According to Rogers, each individual symbolizes his experiences for remembrance. Since experience is filtered, however, through one's value system (self-image), incongruencies between this internal system and objective reality will tend to distort experiences, causing further divergence from reality. If, however, an individual is open to new experiences, trusts them, and interprets them in light of his own independent, congruent value system, he can accurately perceive reality and can appropriately respond to his environment. With such undistorted feedback, an individual can adjust to previous incorrect responses and adapt to changing environmental conditions. His congruence with reality yields immunity to threats to his self-image, because all of his experiences are accurately available to his awareness and in congruence his problem-solving ability gradually grows.

Such an individual responds to his own inner reactions despite social pressures, and he is not likely to twist reality, via defense mechanisms in an attempt to reconcile it with a preconceived self-structure. His self-perception configuration is a fluid gestalt, reflecting his own immediate, evolving feelings. Utilizing *his own* "locus of evaluation" and effective reality testing, he will ignore invalid praise or criticism. The attainment of unconditional, positive self-regard and rejection of external conditions of worth will allow him the formation of reciprocal positive relationships with others. People freed from defensive reactions will establish harmonious relationships based upon the logic of interdependent needs and mutual regard. Each *individual* will be free to self-actualize, reach for his true potentials, and choose the challenge of personal creativity. He will be rewarded by a dynamic, meaningful, vivid, rewarding, existential form of living rather than a static, anxiety-laden existence. Such individuals, representing increased consciousness, survival ability, and adaptability, comprise the vanguard of human evolution.

Consistent with his ideal of human potential, Rogers focuses therapy not upon a client's specific complaint but upon the client himself. The purpose is to free him to integrate his own ego so he can consciously seek self-evolution. Since the client is typically unfree of unconscious influences and deterministic attitudes causing inconsistent behavior, the therapist must be quite gentle and empathetic. Encouragement and permissiveness, not criticism or exposure of hidden motives, are conducive to self-analysis and growth. To generate such an atmosphere, trust and concern are imperative in any encounter with the client. The therapist, therefore, must be a person of high quality, possessing an integrated and well-balanced personality, as well as a high degree of specialized training. Through nondirective therapy the practitioner aids the client to express and accept his feelings without fear, initiating a metamorphosis of self-image to a more congruent state. The therapist thus stimulates the client's positive, constructive tendencies, teaching him how to evaluate and solve his own problems.

Rogers' approach to human psychology is inductive rather than deductive. He thus avoids the behaviorists' "tunnel vision" and their deterministic conclusions about human nature. To him, the individual is more than the algebraic sum of his parts as in the approach of the Gestalt psychologists.

Despite vast acclaim, nondirective therapy has been accused of being quite ineffective in the treatment of deep emotional difficulties, albeit successful with milder neuroses. Rogerian influence has been nonetheless very strong. In increasing numbers, people are realizing that, as Rogers asserts, one *chooses* to be free and that this freedom is the key to individuality, creativity, and meaningful living.

Viktor Frankl: Logotherapy.   Viktor Frankl's views parallel those of Rogers in many areas. Logotherapy, as its name implies, is concerned with the patient's sense of the meaning of life. Frankl (1962) holds that the Will to Meaning is a primary function whose frustration leads to a different kind of neurosis: noogenic neurosis. Such neuroses involve value conflicts rather than drive or instinct conflicts. Since one's life mission is unique and one's values, goals, and meanings are personal, the therapist's goal is to pilot the client through his existential crisis toward growth, development, self-realization, and discovery of the meaning of life. To Frankl, such life meanings are of three types (with corresponding life styles): (1) active life—gains through creativity (doing); (2) passive life—gains through enjoyment of beauty (love, nature, culture); (3) restricted life—gains through suffering.

Love, however, is the ultimate goal, and inner values are enhanced through spiritual things. Love implies the full awareness of another being, which enables the individual to help actualize another. Sex becomes the vehicle for ultimate togetherness. Thus self-actualization is not the aim of human existence but rather a prerequisite for self-transcendence. Paraphrasing Kennedy, Frankl states that one should not ask what he expects from life, but rather what life expects from him. Sidestepping the abstract question of the Meaning of Life, Frankl establishes responsibility to life as his guiding principle.

Frankl's views on suffering, stemming from his own concentration camp experiences, are of great importance to his philosophy. Suffering is considered ennobling, not degrading. Actualized experiences are saved as a part of one's being, so that suffering becomes an achievement. Frankl accepts the existentialist view that suffering is part of life, but he agrees with Buddha that there is purpose in suffering. Ironically it is one's life purpose which upholds him in his suffering. Since one grows through adversity, suffering strengthens him in his purpose. Antithetically, a belief in the normality of happiness increases one's unhappiness, since such a state cannot be maintained: pleasure is a self-spoiling goal (actually a by-product rather than a legitimate goal). Similarly, fear causes that which is feared. In this instance, Frankl proposes "paradoxical intention" as the cure: intend what you fear in order to cure the fear and accomplish your goal. Furthermore, ignoring, ridiculing, or laughing at one's anticipatory anxiety and obsessive-compulsive or phobic conditions will alleviate one's neuroses.

Such neuroses tend to occlude one's full awareness of life and one's life task. The fundamental function of the logotherapist is to expose to the patient his own life meaning and mission. Frankl feels that cultural depersonalization and individual loss of values can be counteracted by emphasizing man's capability for self-determination and his inherent human dignity. Frankl decries the "Pan Determinism" of many educators and religious leaders but extols the potentially fulfilling aspects of their respective fields and institutions, begging them to fill the "existential vacuum." Conformity only impedes one's need to strive, which is requisite for psychological health. Since, as Fromm has asserted, Paradise is closed forever, Frankl focuses on the future—a future of fuller consciousness in which one overcomes one's own neuroses through fulfillment of the "search for meaning."

To Frankl, meaning is a primary motivational force (as pleasure is to Freud and power to Adler). Various surveys have substantiated the prevalence of the "Sunday neurosis" which leads to delinquency, suicide, alcoholism, and so forth, all apparently due to the lack of meaning in life. While Frankl gladly accepts the views of Freud and various existential psychologists, he places primary emphasis upon the patient's values. Thus, like Rogers, Frankl refrains from imposing value judgments on the patient. Rather, he utilizes methods such as "deathbed analysis," through which the patient can analyze present alternatives from a future perspective. With his goal established, the patient can face life's difficulties with confidence and determination.

Abraham Maslow: A Self-actualization Psychology. Maslow's eclectic approach to psychology led to the formation of his famous Hierarchy of Needs. In accord with Lloyd Morgan's canon, Maslow (1968) arranged needs (physiologic, safety, love and belonging, esteem, and self-actualization) in order of their motivational strength. Though these needs do overlap, one usually dominates. While lower order needs are initially dominant, satisfied needs no longer motivate. Thus, in an affluent society, most people are usually motivated only by higher order needs. Frustration of these needs, however, can result in need substitution. Similarly, neuroses may invoke lower order needs through unconscious motivation (control). Thus Maslow's theory tends to integrate the earlier theories of Freud, Adler, Fromm, and others into an inclusive whole. Significantly, Maslow chose to explore the nature of his highest order need, self-actualization. This need had been greatly neglected, especially by behavioral scientists mostly concerned with neuroses and other illnesses. Maslow, however, focuses on the healthy individual who in our society should come under the increasing influence of his self-actualization needs. It would seem that democracy and prosperity do not solve one's value problems; instead, they intensify them. The individual must transcend his old values and establish new ones. He must overcome his actuality/ potentiality discrepancy through the formation of *internal* values which can guide him toward self-fulfillment.

In researching the nature of this state and its inherent values, Maslow studied various creative individuals, including Lincoln, Einstein, Spinoza, and Schweitzer. He correlated their individual approaches to life, obtaining a psychological picture of the actualized individual. All such people perceive and accept reality, accept themselves and others, are highly spontaneous, and are problem-centered rather than self-centered. They are also relatively independent of their environments, have a need for privacy and detachment, identify with mankind, are creative, and have a well-developed sense of humor. Generally they tend to be nonconformist, have deep interpersonal relationships with others, and experience profound mystical states at times. Maslow termed the latter "Peak Experiences," which appeared to heighten the individual's creativity and self-integration. Interestingly, psychiatrist Richard Bucke (1974) conducted a similar study with similar results. Indeed, Bucke theorized a physical evolution of mankind beyond self-consciousness to a higher state that had already been reached by certain individuals.

Such theories closely agree with those of Rogers and May. Indeed, much of Maslow's theory coincides with that of Adler, Fromm, Taoism, and Zen Buddhism. Strangely, however, though peak experiences are therapeutic and have ennobling and beautifying effects on the character and on one's world-view, they are not always accepted by the individual and do not always counteract fear, hostility, and the misery of life.

Thus Maslow calls normality the "psychopathology of the average," decrying phoniness, illusion, and fear. To Maslow, self-actualization is the answer to man's uniqueness, which had been ignored by previous behavioral scientists. He extols its qualities of intuition, empathy, love, altruism, and profundity. Thus tragedy becomes therapeutic, as with May and Frankl, and the emphasis is on a dynamic future.

Maslow asserts that such a view is obtainable by all, that belief in a shepherd/sheep dichotomy of mankind is a self-fulfilling prophecy. Rather, man must be what he *can* be. One's capacities clamor to be used; otherwise they atrophy or become diseased. Thus, Maslow defines new diseases of the psyche—valuelessness and stunted growth—which resemble Frankl's existential frustration and noogenic neurosis. The quality of disease thus becomes a blocking of positive potential rather than an invasion of the negative. Indeed, Maslow depicts the healthy individual as an integration of various dichotomies (such as Jung's male/female archetypes), so that the unconscious becomes utilized by the individual in effecting the nonrational and intuitive gains of creativity.

While stressing a nondeterministic future for a self-determining mankind, Maslow nevertheless values a balance of spontaneity and control, though he asserts that our culture is presently unbalanced in favor of the latter. While self-fulfillment is achieved through gratification, not frustration, tolerance is necessary for empathy development. Such a frustration development should, however, be gradual, graded, and nontraumatic. Such challenges and failures are necessary for growth. One can only perceive at one's own level, but as lower order needs are satisfied, Deficiency Cognition should yield to Being Cognition, that of self-actualization. Being cognition is more accurate, mature, and authentic and less abstract, selfish, and fearful. While growth does involve pain, loneliness, separation, unfamiliarity, and even danger, it is ultimately exhilarating and strengthening. To Maslow, hostility is reactive, not instinctive, so that uncovering the self releases one's intrinsic positive value. Thus, in reaching one's "idiosyncratic potential," one achieves correct spontaneity and self-transcendence, becoming (in Buddhist terms) "one with the law."

Rollo May.   May (1953) wants to find a center of strength within man in order that he may achieve goals which can be depended upon at a time when very little is secure. To this end he has developed a theory of six ontologic processes in which each person (1) is centered within himself, (2) has a need to affirm and preserve his self-centeredness, (3) has the need (and possibility) to go out from his self-centeredness to participate with others, (4) has subjective awareness, (5) has a uniquely human self-consciousness, and (6) has the ability for self-confrontation to overcome illusions and rationalizations (May, 1969). This structural system is in agreement with those of many other psychologists, but May applies it to sociologic developments, as did Fromm with whom May greatly concurs. According to May, one's excursion from self-centeredness involves a dual risk: stagnation if one does not go far enough, and conformity if one goes too far. This results in two types of neuroses (as Maslow affirmed) and in two types of individuals—Riesman's inner-directed and outer-directed types. While one always needs more than just one's own self, the degree of involvement is important. In Freud's time, people did not go out far enough, but in the United States today, conformity is rampant. The resulting second type of neurosis requires a different therapy.

Such conformity results from our lack of direction due to the loss of instinct and tradition. Consequently, the United States is immersed in an Age of Emptiness filled with "hollow men." The dehumanizing effects of modern science and the anxiety of the nuclear threat exacerbate this situation. The conformist or "radar-directed person" has lost the meaning in his life by surrendering his own personal values and accepting those of society (collective emptiness). He has lost the meaning of the very terms describing his lost values: love, courage, freedom, responsibility, and integrity. Indeed, "comformity is the great destroyer of selfhood" (May, 1953). Thus man has thrown away his weapons against anxiety: courage, direction, and problem-solving ability. The conformist, therefore, "serves" time rather than utilizing it for his purposes; May, quoting Jung, asserts that a person is afraid of growing old to the extent that he is not living in the present. The conformist has become a prisoner within his own prison.

According to May, self-consciousness is the foundation of psychological freedom. Within limits, one *is* his choices. One can choose his values and ideals over pleasure or even death. Indeed, tragedy can prove cathartic, and death can provide impetus and meaning to life. Thus the tragedy of the present can provide the evolutionary impetus to mankind. Man's consciousness is still evolving. May entitles the next stage which goes beyond self-consciousness "creative consciousness"; Bucke (1974) called it "cosmic consciousness"and it is similar to Maslow's concept. May points out examples of it among the various saints. Interestingly, the ethical prophets railed against the conformist, conservative, religious institutions. To May, evolution is a process of differentiation. Thus his most fulfilled state is the epitome of individuation. Nevertheless, as with Maslow's description it is simultaneously self-transcendent.

As the ultimate eclectic, May absorbs much from other existential psychologists. He is, perhaps, more vehement in his reviling of present trends and is much more specific in his forays. He ascribes drug use, alcoholism, and religion used as an opiate to the effects of conformity in a rather unique manner, consistent with his overall view. Similary, his views of therapy go beyond those of his more wary colleagues. He espouses individualistic therapy; he asserts that to understand art (which accurately reflects psychological conditions), one must understand the artist; he states that therapists are born and not made though they can learn. May recognizes the validity of Iteration Theory, whereby different stimuli may elicit identical responses and identical stimuli may elicit different responses from individuals. Man can utilize his consciousness and freedom to break the S-R chain. May decries any technical dogma in the relationship between patient and therapist. Indeed, he accepts the validity of empathetic and telepathic communications between patient and therapist and believes in the treatment of drug addicts by people such as Dr. Ramirez who apply principles of existential psychology in the process.

Furthermore, May acclaims the forgotten value of positive conscience, art and literature, the wisdom of the unconscious, self-revelation through dreams, contemplation and meditation, solitude, and cooperation. He gives new meaning to love, courage, freedom, responsibility, and integrity and condemns overestimation of the value of work, material goods, and competition. He even goes so far as to praise Zen Buddhism for its emphasis on meditation and to call schizophrenia a "strategy of adaptation."

While debate still rages among the three schools, it is becoming apparent that the eclectic-inclusive approach of the humanists must triumph. The need for an inclusive, generalized theory of human psychology is increasing. Though existential psychology is founded largely upon conjecture and observation, scientific methods of evaluation are being developed. They appear to uphold what has been considered speculation by some. The new era, in summary, establishes man as a potentially unique, creative individualist who relies upon his own awareness and self-established values to guide him in his decisions. He has evolved his own life mission, which he consciously pursues, and he is progressing toward an even higher state wherein his self-actualization becomes self-transcendence.

WIDESPREAD INTEREST IN HUMAN BEHAVIOR

Much of this advancement has arisen out of clinical experience, particularly with sensitive individuals who are more quickly affected by conflict with society. Much has been written about the technocratic society, impersonal mechanistic organizations, and man's dehumanization (i.e., becoming a cog in a machine or a number on an IBM card). Job enlargement and job enrichment have been proposed as possible solutions to the problem of man's separation from the product of his labors, and Berle (1969) has noted the separation of ownership from control in large organizations. It has become an era of big business, big labor, and big government. Entrepreneurship has almost become a thing of the past. The individual feels a terrible loss of power over his own existence. Meanwhile, relative prosperity has enabled him to satisfy his basic needs, but society is not conducive to the satisfaction of his higher level needs. While some turn to hobbies or other extracurricular activities beyond the dissatisfying work situation, others are more vocal. The number and variety of influences upon these trends are phenomenal and increasing.

Literature

As May has stated, art and literature reflect the psychology of the day. While May mentioned such greats as Ibsen and Cezanne, many other lesser known writers and artists reveal similar insights. Times of stress appear to allow or encourage rebellion from preestablished norms and growth in previously discouraged areas. During and immediately following World War II, there occurred a revival of general interest in mysticism. The teachings at the time by scholars such as White (1943, 1945, 1948) not only were philosophical but also formed the foundation of recent developments in the behavioral sciences. White contends that material goods are transitory and unreal to man's nature. He emphasizes instead the meaning of life and honest relationships between people. His work gave impetus to a flood of publications which dealt with the same subject matter.

Periodicals as well as books explored the area of psychological self-knowledge. They came from many quarters: the editor of the prestigious *Electronic Design* wrote about the psychology of lying (Rostky, 1974) and *Datamation* published an article entitled "The Inverse Peter Principle." Likewise, television and motion pictures develop the same psychological themes, as witnessed by *The Three Faces of Eve* (a true case of schizophrenia), *Psycho, Shock Treatment*, and *Bob and Carol and Ted and Alice*. The latter movie, which begins with an encounter group session, was adapted as a weekly television series. There exists, therefore, a plethora of such influences on the public. It is no wonder that such terms as repression, ego, id, schizophrenia, paranoia, phobia, nymphomania, introversion, and sibling rivalry have become household words. While such influences are quite pervasive, many individuals have become more deeply involved with the search for themselves in a situation other than the formal therapeutic one. At a time when the patient indubitably learns much about psychology and about himself, nonpatients are seeking answers to psychological questions and learning also.

Involvement

Transcendental Meditation.   The followers of Maharishi Mahesh Yogi constitute one of the fastest growing groups in the United States. Although meditation itself is perhaps too ancient to be dated, Western interest, except at the scholarly level, is extremely recent. While there are many different techniques of meditation, they all have certain common characteristics. In fact, the very prevalence of meditation in virtually every mystical movement is probably its most important characteristic. Proponents of T.M. (transcendental meditation) are merely joining the ranks of mystical groups practicing various forms of meditation. Easterners such as Hindus and Buddhists have practiced meditation for centuries; some of these and related groups have made inroads into American society. The Zen Buddhists are of particular note in California and have made themselves felt through the works of Alan Watts and D. T. Suzuki. Less obviously, more Western-oriented groups, such as the Rosicrucian Order AMORC which takes much of its traditions from Ancient Egypt, instruct members in meditation methodology. Indeed, the A.R.E. (Association for Research and Enlightenment) not only espouses meditation for its members and society in general but also publishes its own books on this subject and made a movie called *Venture Inward*. Of course, the IMS (International Meditation Society) and the SIMS (Student's International Meditation Society) assert that T.M. is different from and superior to the other types of meditations such as that practiced by the IYI (Integral Yoga Institue), even though T.M. is yogic in origin. Nevertheless, the impact of meditation is greatly enhanced by this diversity of concerned and sometimes evangelistic societies.

The IMS/SIMS group (the proponents of T.M.) is perhaps the best known meditation group in that it identifies itself primarily, if not exclusively, with meditation and its ramifications, being typical in its external approach. While it is true that the IMS is uniquely scientific in its appeal, its true purposes involve strong mystical-developmental aspects. As with certain other basically Eastern approaches, IMS makes its initial appeal on a somewhat materialistic level. Evidence is presented as to the scientifically proven efficacy of T.M. in a physiologic sense. T.M. is shown to be extremely relaxing in terms of heart rate, lactic acid level, respiration rate, and skin resistance, much more so than sleep. Further, it is asserted that this increased rest will enhance one's energy level throughout the day. Thus it may appear to the casual observer that T.M. adherents are not searching for more meaning to their lives but are only trying to make life a little easier and more enjoyable. Not so, since the IMS is a die-hard proponent of Consciousness Expansion. It is stated that T.M. not only will improve one's vitality but also will change one's character and personality for the better, improving interpersonal relationships and simultaneously increasing one's awareness of the totality of life by enabling one to attain a higher state of consciousness.

In other words, the true underlying purpose of T.M. is to develop one to the highest possible state of existence—a truly metaphysical aim. Indeed, this is the stated aim of *all* mystical organizations and of nearly *all* religious organizations, although the terminology differs. To further this aim, the IMS teaches courses in the Science of Creative Intelligence, gives lectures, movies, residence courses, teacher training courses, and so forth. It has even established the MIU (Maharishi International University). Individuals taking the T.M. course come from all walks of life. Indeed, a short course in the effectiveness of T.M. for workers was recently given to extol its benefits to management. The contention is that employees who practice T.M. will become better workers and will achieve greater satisfaction from life.

The IMS contends that experiments have indicated that the 40 minutes per day T.M. experience does carry over into the rest of the day, and that follow-up tests have shown more adaptive behavior from T.M. practitioners under stress.

Many famous people have spoken at SIMS-sponsored symposia. Permission was granted to teach SCI in the Ethiopian school system. T.M. was also installed into the Eastchester, New York, school system. The State of Illinois House of Representatives passed a resolution encouraging T.M. in that state. It is obvious that the popularity of the new trend is on the rise.

Mystical Societies.   Mysticism, often grouped with magic by the general populace, is in reality the basis of nearly all religion. It may be defined as the study of cosmic law in order to determine why the universe exists and how an individual should conduct his life. Undoubtedly people have greatly varying answers to these questions, and the human need for these answers will persist indefinitely.

Mystical groups may be divided into formal and informal types. The informal types do have their own formalized teachings and a degree of religious bias, but they are not bodies of worship and do not have churches, though they may have rituals. They are generally open-membership groups, in contrast to the closed society of the formal groups. It is impossible to determine the number of small local groups, but there are a great many national and international societies. They range from the scientifically oriented borderline groups, such as the British Society for Psychical Research, to the religiously oriented Spiritual Frontiers Fellowship. Their common ground, however, lies in their quest for answers, for the truth. In order to determine how to act, man must have reference to some kind of moral or ethical code. Mysticism extends beyond this code to its origin. Only the "why" can tell us the value of the code. The true mystic wishes to study and explore the science of religious thought.

This has applicability to the work situation in that many workers might well be members of these societies, or larger religious bodies, which remain under the influence of the former groups. Many of these groups instruct individuals in self-development, and many utilize meditation in this regard. An important aspect of the teaching is the necessity of knowing oneself as a basis for developing to one's maximum potential. In this respect mysticism correlates well with many trends in Behavioral Science, and one could almost categorize Carl Rogers and Abraham Maslow as mystics. Although the idea may seem far-fetched, to a great many mystics and others, the ultimate reality of the Cosmic Force or God is internal, *not* external.

Workers inculcated with the idea of self-development are likely to exacerbate their demands for more meaningful work in the quest for greater individual fulfillment through the use of personal abilities and interests. The potential impact of such demands on the present state of American society and business is self-evident. Many people would dismiss such groups as small, ineffectual and fanatic minorities. Rationalizations of this sort are futile, since the membership tolls of such bodies are extensive and growing. Moreover, their membership consists to a great extent of intelligent, influential individuals most of whom are independent thinkers rather than conformists. Membership includes doctors, lawyers, and scientists as well as housewives, truck drivers, and assembly-line workers.

Religious Groups. While almost all religious organizations are mystical in origin, the so-called major religions have greatly departed from these roots. Having ignored mystification they are failing to answer sufficiently the questions asked so vehemently by today's youth. Thus there is a great exodus from the churches of the "old" religions and a proliferation of new more relevant beliefs. In Japan alone there are over 150 new religions, and naturally enough the United States also is in the forefront of these movements. Similar to the mystical societies, many of these new religions stress self-fulfillment and human obligation to one's fellows. Their members are dissatisfied with the old clichés. They want results. While to many the practices of the so-called "Jesus Freaks," "Hare Krishnas," and Zen Buddhists seem extreme and fanatical, some of these new religious groups represent an increasing collection of people in the United States and the world over. Both Bahai and Nicheren Shoshu of the United States, for instance, claim to be the fastest growing religions in this country. The Soka Gakkai of Japan (from which Nicheren Shoshu of the United States sprang) claims an amazing number of daily conversions. The entire organization has grown from virtually nothing in 1945 to well over 20 million today, with 100,000 to 200,000 members in the United States. Admittedly this represents only 0.1 percent of the American public at most, but the trend indicates *increasing* numbers.

These groups are highly evangelical. How can they attract new members? The promises are dualistic in nature: total self-fulfillment and world peace. These purposes are simultaneously identical and antithetical. Nicheren Shoshu's initial approach is purely materialistic. Self-development is featured in its most crass form. By chanting NAM-MYOHO-RENGE-KYO one can obtain almost any material benefit. One cannot, however, attain these benefits by chanting against another. There is more to this Buddhist sect than appears on the surface, however. What, after all, is the real purpose of chanting? How does it change the adherent? Daisaku Ikeda, President of the Soka Gakkai, the lay organization associated with an orthodox Buddhist sect, explains all by the term "human revolution." Strangely enough, these apparently total materialists eventually get to the point of human development. It is not the initial conspicuous material benefits that really matter, but rather the "inconspicuous" (psychological) benefits later on. The real object of the whole movement is enlightenment, which is the ultimate in self-development. It is an orthodox Buddhist doctrine. The Ceylonese sects, called Hinayana sects, aim for it, as well as many of the Japanese sects. Nicheren Shoshu, as a Mahayana sect, affirms that it is not enough to be enlightened to achieve Buddhahood; one must be a Bodhisattva and help others achieve it also. Kosenrufu is that state in which enough people have reached a high enough stage that world peace is achieved. Thus the most materialistic means are used to achieve a most idealistic end.

These dynamic groups, often referred to as militaristic by their critics, carry forth their influence into the place of work. These Buddhists sell their newspaper, *The World Tribune,* at places where people work, to employees and supervisors, as often as they do on the street. The membership is greatly varied, including, in places, computer programmers and trained psychologists. All are welcome, and no race, nationality, or background is discriminated against. Buddhism is almost nonsectarian, and atheists are welcome also. In fact, Buddhism is on the borderline between pure mysticism and religion. According to Huston Smith (1958), it is the one religion which does not have the basic qualities of religions.

Occultism.   Paralleling the upsurge of interest in mysticism and mystical religions is the reawakening of interest in the occult. While it is true that many of these areas, e.g., palmistry, magic, spiritualism, have little effect on the complex business organization, some, such as astrology, are actually being employed in business. Authors of books on astrology claim that it is being used to detect periods of poor telecommunications by major electronics corporations or to choose among applicants for jobs. The value of astrology is not in question here, but its use and increasing following must be considered if present trends continue. All too often, one's preconceptions veil the truth. The layman's view of astrology as deterministic, for instance, is incorrect, and any reasonable astrologer will assert that astrology depicts the situation into which one is plunged, but the outcome is determined by what one does with what is at hand. It must be remembered that Jung correlated astrologic views on marriage with those of psychology, and that William James was a respected psychologist as well as a parapsychologist. In relation to the work situation, it is not suggested that the manager should run out and immerse himself in the mystical and occult, but it is definitely desirable for him to be objective toward things with which he is unfamiliar and to be a little more informed about trends in which his employees might be involved.

The Drug Culture.   Another related trend developing in recent years is the use of drugs, and managers must also take cognizance of this. Admittedly the term "Drug Culture" as used here is misleading, since many of its members are not active or consistent drug users; they are, however, supporters (if only morally) of drug use, especially the use of marijuana.

Although some present-day mystics attempt to treat drug use as a poor relation in terms of mystical development or as a stepping stone in this regard, LSD in fact has been known to induce a state of mind characterized by a feeling of oneness with all the universe, of goodwill and love, very similar to that of mystical religious states. One experiment showed that theological students reported the most extraordinary religious experiences of their lives while attending Good Friday service after ingesting psilocybin. Even the term "drug abuse" directly implies that drugs can be beneficial if used properly. These benefits are not necessarily restricted to the treatment of alcoholics with LSD. While it is certainly true that drugs can be used merely as an escape mechanism, they can also be used to achieve a "religious experience or 'instant' creativity." Certain Indian cultures have used hallucinogens for this purpose for ages.

In the new age, however, drug use is becoming more widespread, according to Dr. Stanley F. Yolles, Director of the National Institute of Mental Health. It was found that acceptors of LSD perceived their problems as strictly internal, while rejectors perceived their problems as external. This concurs with the generally accepted mystical belief that one's problems are within oneself and not without. Buddhists call this relationship ESHO FUNI, oneness of self and environment, and state that to change one's life situation, one must change oneself. Many authorities, including nearly all mystics, have concluded that American life is too materialistic, aimed primarily toward the external environment, and not spiritual enough to be turned inward. It is doubtful that one could find many psychologists or behavioral scientists who would dispute this view.

Many adherents of the "drug culture," even those who take drugs for other reasons, take the external point of view. It must be remembered, however, that mystics also profess the need for service, the external application of internal expansion. While it is true that many users of drugs, especially narcotics, are merely retreating from their problems, many members have, indeed, rendered service to society through external application. As with drugs, the young have always been in the forefront of change, and they have also experimented with the idea of communal living. In addition, community action groups have increased drastically, as well as community cooperative markets. Co-ops, such as Stone Soup in Washington, D.C., offer healthy natural foods, e.g., wheat products made of unbleached flour, at very cheap prices. These results are achieved through bulk purchasing, simple packaging, self-service, and free *volunteer help*. Better publicized, however, are student strikes and public boycotts. Some criticism by students, such as at UCLA, has been applauded by the authorities. Effective or not, grape and lettuce boycotts have illustrated the involvement of the new culture. The basic values of society and resulting behavioral norms are being challenged and rejected. Interestingly enough, the older generation has also found these techniques to be effective; hence the rise in apartment co-ops and condominiums. Housewife picketing and boycotting of meats and church-sponsored food co-ops for elderly pensioners are all signs of new trends.

Sensitivity Training Groups. Carl Rogers (1970) has called sensitivity groups the most rapidly spreading *social* invention of our time. Such groups are of several different types: training groups (T-groups), which emphasize human relational skills; encounter groups, which emphasize personal growth and development; sensory awareness groups, which emphasize personal growth and development; sensory awareness groups, which emphasize physical awareness; creativity groups, which emphasize freedom and spontaneity; organizational development groups, which emphasize leadership skills; gestalt groups, which emphasize diagnosis and therapy; and synanons, which emphasize rehabilitation for drug addicts.

While T-groups evolved outside of the establishment, they are increasingly noticed by organizations. Schein and Bennis (see Hampton et al., 1973) have described the organizational approach to T-group meetings, which are interspersed with theory sessions, focused exercises, and informal discussions. Such groups, which previously stressed interpersonal skills, have recently incorporated some of the personal development aspects of encounter groups. Thus their benefits now include learning how to learn, more objective analysis of behavior, increased awareness of one's impact on others, acceptance of differences between individuals and their needs, intellectual understanding of behavior, and practice in the art of giving help.

Encounter groups rely more on the intensive group experience. They focus on the Rogerian ideals of self-understanding and congruence. Their unstructured nature causes a series of sequential processes to occur, resulting in a "journey to the center of self" (see Rogers, 1970). The climate of safety which develops from these processes includes mutual trust, freedom of expression, self-acceptance, increased risk-taking, and decreased defensiveness among the participants. Such an atmosphere fosters personal independence, openness, and integrity. It is presumed that changes in self-perception will eventually change behavior. Hopefully the participant will learn to comprehend and be himself (Rogers), seek his creative potential (Maslow), develop more meaning in his life (Frankl), and form his own individualistic value system (May). Indeed, these groups are by their very nature experiential/existential.

Naturally, these effects are an anathema to conformist, conservative groups, who are against change such as that initiated by encounter groups in their attempt to break old ties and habits. The critics base their arguments on the subsequent failure of some encounter group members, who slip back into old patterns of behavior, or who become estranged from their spouses because of their newly found congruence and development. Objectively speaking, the greatest danger of encounter groups lies in the attitude of the facilitator, who must refrain at all times from imposing control or specific goals upon the group members. Realizing the danger of too much manipulation, universities such as NYU, which awards an M.S. in sensitivity training, and the Center for Studies of the Person provide training for facilitators. The latter provides weekend groups at La Jolla where the facilitators in training can practice. Eight thousand volunteers participated in these practice sessions. These and similar groups are growing rapidly and are extending to business organizations, churches, and schools. The Louisville, Kentucky, school system has based its Project Transition, financed by the U.S. Office of Education, upon Rogerian ideal and encounter groups. Indeed, the U.S. Navy has conducted Racial Awareness Seminars as part of its Equal Employment Opportunity (EEO) program. These seminars involved a fusion of gestalt and synanon group techniques, which were used to reveal and counteract participants' prejudices and discrimination patterns. Participants who were part of a teacher training program would, on completion, train government managers in EEO principles and techniques.

While there are other possibilities in the future for lessening international and racial tensions and revamping the traditional educational system, sensitivity groups provide an answer to the "silent scream" of people at present. Whether left-wing extremism will destroy their influence or right-wing repression will in the future drive them underground is unknown, but sensitivity groups provide a unique and effective means of attaining personal involvement and growth today.

IMPLICATIONS

Modern behavioral science has reached a point at which the jigsaw puzzle of the human psyche is beginning to take shape. Man is finally starting to understand himself and others and thus his place in the universe. Man's values, therefore, are changing; he wants and expects more out of life. Since work is one of man's major endeavors, it must provide a continual opportunity for psychological and emotional growth, health, and development, and this is of increasing value to him. Management must recognize these changes and trends and develop appropriate strategies in order to cope with them. It has become obvious that corporate ownership has become a legal fiction and that the corporation is a social entity. Top management must integrate social responsibility into the corporate structure; otherwise, bright young people will not be attracted to it.

Youth is in the forefront in the concern for human values. Management must realize the interdependence of human values and productivity and the fragility and vulnerability of both. Instead of censuring student protests, executives should attempt to understand them. Management must comprehend the questioning of assumptions regarding values in reference to knowledge and wealth and its uneven distribution. Organizations, however, resist change, but management *must* adapt to the new values of the 1970s instead of clinging to those of the 1930s. They must introduce "participating democracy" into their institutions. Decisions can no longer be made exclusively "at the top." Corporations must recognize the evolving human needs of personal identity, community membership and responsibility, self-regulation, and creativity. Indeed, sophisticated management must be in the avant-garde and provide leadership for *tomorrow's* society, the so-called postindustrial society, which it helped to create.

BIBLIOGRAPHY

Athos, A. G.: Is the corporation next to fall? *Harvard Business Review*, Vol. 47, July–Aug., 1969, pp. 154–163.

Belkowitz, B.: *How To Be Your Own Best Friend*. New York: Random House, 1973.

Bell, D.: The corporation and society in the 1970's. *The Public Interest*, No. 29, Summer, 1971, pp. 5–32.

Berle, A. A.: *The Modern Corporation and Private Property*. New York : Harcourt, Brace Jovanovich, 1969.

Berne, E.: *Games People Play*. New York: Ballantine Books, 1964.

Branden, N.: *The Disowned Self*. Plainview, N.Y.: Nash Publishing, 1971.

Bro, H. H.: *High Play*. New York: Coward, McCann & Geoghegan, 1970.

Bucke, R. M.: *Cosmic Consciousness*. New York: Causeway Books, 1974.

Campbell, A.: Towards pinning down meditation. *Hospital Times*, May, 1970.

Cayce, E. A.: *A Search for God*. Vol. I. Virginia Beach: ARE Press, 1942.

Cayce, E. A.: *A Search for God*. Vol. II. Virginia Beach: ARE Press, 1950.

Cayce, H. L.: *Venture Inward*. New York: Harper & Row, 1964.

Cerminara, G.: *Insights for the Age of Aquarius*. Englewood Cliffs, N.J.: Prentice-Hall, 1973.

Chaplin, J. P., and Krawiec, T. S.: *Systems and Theories of Psychology*. New York: Holt, Rinehart, and Winston, 1968.

Culbert, S. A., and Elden, J. M.: An anatomy of activism for executives. *Harvard Business Review*, Nov.–Dec., 1970, pp. 131-142.

Das, Baba Ram: *Be Here Now*. New York: Crown Publishers, 1971.

Driscoll, F.: Transcendental meditation as a secondary school subject. *Phi Delta Kappan*, Vol. LIV, Dec., 1972, pp. 236–237.

Drotning, P.: Why nobody takes corporate responsibility seriously. *Business and Society Review*, No. 3, Autumn, 1972, pp. 68–72.

Frankl, V. E.: *Man's Search for Meaning: An Introduction to Logotherapy*. Boston: Beacon Press, 1962.

Frankl, V. E.: *Psychotherapy and Existentialism*. New York: Simon & Schuster, 1967.

Frankl, V. E.: *The Will to Meaning.* New York: The New American Library, 1969.

Gaddis, P. O.: Winning over indifferent youth. *Harvard Business Review,* Vol. 47, July-Aug., 1969, pp. 154–163.

Graham, E.: Transcendental trend. *Wall Street Journal,* August 31, 1972, p. 1.

Hall, C. S.: *A Primer of Freudian Psychology.* New York: The New American Library, 1954.

Hampton, D. R., Summer, C. E., and Webber, R. A.: *Organizational Behavior and the Practice of Management.* Glenview, Ill.: Scott, Foresman and Co., 1973.

Harris, T.: *I'm O.K.—You're O.K.* New York: Avon Books, 1973.

Hicks, H. G.: *The Management of Organizations.* New York: McGraw-Hill, 1972.

Hyde, M. O. (Ed.): *Mind Drugs.* New York: Pocket Books, 1971 (previously McGraw-Hill, 1968).

Jones, E.: *The Life and Work of Sigmund Freud.* Vol. I. London: Hogarth Press, Basic Books, 1953.

Kaam, A. von: Reprint from "Existential Psychology as a Comprehensive Theory of Personality." *Insight,* Vol. II, Spring, 1964, pp. 1–9.

Levine, P. H.: Transcendental meditation and the science of creative intelligence. *Phi Delta Kappan,* Vol. LIV, Dec., 1972, pp. 231–235.

MacDonald, J. D.: *The Damned.* New York: Fawcett World Library, 1952.

Mann, J.: *Encounter.* New York: Grossman Publishers, 1970.

Marx, M. H., and Hillix, W. A.: *Systems and Theories in Psychology.* New York: McGraw-Hill, 1963.

Maslow, A. H.: *Toward a Psychology of Being.* 2nd Ed. New York: Van Nostrand Reinhold Co., 1968.

May, R.: *Man's Search for Himself.* New York: W. W. Norton & Co., 1953.

May, R. (Ed.): *Existential Psychology.* New York: Random House, 1969.

Morgan, C. T.: *Introduction to Psychology.* New York: McGraw-Hill, 1961.

Murphy, G.: *Historical Introduction to Modern Psychology.* New York: Harcourt, Brace and Co., 1949.

Nonymous, A.: The inverse Peter Principle. *Datamation,* Vol. 20, Barrington, Ill.: Technical Publishing Inc., April, 1974.

NSA Quarterly, World Tribune Press, Santa Monica, California, Spring, 1973.

Olson, R. G.: *An Introduction to Existentialism.* New York: Dover Publications, 1962.

Perceiving Behaving Becoming. Association for Supervision and Curriculum Development, NEA, Washington, D. C., 1962.

Pothier, D.: Arguing with officer? Watch audience. The *Miami Herald,* April 25, 1974, p. 24-A.

Richards, M. D., and Nielander, W. A.: *Readings in Management.* Cincinnati, Ohio: South-Western Publishing Co., 1963.

Rogers, C. R.: *On Becoming a Person,* Boston: Houghton Mifflin Co., 1961.

Rogers, C. R.: *Client-centered Therapy.* Boston: Houghton Mifflin Co., 1965.

Rogers, C. R.: *Carl Rogers on Encounter Groups.* New York: Harper & Row, 1970.

Rostky, G.: We lie a lot. *Electronic Design,* April 26, 1974, p. 51.

Rubottom, A.: Transcendental meditation. *Yale Alumni Magazine,* Feb., 1972.

Scientific Research on Transcendental Meditation. Los Angeles: MIU Press, 1972.

Skinner, B. F.: *Beyond Freedom and Dignity.* New York: Alfred A. Knopf, 1971.

Smith, H.: *The Religions of Man.* New York: Harper Colophon Books, Harper & Row, 1958.

Smith, H.: Do drugs have religious importance? *The Journal of Philosophy,* Vol. LXI, Sept. 17, 1964.

Statistical Abstracts of the United States, Bureau of the Census, United States Department of Commerce, Washington, D. C.: Vol. 92, 1971; Vol. 93, 1972; Vol. 94, 1973.

Venture Inward, ARE Tape Library, Box 595, Virginia Beach, Virginia 23451, 1973.

Wallace, R. K., and Benson, H.: The physiology of meditation. *Scientific American,* Vol. 226, Feb., 1972.

White, S. E.: *Anchors to Windward.* Mt. Vernon, N.Y.: E. P. Dutton & Co., 1943.

White, S. E.: *Across the Unknown.* Mt. Vernon, N.Y.: E. P. Dutton & Co., 1945.

White, S. E.: *The Job of Living.* Mt. Vernon, N.Y.: E. P. Dutton & Co., 1948.

Woodworth, R. S.: *Contemporary Schools of Psychology.* New York: The Ronald Press, 1948.

CHAPTER
IV

EDUCATION AND VALUES

||||||||||||||||||||||||||||||||||||||||||||||||||||||||||||||||||||||||||||||||||||||||||||||||||||||||||||||||||||||||||||||||||||||||||||||||||||||

INTRODUCTION

Education, being one of society's classic institutions, has always been regarded as significant, desirable, and essential for civilization. In the United States, education has historically been regarded as an institution in which all the citizenry must take part—hence the growth and development of compulsory education, the purpose of which is to strengthen and perpetuate a democratic form of government. Critical importance has been attributed to an "informed" body of citizens who know and are willing to pass on the cherished values of the society so that it will endure.

All of these ideas are well known to those of us today who have gone through various schools, colleges, and universities. We have heard the preachings and teachings of countless pedants and read volumes of literature emphasizing the value of "a good education." Yet education has come under constant attack. It has been the subject of raging controversy, and its houses have been the battlegrounds for thousands of students over the past 15 years. There are many reasons for this, but certainly one of them is that institutions of learning are places where ideas collide and values clash. In our attempt to learn more, we learn how little we really know. We confront those who oppose us and those whom we oppose. We find out that education is a serious undertaking in the twentieth century, and that even though it is regarded as extremely important for getting ahead in the world, it often lags sadly behind what is really going on in society. Reconciling the cultural lag, responding to the needs of its students, and somehow maintaining itself as an institution as well as an enterprise are all problems facing educational organizations and salient issues of consideration for educational administrators and personnel throughout this country. The products of our schools, the students, go on to exert enormous pressures on many other institutions of society—indeed, on society itself.

The major corporations have felt and still seem to feel that the discontent, frustration, and turmoil experienced by other organizations (i.e., schools and churches) will never reach them. They ignore the possibility that the problems faced by campuses and churches will ever confront them, that traditional business values and authority can be challenged. It is time to look at the position and role of education in the United States today and to see what implications education has for those who feel that their corporate seats will never be heated. Education, almost by definition, deals with, teaches, challenges, and exposes values. Many of the values once held have changed and are changing, and the ramifications for industry could be monumental.

THE PRESENT POSITION OF EDUCATION

Grant (1972) offers some evidence that education is still a very basic and important force in the United States, it employs some 6.4 million people and operates on quite a large budget. Recent figures clearly demonstrate these facts: "total expenditure for public and non-public schools at all levels of education from kindergarten through the graduate school amounted to approximately $84.7 billion during the 1971–1972 school year" (Grant and Lind, 1974, p. 25). The total population of the United States was about 213,631,000 on July 1, 1975, indicating in global terms the reasonably high ratio of people employed in the field (Current Population Reports, 1975a).

The drive for education has continued to grow throughout the country's history until today only one state, Mississippi, does not have some form of compulsory education (The Columbia Encyclopedia, 1956, p. 592). The rise in educational experience over the last 50 years has been tremendous. For example, the 1940 census showed that three-fourths of the white population age 65 and over who would have graduated from high school prior to the turn of the century had gone no further than the eighth grade. Some 95 per cent of the nonwhite members of this group had completed eight years or less of formal schooling. Only 15 per cent of the whites had received some high school education, and of these a little more than half actually graduated from high school. Among the nonwhites, 3.5 per cent attended high school, but only about one-third of them ever graduated. About 15 per cent of all high school age students in 1900 actually graduated from high school. About 20 per cent of the white population and 10 per cent of the nonwhite population finished high school and entered college in 1935.

To show how education has grown even more dramatically in recent years, Withey et al. (1971, pp. 2, 3) indicate that the total number of college graduates in the United States in 1940 was less than the approximately 7.5 million students enrolled in 1971. In 1974 the number of persons under 35 enrolled in college was 8.8 million (Current Population Reports, 1975b, Table 1, p. 3). Almost half of all high school graduates now go on to college, and during the last three decades the number of colleges and universities has almost tripled. In 1940, only 38 per cent of the 25 to 29 year old population was made up of high school graduates. In 1969, about twice that proportion finished high school. The figure for the same age group in 1974 was 82 per cent (Current Population Reports, 1975b, Table 1, p. 15).

Among blacks, the rise in educational attainment has been even more pronounced. In 1940, only 12 per cent of all Negroes in the 25 to 29 year old age group had completed high school. By 1969, 56 per cent of this age group were high school graduates (Withey et al., 1971, pp. 2, 3). By 1974 the proportion had risen to 68.3 per cent (Current Population Reports, 1975b, Table 1, p. 15).

In 1940, 36 million of the 75 million people who constituted the adult population of the United States did not finish elementary school. Over 3 million adults were completely illiterate (Adams, 1940). At that time, the average male worker had about 8.7 years of schooling. However, by 1952 the average male worker had 10.4 years of schooling; by 1962, 12.1 years; by 1967, 12.3 years; and by 1974, 12.5 years. The U.S. Department of Labor stated that by March 1975 all *laborers* under the age of 25 had an educational attainment of 12.7 years. The 25 to 44 year old age group had reached 12.7 years of schooling in 1974 (Current Population Reports, 1974, Table 1, p. 15).

Table 4–1 illustrates the upsurge in white-collar positions since the turn of the century and indicates that the number of these jobs will continue to grow and permeate all sectors of the labor force.

TABLE 4–1

Occupational Group	1900	1947	1960	1975 (Est.)
White-collar workers	17.6*	34.9	43.1	48.5
Blue-collar workers	35.8	40.7	36.3	34.0
Service workers	9.0	10.4	12.5	13.8
Farm workers	37.6	14.0	8.1	3.2

* In millions.

We are also seeing that over a wide range of occupations job entry and upgrading are increasingly a matter of education. The relationship between educational achievement and occupational entry and promotion is demonstrated in Table 4–2 by the median years of schooling of workers within the major occupational groups.

TABLE 4–2.   Median Years of School Completed as of October 1952, March 1962, March 1967, and March 1974 by Major Occupational Groups*

Occupational Group	Median Years of Schooling			
	1952	1962	1967	1974
White-collar workers				
Professional and technical	16+	16.2	16.3	16.7
Managers and proprietors	12.2	12.5	12.7	13.3
Clerical workers	12.5	12.5	12.5	12.6
Sales personnel	12.3	12.5	12.5	13.3
Blue-collar workers				
Craftsmen and foremen	10.1	11.2	12.0	12.3
Semiskilled operatives	9.1	10.1	10.8	11.8
Laborers (exclusive of farm and mine)	8.3	8.9	9.5	10.3
Others				
Service workers	8.8	10.2	11.0	12.2
Farm workers	7.5	8.5	8.6	8.1

* The figures up to 1974 are taken from Grant (1972). For 1974 they are taken from Current Population Reports. *Population Characteristics.* "Educational Attainment in the U.S.: March 1973 and 1974." Series P–20, No. 274. Issued December, 1974 (Table 11, p. 53).

It is apparent that years of schooling are on the upswing, but more than that, the educational requirements for young people entering occupations today are greater than ever before. A high school diploma is now a prerequisite for most production worker positions, and a bachelor's degree, often in engineering, is required for foremen and supervisors. A college education has become the only ticket for entry into the professions, with graduate study often becoming a necessity for advancement. The technical, skilled, and semiprofessional occupations all demand substantial amounts of postsecondary education for entrance and retention as a result of the accelerating job upgrading process of technology. In summary, education has become a key to rewarding positions in business and in society.

Another aspect which must be considered when we discuss education as a basic societal force is the integral meshing of education and technology. Education is the means by which one can climb above the masses, realize new heights, and attain higher goals. Simultaneously, business is becoming more and more complex and specialized. To be able to perform many of today's jobs, a higher level of education is needed, particularly in jobs with prestige leading to high self-esteem. Technology and automation have been responsible for the phasing out of thousands of lower level work positions over the last four or five decades. Certainly a steady increase in job dislocation can be predicted as the nation accelerates into even more technological areas. This onset of technology makes education one of the primary requisites for the individual who plans to take control of his wants, desires, and lifestyle. Education is the means through which many people find the ability to secure the "good job" and all that goes with it.

Education's impact is still very real to the average American wage earner, especially if he or she has not attained a high school diploma or some exposure to higher education. A person's income is generally related to his educational attainment, as shown by Grant (1972). Of all employed men aged 24 to 64 without high school diplomas, 33 per cent had yearly incomes of less than $6000 in 1971. Only 13 per cent of this age group with diplomas had incomes below $6000 a year. Looking at it from another vantage point, only 6 per cent of the men without high school diplomas had yearly incomes over $15,000, while 22 per cent of the men with high school diplomas had yearly incomes over $15,000, and 43 per cent of those with college degrees were in the same category.

Figures for 1973 tell the same story more convincingly. Of all employed men aged 25 to 64 without high school diplomas, 46.5 per cent had yearly incomes of less than $6000. Only 19.9 per cent of this age category with diplomas had yearly incomes below $6000, while only 14.5 per cent of the men without high school diplomas had yearly incomes over $15,000. At the same time 49.2 per cent of the men with high school diplomas had yearly incomes over $15,000, and 37.6 per cent of those with college degrees were in the same income group (Current Population Reports, 1975c, Table 58, p. 122).

Also directly connected with these income figures is the type of work done by those who finish high school as compared with those who do not. In 1972 only 9 per cent of those without diplomas were working in professional, technical, or managerial positions. Of those with diplomas, 21 per cent held positions of this type, and college degree personnel were in control of about 80 per cent of the top white-collar jobs (The World Almanac and Book of Facts, 1974). Only 7.5 per cent of those people without high school diplomas were working in professional or managerial positions. Of those with the diploma aged 25 to 64, 37.2 per cent held positions of this type, while college degree personnel were occupying 79.7 per cent of this type of white-collar work (Current Population Reports, 1974).

Table 4-3 illustrates the important relationship between educational attainment and level of family income.

TABLE 4–3*

Education of Family Head	Mean Income in 1974	Total	Less than 3000	3000 to 4999	5000 to 7999	8000 to 9999	10,000 to 14,999	15,000 or more	Number of Cases	Median Income in 1974
0–7 Grades	8685	100	13.5	19.6	23.8	10.5	17.9	14.4	4764	7008
8 Grades	10,771	100	7.2	13.5	21.4	12.2	23.5	22.2	5065	9266
9–11 Grades	12,353	100	5.3	9.1	15.3	11.2	29.8	29.3	6771	11,359
12 Grades	14,557	100	2.9	4.6	10.5	10.3	31.2	40.6	15,353	13,464
College, no degree (completed 1–3 years)	16,417	100	2.3	3.9	8.3	8.1	27.6	49.9	5747	14,974
College, degree (completed 4 years)	20,100	100	2.0	2.5	5.0	5.1	20.7	64.7	4085	18,612
College, plus (completed 5 or more years)	23,155	100	0.9	1.8	3.9	4.1	17.6	71.7	3472	20,640

*Current Population Reports. *Consumer Income.* "Money Income in 1973 of Families and Persons in the U.S." Series P–60, No. 97. Issued January, 1975 (Table 58, p. 122).

There are some interesting aspects to the "importance of education" concept. Higher educated individuals are less subject to the risk of unemployment, illness, or the obsolescence of skills or experience. They have far more job opportunities and are better equipped, intellectually as well as motivationally, to utilize or take advantage of them (Withey et al., 1971). Moreover, they are more frequently able to plan ahead to provide for the future, and to profit from any special provisions they have made in the past.

Education has seen incredible growth both in terms of the levels of educational attainment of those in the working force and in terms of its influence as a major force in society. Higher levels of education are encouraged for all individuals who seek stable, rewarding, fulfilling employment. The importance of education in our technocratic culture is bolstered and perpetuated. We are now witnessing the creation of new environments and experiences by educational institutions and settings which inevitably will affect and influence the young people entering the working world.

EDUCATION AND ATTITUDES TOWARD WORK

Education has been directly associated with earning power and income, but there are other aspects of work which can be and are influenced by education. For example, job satisfaction correlates closely with education, as found in a survey conducted by Mueller (1969) of the University of Michigan. Results indicate that college degreed people found their jobs enjoyable in 89 per cent of cases, while subjects with up to 11 grades of schooling found it so in only 70 per cent of cases. One conclusion that can be drawn from this finding is that those with higher levels of education tend to feel more secure in their positions. Their jobs and places of employment provide room for growth and give a sense of personal worth. Owing to the benefits derived from higher education, working-class parents push education for their children and stress the importance of attaining levels of education higher than their own.

Higher education is also sought because it eliminates the common hazards of occupational life, such as unsatisfactory rates of pay, uncongenial workmates, and lack of control over working conditions. Sick leave, insurance plans, physically less demanding work, and more secure tenure are all typical of jobs involving higher education. Apart from job-related benefits, the general value of higher education cannot be disputed because of the influence it has on the individual as a whole.

The Worker and His Changing Values

Increased education has brought about changes. The younger generation and recent college graduates are coming forth with new philosophies concerning work, corporate loyalty, and lifestyles. This potential manpower is a force to be recognized and one which can have serious implications for the operations of the generally inflexible corporations.

Corporations most frequently view new college graduates as overambitious and unrealistic in their expectations about advancement and responsibilities. They are seen as too theoretical, idealistic, naive, immature, and inexperienced. Instead, the corporation wants the employee to possess the values and modes of behavior listed in Table 4–4.

TABLE 4–4.   The Right Values for Business*

1. Join only when convinced that the organization itself represents a form of discipline or art.
2. Accept the idea of hierarchy of power if based on intellect or talent.
3. Accept the use of power when it stems from ability and attainment that they can recognize.
4. Seek praise from superiors in power because they are respected.
5. Prefer life of action to life of reflection (there can be no compromise on this value).
6. Combine judgmental and analytical thinking.
7. Get the job done and see it through to the end.
8. Accept organizational realities.
9. Show loyalty and commitment by placing goals of the organization ahead of own.

* Condensed from Fielden (1961) and Schein (1964).

The question arises whether or not corporations today can find such individuals in view of the fact that more college graduates are challenging the values of business than in past years. More importantly, those young people who do enter the business world at present bring new philosophies with them which are often contradictory to those just mentioned and to the traditional stance of the enterprise. The results of some recent research demonstrate that newly graduated students express deep dissatisfaction with the desire for wealth and its status symbols and want to substitute a free and unrestricted life both on and off the job.

Education has effected a sense of awareness in young people, engendered a sense of curiosity and inquiry, and stressed theoretical and philosophical points of view often quite contrary to those of the real world of a business enterprise. Young graduates frequently have a bad image of "corporation life" and are aware of the dangers which corporations can pose for society, e.g., blind faith in executive leadership, economic recession, exploitation of consumers, price inflation, and inferior products. The "bad image" of business has been exposed, expounded, criticized, and analyzed, and a person with a higher level of education cannot avoid becoming immersed in the flood of critical documentaries. Furthermore, students today view the corporations as moral wastelands in which the work is dull and coercive. They are not anti-business as much as anti-management because they fear being managed or manipulated.

The so-called "new organization man" is concerned about self-fulfillment, a factor quite alien to the older generation of managers. According to Hanan (1971), the newer employee ranks his priorities as follows:

1. His own personal desires
2. His professional field or discipline
3. His social belonging
4. His corporate belonging

This new organization man seeks more equity in the corporation through stock options and more leadership control by serving on corporate committees. He is much more socially aware and concerned than businessmen of the past, and his social-mindedness encourages a dual career, one centered around his corporate responsibilities and the other centered around his community. Consequently, he expects the corporation to be more socially oriented and to participate in community developments, in minority education, and in the control of environmental pollution. It is a tall order, and business establishments throughout the country will have to prepare themselves to meet the new challenges, accept the new styles, and recognize the new concerns.

NEW FORCES IN EDUCATION

We are constantly reminded that "education is a lifelong process," that we never stop learning and must keep ourselves open to new ideas and developments. Nevertheless, there are still vast numbers of working people who sincerely feel that their learning days are over and that their responsibilities lie in the areas of paying the bills and raising families. This position is acceptable if we recognize that for decades schools propagated these responsibilities as the primary concerns for everyone. As noted earlier, many thousands of people never had opportunities for education beyond high school until recent years. The purpose of education until after World War II was, for the most part, to teach "the basics" so that people could get jobs and raise families. Things are changing drastically, however, and children today are being confronted and provided with some educational developments previously unknown: alternative school, Montessori schools, special career education centers and programs, "schools without walls" and so forth. These educational ventures will greatly change the nature of learning in this country and will have various implications for industry and commerce once these young students enter the labor force.

There is, of course, tremendous controversy in some sectors about the "new," "liberal," or "inquiry-oriented" approaches to education, decried by parents who are quite satisfied with their own scholastic achievements. Their children, however, are deeply antagonistic toward the old methods of teaching, as witnessed by their lack of pride in and respect for their schools and their teachers. These value changes remain unrecognized by the school authorities.

Many communities have heeded the cries of their youth and established alternatives to the old school system; to show their cynicism they have called the new establishments "alternative" schools. The objective of the new schools is to revitalize the child's interest in learning, to regenerate his desire to grow and to find direction in life. Traditional schools have been criticized for their neglect of these objectives and attacked by students and more enlightened teachers for imposing older value systems on a populace which no longer accepts them. In view of the developing trends, the repercussions for business enterprises are self-explanatory.

For years our schools were modeled after the industrialized, highly structured, mechanized work environments created by depression economics and a wartime production ethic. People were deeply concerned about security, and security required some semblance of order and discipline. Schools were seen as training grounds for the society's capitalistic work ethic, places where our youth was taught "respect" for authority, pride in work, and discipline. Bells rang, teachers spewed forth "knowledge" which was captured in three-ringed notebooks, and there was a proper time and place for everything. In a growing nation threatened by outside forces, e.g. communism, war, depression, foreign entanglements, every person had to share in the responsibility to make the country strong. Work was important and desirable in order to ward off "laziness," provide for the country's needs, and accrue an income that would ensure a comfortable standard of living. School philosophies have been and are still based on the premise that every student should be made a responsible and productive member of society. Productivity has always been one of our most treasured values, and the purpose of schools was to make sure that these values were transmitted and accepted.

As productivity increased, prosperity became the norm in millions of homes. Children saw their fathers working at less strenuous jobs with fewer hours of work and yet receiving more income. What money could buy, they had. United States capitalism during the sixties was enjoying the spoils of a victorious economy, and this was an era of unprecedented spiraling prosperity. Shades of depression, fear of recession, and thoughts of going back to the postwar days were fading rapidly. Values were changing along with this prosperity. American youth, however, could not realize or conceptualize the factors which had caused their parents' materialism. They were asking questions which the establishment could not always answer, such as why work, why commit your life to a company?

Schools began to be seen as outdated and unresponsive to their present needs, as ignoring recent conflicts and issues. Traditional subjects and discipline have become less and less acceptable to youth whose values have by now changed from those held by older generations. Responding to bells, following "authoritarian" policies, e.g. dress codes and rules of conduct, or following a prescribed curriculum have become increasingly intolerable. Young people have been pressing society's institutions to explain the need for many of the patterns they prescribed: Why classrooms? Why church on Sunday? Why conjugal families? Attacked from all sides, the schools have found themselves to be victims of a cultural lag, of values and patterns that in many cases have long been discarded by young people.

One response to this plea by students is the growth of alternative forms of education. As stated earlier, this concept poses some interesting questions, but it is nevertheless a very real force in education and one worthy of recognition. In the last seven or eight years, hundreds of "alternative schools" have emerged around the country—in people's homes, renovated warehouses, old one-room schoolhouses, and even parts of college campuses or industrial parks. Many programs have formed coalitions and are sharing resources, staff, and students. There is a definite thrust toward the nontraditional. Students are involved more in their own personal goal-setting; new methods are being tried and tested; little emphasis, if any, is placed on dress codes or appearance (hair length, beards, and so forth); bells do not dictate movement between classes; and policies are rarely established without student body consent. In many cases, students share the same decision-making/voting power as their teachers with regard to policy. As a result value conflicts are inevitable between the young and old. Students who have learned to question and who have been given a voice and influence in their learning environment will now come face to face with employers who have always looked upon their employees merely as subordinates.

There are signs that things are changing in the traditional establishments too. Some educational authorities are beginning to look within and are attempting to reorganize their approach to education in its wider ramifications. For example, the Pennsylvania Board of Education has stressed as a matter of policy that school children in that state should, in addition to ordinary school subjects, be taught self-esteem, citizenship, creativity, familiarity with vocational options, appreciation of human accomplishments, and adaptability to a changing world. However, scores on state-wide tests to measure these qualities reveal that suburban students are low on citizenship, exemplify a disrespect for authority, and possess easily shaken values. Such findings startle many middle-class, and upper middle-class adults who have been secure in the belief that their children were going to the "best" schools and developing into "productive citizens."

Neglect and rejection of traditional values, disgust with conventional schools, changing values regarding "important" elements in learning, and reassessment of the basic concepts of public education are the new forces to be reckoned with in the future.

Ralph Weill (1971) summarizes some personal views on adolescents and young adults which might lend further perspective to the whole issue of generation differences and change:

> Questioning of values and authority—parental values are not accepted on faith or by authority. Rejection of materialism; commitment to tolerance, this generation of students, compared to ours, is much more liberal in its attitudes on sex, drugs, or religion—there is no doubt that this generation of college students is more idealistic and more genuinely honest with regard to the need for righting the wrongs of society; challenging the older establishment, students with youthful vigor enjoy challenging the older generation's assumed virtues; the trend to one-way communication: we hear a great deal about the need for communication when the older generation [shows] unwillingness to listen—youth tends to listen, but youth tends to be intolerant of the other fellow's point of view. As far as the young are concerned, "listening" frequently means agreeing with their values. (pp. 246, 247)

These are characteristics which the current educational system has both produced and opposed, provided for and then rejected simultaneously. If educational institutions have been creating their own Armageddon, then it is little wonder that the industrial complex wants to hold so firmly to its values and its procedures. The forces are changing, and our strength may be determined by our willingness and capability to effectively use the forces which our youth are going to represent as they move on to work and live in our twentieth century world.

Modern Programs—Education and Business

Many of the potential problems, difficulties, and differences arising from increased education have been highlighted, but there is a positive side to the relationship between educational institutions and businesses. Many businesses and industries are aiding and contributing to the education of students through cooperatively planned programs.

The work-study or work experience approach to learning is one way that both business organizations and schools can mutually provide services for one another. While the students are still at school, they are usually paid a small stipend to enter the organizational environment, which provides a realistic setting away from the theory-textbook-classroom approach. Students are able to explore occupational settings and experiences while actually being involved with the machinery, equipment, materials, and procedures of the enterprise. This technique enhances vocational/occupational awareness and ostensibly acquaints young people with the values of business and vice versa.

In Newark, New Jersey, the Western Electric Company sponsors a partnership program in the public schools. In addition, it provides financial assistance and instructional equipment to be used as aids in the technical courses given.

In Dallas, Texas, the Skyline Center for Career Development was established through contract between the Dallas Independent School District and the RCA Corporation. The Skyline program is a career education program which is designed to increase rather than decrease vocational and career options. Whereas vocational school is basically a one-way street, students in the career education program avoid training for a specific skill (e.g., drill press operator) in order that they may be trained in broad fields encompassing that job. The course offerings range from horticulture and cosmetology to computer technology and aeronautics. Students may choose from 24 clusters, of which 12 were developed by the Dallas Independent School District's own staff, and 12 of which, described as technical fields, were developed and written by RCA Educational Systems. Some 200 businessmen donate their time and talents to Skyline students, overseeing operations and teaching classes. The entire program has been geared toward ensuring the following: (1) a curriculum relevant to the business community; (2) a curriculum relevant to each student's future needs; (3) the development of an interface between the school experience and the world of work; (4) the establishment of a validating procedure for course and program goals.

Both the Chrysler Corporation and Michigan Bell Telephone Company are involved in programs with the Detroit secondary schools. Work experience courses and instructional aid for students are cooperatively planned, designed, and implemented. These corporations offer remedial reading, tutoring, and professional counseling.

The Michigan Consolidated Gas Company offers a program for about 100 secondary students, while Campbell-Ewald Advertising Agency opens its doors to summer workers from surrounding schools.

The Aetna Life and Casualty Company aids a high school in Hartford, Connecticut, by assisting students who are involved in the making of their newspaper. In Philadelphia, this same company provides on-the-job training for a large adult manpower training program. In Chicago, the Ford Motor Company cooperates with the Chicago Board of Education by providing work experiences for high school students. The Prudential Life Insurance Company uses its employees to help students in a variety of subject areas.

The list could go on, but the point is that there are new training opportunities and corporate involvements developing each day. Both educators and businessmen have been experiencing deep concern over new employees, whose feelings of confusion and helplessness struck them forcibly. Education and business are attempting to work together to resolve the problems of disenchantment with traditional education, lack of knowledge of a working environment, and lack of any career consciousness on the part of students entering the labor force. As our society expands and increases in complexity, there will hopefully be many opportunities for growth in both the education and business sectors. However, the problems will be proportionately large and necessitate the mutual efforts of all society's institutions. No longer can parents, businessmen, or citizens rely on one institution to take care of certain issues to the neglect of others. The entanglements are many and require a broad, cooperative network of interacting forces if our society and its institutions are to progress. The synergism between the educational establishment and the business community must continue and proliferate if both sectors are to succeed. An openness and a sharing of resources, accommodations, and personnel among all components of society will have to evolve. The children of today are acquiring the values and habits which will intensify the demands upon the schools and businesses of tomorrow.

Open Education

American "culture" has become increasingly "open" or "permissive" in the last two decades, emphasizing individual freedom, choice, personal "happiness," self-fulfillment, and satisfaction in life. This "open" policy has permeated our institutions and influenced our thinking, our acting, and our value system. We now proceed to "open education"—a term used to describe an informal approach to learning characterized by certain philosophical principles and classroom practices.

Its purpose is to meet the unique needs of each child within the learning situation. The curriculum, the classroom organization, and the teacher's expectations for each child's achievement are tailored to the needs of the individual child rather than the child being molded to fit into the educational structure.

Open education in the United States since 1970 has made considerable progress. Numerous articles have been published since then concerning open education in England and Europe. In the United States the teacher's dissatisfaction with the traditional classroom and the civil rights movement as it regards the equalities of education form the main explanation for the advancement. The belief of open education is that a child learns by understanding the "process" of how he learns. The process itself is the most important element, while the product becomes secondary. Open education views the child as an active learner and not a passive subject. The learner explores and manipulates the world around him with a minimum of guidance and direction. This concept has become increasingly pronounced in schools since the implementation of the modes of instruction of many behavioral scientists. Such men as Carl Rogers and Abraham Maslow have had a significant impact on education for the past 10 to 15 years and are now being regarded more and more seriously in industry and commerce. These developments reflect in some ways an extension of the "learning by doing" theories of John Dewey earlier in the twentieth century.

There are some aspects of the "open education" technique which managers are well advised to learn in order to be better prepared to meet young employees of the future. Although competition is a way of life in American society, it is frowned upon in the open classroom. Teachers direct students toward activities which they can successfully perform, spontaneous discussions are enhanced, students are directed toward some conclusions, but the teacher never completely answers or gives a solution to the problem or issue at hand. The idea of inquiry has permeated the educational methodologies, and in practically all schools today open education has progressed from concept to practice. Discussing, voicing opinions, and reaching personal conclusions are all parts of the learning process. Should we really expect such behavior to discontinue once the child becomes an adult employee? Unfortunately, it is often being demanded by the leaders of our enterprises, and the incongruity between the experiences gained at school and those at work widens measurably.

Time in the open learning setting is flexible. There is no specific schedule by which groups and individuals proceed from one activity to another in prescribed fashion. The integrated day allows for more effective use of time because it is topically based, crossing subject lines intermittently. The approach is interdisciplinary, with the children being helped to understand the relationship between different subjects and given topics.

In the open school, multi-age groups and groups with different skills and different learning levels are found. There is no special rank or grade level, no designation of superiority, but rather a sharing of talents and ability. Children are allowed to move about physically in order to interact with their whole environment.

In the open classroom freedom of choice and thought are encouraged, and this provokes free expression of feeling and facilitates unrestricted interaction. The teacher's sole role is to find constructive ways of directing the pupils' emotional and intellectual growth and development, unlike the work situation in which both are often stifled by management.

Individual differences are the main focus in the open school, each child being granted the privilege of remaining unique and himself. The preservation of individuality is a policy which should be continued at work to enable every employee to use fully his talents and the abilities he possesses. In summary, Oswalt (1970) feels that adoption of the open classroom approach will produce the following:

1. Happy children who feel successful and confident.

2. Self-disciplined children who have a wholesome attitude toward life and learning.

3. Independent thinkers who are self-propelled and continuing learners.

4. Readers who are increasingly fluent and who enjoy reading for purpose and meaning.

5. Children who write because they need to record and convey thoughts.

6. Competent students able to cope with the fundamentals of math, science, and social studies concepts because they are necessary to answer important questions and to solve problems.

Certainly these concepts have potential significance for both schools and business environments. The more children experience open learning approaches, discovery techniques, and the freedom to choose or reject curricula, the more attitudes toward education will change. The focus of the concept of responsibility will change, with emphasis being on personal rather than corporate responsibility. Students as future employees are taking much more into their own hands when it comes to decisions that will affect their working lives.

College, Graduates, and Work

The impact of educational trends on the American system of enterprise cannot be underestimated. From elementary school through college innovations and alterations have been made with increased frequency and complexity. Even so, many colleges of so-called higher learning have lagged neglectfully behind in the purpose of preparing young adults for the world in which they are to live and work.

For years colleges were under little or no compulsion to evaluate their curricula and policies until suddenly they were faced with an eruption of student revolt and dissent. The Carnegie Commission on Higher Education (Dunham, 1970) conducted a study and made recommendations to the system of education based on its findings. The following list reveals some of their recommendations:

1. Shorten the length of time in formal education.
2. Provide more options.
3. Make educational opportunities more appropriate to life interests.
4. Make certain degrees more appropriate to the position to which they lead.
5. Make educational opportunities more available to more people.

The word "college" has meant four uninterrupted years of attendance at one institution removed from the diversity and pressure of ordinary life. It conjures up nostalgic memories of classroom lectures, fraternity and sorority parties, glee clubs, term papers, football weekends, and hundreds of other things unique to it. More recently, however, it has meant protests, extracurricular volunteer work, community involvement, and concerts with Pink Floyd or Joe Cocker.

Traditionalism is still evident on many college campuses, but the activities have changed somewhat. Sit-ins, political activism, and demonstrations are taking place. Fraternities and sororities still keep their traditions, but many students view them as threats to their individuality and avoid them. As a consequence, the social power of these organizations is gradually diminishing.

Colleges, being under pressure, are now offering credits and degrees to students who not only live off campus but also in many cases do not attend classes. Courses via television, correspondence courses through the mail, and independent study projects have taken on a new popularity, even among people outside of the college milieu. This has led to a university without walls, which allows students to earn a degree without participating in the formal setting of the college classroom. Courses are arranged and agreed upon by the student and his advisor, and the student may attend classes at any campus provided he fulfills the requirements agreed upon. The New York State Education Department has created an academic program in which a student is free to utilize the resources of the entire state university system—a combination of home study, off-campus work-study experiences, educational films and cassettes, and correspondence courses. Independent studies are quite acceptable.

The community college system, which has been burgeoning throughout the United States, represents another prominent approach to meeting the ever increasing demands of society. Its philosophy, as its name implies, is to meet the needs of the community, and this educational approach is described by Tatten (cited by Saxe, 1972) as follows:

> The learner has a part in determining "what" is important for him to know; "where" he learns what he needs to know is not important. It may be in a school house or somewhere else in the community. Only the learning can determine "when" learning experience can be most meaningful to him. For example, the second shift factory worker who needs to improve his skill in blueprint reading, either to hold his job or to qualify for another, must be able to have this learning experience after eleven o'clock at night. Community college encourages self-examination. It challenges all learners to know "why" they should engage in a particular learning activity. The fifth of the honest service is "who." Community college education puts the self at the head of the list of those who contribute to one's learning. (p. 215)

Colleges and businesses have also been concerned with demographic factors and school enrollments. Changes in family size and in birth and death rate patterns due to technology and medical advances, and societal change regarding early marriage have all affected school enrollments over the last four decades. The number of elementary schools has steadily decreased from 247,581 in 1930 to 81,249 in 1970 and to 80,172 in 1971. The number of secondary schools has increased from 27,188 in 1930 to 30,482 in 1970, but a decrease is noted for 1971 when the number dropped to 29,122. Higher educational institutions, however, show a dramatic increase from 1409 in 1930 to 2556 in 1971 and 2665 in 1973 (Statistical Abstracts, 1974).

More recently, the concern has been over decreasing enrollments in higher education as well. Many colleges have reported decreases in student population as high as 40 per cent between 1970 and 1974. Whether or not this trend is to continue remains a moot point. It seems extremely likely that as public education continues to wane as a relevant force, students will increasingly turn toward work-study programs, alternative forms of education, open education programs, "schools without walls," and the like. Unless educational institutions take more significant positions in terms of shaping and preparing young people for the future, rejection of the educational system at all levels by our youth is likely to continue.

In terms of employment opportunities for the qualified, some writers feel that things will sail along on an even keel once the balance in our economy is restored. Alexander (1972) stated that it has been possible in the United States to absorb all college graduates in recent years, and a study by the Bureau of Labor Statistics (BLS) predicts that until 1980 the supply of graduates will balance the demand for manpower. Unfortunately, we are seeing thousands of college graduates unsuccessfully seeking jobs or accepting jobs not commensurate with their training or interests. Many of them, under the circumstances, see little merit in a college education.

Concurrently, the concept of work has changed, and with the change comes a new challenge for business, industry, and management. Work for thousands of Americans is no longer just a vehicle toward financial security. It is now a daily activity which is intended to provide self-actualizing opportunities and growth-inspiring experiences for the individual. Personal satisfaction in a particular job may vary from person to person, but basically it is a function of one's needs. As these needs change or are perceived to change, the individual's attitudes toward work may also readily change.

According to Sykes (1971), "work for far too many has lost all meaning except as an effort to satisfy the material needs engendered by compulsive consumption; and the prediction for automation contains as many threats as promises" (p. 1). This may be true, but what happens when compulsive consumption wanes or is greatly satisfied by increased availability of products and the affluence to obtain them? What happens when the money earned at work has satisfied almost all of our material desires? Do we just quit? Certainly the job must represent something more than just the vehicle to material needs. Blood (1969) states that "the way a person evaluates work in general should be related to his attitudes toward his particular job. Someone who thinks that all work is an abomination to be undertaken only when all other strategies fail will likely be unhappy even in the most pleasant work situation. On the other hand, a person who feels that a personal satisfaction results only from self-sacrificing work or occupational achievement would likely derive some satisfaction even in a demanding menial position" (p. 456).

Since satisfaction with work is intertwined with individual needs and values, there is little merit in training programs as instituted by companies. This is a point made by Drucker (1965), who claims that graduates at present have ample schooling, but what they need most is meaningful employment. Corporations are therfore called upon to utilize the high standards of education of their future employees by offering them challenging work in order to make them valuable corporate personnel.

FUTURE IMPLICATIONS FOR EDUCATION AND BUSINESS

Madden (1972) states that "during the 1970's, the U.S. educational process will be subject to increasing scrutiny as the nation moves in search of a new, part-renaissance world view. The fiscal bind of education, the revolt of students, the bureaucracy of teaching, the technological revolution of electronics, the increasing isolation from society of the educational process, and the sheer increase in numbers and proportion of highly educated young will continue to call for instructive change" (p. 95). Further, it is claimed that by the year 2000 education will be broken down into various components, but predictions are that two basic categories will emerge—namely, education for the affluent elite and education for the poor. The elite will take part in a "liberal education" concomitant with their resources, leisure time, and wealth. The majority of the poor people will partake of vocational education in preparation for the productive needs of society. This sounds quite similar to ancient Greek philosophy—that is, separation of the population into distinct classes.

Others maintain that the schools in years to come will be much more explicitly concerned with values than they presently are. Instead of preparing our young people to take their places obediently on the production lines, schools will have to prepare them to become superior decision-makers. Through experiences and activities that enhance self-knowledge and self-awareness, schools will have to help students to clarify their own values and to understand the social consequences of their choices.

It is said that the educational system of the future will be required to provide more knowledge in less time to more people. As scientific discovery and technological change continue at a rapid pace, man's control over and mastery of his environment will be determined by his store of knowledge and the wisdom with which he uses it. His reservoir of knowledge is expanding tremendously, however, and it is increasingly difficult if not impossible to acquire or transmit all of the information that is needed. Therefore, educators will realize that their primary role as teachers is to guide students in the process of seeking, locating, and analyzing information.

George Steiner (1971) has forecast some other trends relative to education as well as business and society.

> In 1980 and beyond—much more of a learning society. Education will be continuous throughout the lives of most people. Individuals will have double and even triple careers.
>
> The rapid expansion and improvement in the educational system will continue.
>
> Degree credit enrollment in institutions of higher learning will reach 11 million in 1980 (four times the 1960 enrollment).
>
> Two-thirds of the 18–21 age group will be in college.
>
> Education by 1980 will represent an enormous market for business.
>
> Education expenditures—$38 billion in 1964–65—will grow to $90 billion by 1980.

> Managers in the future will take periodic retraining courses as do
> scientists and engineers today.
>
> Industry will experience a relative decline as the prime motivating
> force in society as government and educational institutions be-
> come more innovative in economic and social life. (p. 290)

New courses and curricula will be needed for our children and
adults in the future, and many programs have already become operative which will grow and acquire new impetus in the years ahead.
Some examples are family life education programs, educational seminars for expectant mothers along with hospital-sponsored clinics, day
care centers with work-study opportunities for secondary youth, job
placement programs with continuous follow-up for graduates of secondary schools, expanded studies at centrally located campus schools,
and community-based adult learning centers, offering everything from
high school equivalency training to Shakespearean drama. Other developments, cited by Alexander (1972), include the following:

> Promotions which would be directional and evaluative, rather than
> yearly hurdles to be scraped over.
>
> Special education and remedial work will cease to be. All educa-
> tion of all learners will be "special," whether it be for the gifted,
> handicapped, or "normal" students.
>
> Report cards, marks, "drop outs" will vanish as education is tai-
> lored to meet specific personal needs and prepare people to ac-
> complish mutual goals and achieve certain performances. (pp. 476,
> 477).

The implications for business are wide and challenging. Business
will have to diminish its interest in "final products" and become more
concerned with its effects on human beings.

The managerial aspect of this is that businesses will be forced to
use better in-service training methods and develop far better programs
outside the corporate structure. Top management will be responsible
for seeing that it can analyze and evaluate information properly and
that it can keep abreast of the "knowledge bank." It will also be responsible for providing an employment atmosphere that is stimulating, rewarding, inspiring, and productive.

It is hoped that business and education will mesh their ideologies
on a sound basis for the benefit of all. Industrial growth can no longer
be allowed to run rampant on an exploitative road to riches, and if
unchecked, young students may well halt such activity in the next few
years.

Business will have to wrestle with the profit motive and submit to
being not only profit-minded but also ecologically oriented and
community-minded. An extension of this theme is that business will

have to respond more favorably and positively to minority groups and women in the future, not in a token way but through actual deeds. As minorities and women make educational progress and gain expertise, industry will not be allowed to overlook their needs.

The forces of education are numerous, varied, and strong. Education in the homes, in neighborhood streets, or in formal institutions is affecting the values of all members of our society and hence, the lives they lead. As we learn to become more aware of ourselves and our potentials, more concerned about the community of man, and more involved in the jobs we undertake, the effects of our education will display themselves to others with whom we live and work. Maslow, Rogers, and other behavioral scientists have contended that man is always striving for greater and greater psychic satisfactions, and that as he achieves certain goals, he is motivated to strive for higher ones, always trying to reach a state of "self-actualizing" or "becoming." As more people desire self-actualization, our institutions will have to keep step or perish. Management must recognize man's needs and values and understand the momentous impact education can have on all people entering the working world. If management fails in this, the consequences could be grave indeed. However, if management heeds the call and discovers the interactions and relationships that can exist with educational institutions, the resultant synergy could be dynamic. The future alone will tell.

BIBLIOGRAPHY

Adams, T. R.: *The Worker's Road to Learning*. New York: George Grady Press, 1940.

Alexander, W. (Ed.): *The Changing High School Curriculum: Readings*. New York: Holt, Rinehart and Winston, 1972.

Appley, L.: *Management News* (AMA), June, 1966, p. 6.

Blitz, B.: *The Open Classroom: Making it Work*. Boston: Allyn & Bacon, 1973.

Blood, M. R.: Work values and job satisfaction. *Journal of Applied Psychology*, Vol. 62, 1969, pp. 456–459.

Bradley, G. E.: What businessmen need to know about the student left. *Harvard Business Review*, Vol. 46, Sept.–Oct., 1968, p. 60.

Brameld, T. (Ed.): *Workers' Education in the United States*. New York: Harper Brothers, 1941.

Chew, P. T.: Relax Charlie. *The National Observer*, February 19, 1972, pp. 1, 23.

The Columbia Encyclopedia. Morningside, New York: Columbia University Press, 1956.

Current Population Reports. *Population Characteristics*. "Educational Attainment in the U.S.: March 1973 and 1974." Series P–20, No. 274. Issued December, 1974.

Current Population Reports. *Population Estimates and Projections*. "Estimate of the Population of the U.S. to July 1, 1975." Series P–25, No. 608. Issued August, 1975a.

Current Population Reports. *Population Characteristics*. "School Enrollment—Social Class and Economic Characteristics of Students: October, 1974" (Advance Report). Series P–20, No. 278. Issued February, 1975b.

Current Population Reports. *Consumer Income*. "Money Income in 1973 of Families and Persons in the U.S." Series P–60, No. 97. Issued January, 1975c.

Dobbins, C. S.: Educational work. *Education Record*, Vol. LIV, Fall, 1973, p. 254.

Drucker, P. F.: Is business letting young people down? *Harvard Business Review*, Vol. 53, Nov.–Dec., 1965, pp. 49–55.

Dunham, E. A. (Ed.): *Colleges of the Forgotten Americans. A Profile of State Colleges and Regional Universities.* For the Carnegie Commission on Higher Education. New York: McGraw-Hill, 1970.

Fielden, J. S.: The right young people for business. *Harvard Business Review*, Vol. 39, March–April, 1961, pp. 76–83.

Fielden, J. S.: Today the campuses, tomorrow the corporations. *Business Horizons*, Vol. 13, June, 1970, pp. 13–20.

Gooding, J.: The accelerated generation moves into management. *Fortune*, Vol. 83, March, 1971, pp. 101–118.

Grant, W. V.: *Man, Education and Manpower.* Washington, D.C.: The American Association of School Administrators, 1970.

Grant, W. V.: Education's new scorecard. *American Education*, Vol. 8, Oct., 1972, pp. 4, 5.

Grant, W. V., and Lind, C. G.: Educational expenditure as a percentage of the gross national product. *Digest of Educational Statistics*, 1974.

Hanan, M.: Make way for the new organization man. *Harvard Business Review*, Vol. 49, July–Aug., 1971, pp. 128–131.

Madden, C. H.: Clash of culture: Management in an age of changing values. Washington, D. C.: National Planning Association, Oct., 1972.

Mueller, E.: *Technological Advances in an Expanding Economy.* Ann Arbor, Michigan: University of Michigan Institute for Social Research, 1969.

Oswalt, W. H.: *Understanding our Culture.* New York, Holt, Rinehart and Winston, 1970.

Rathbone, C. H.: *Open Education.* New York: Citation Press, 1971.

Saxe, R. W.: *Opening the Schools.* Berkeley, California: McCutchan Publishing Corporation, 1972.

Schein, E. H.: How to break in the college graduate. *Harvard Business Review*, Vol. 41, Nov.–Dec., 1964, pp. 68–76.

Statistical Abstracts of the United States, Bureau of the Census, United States Department of Commerce, Social and Economic Statistics Administration, Washington, D. C., 1074, p. 106.

Steiner, G. A.: *Business and Society.* New York: Random House, 1971.

Sykes, G. M.: *Social Problems in America.* Glenview, Illinois: Scott, Foresman and Co., 1971.

Weill, R. A.: College youth attitudes today. *School and Society*, Vol. XCIX, April, 1971, pp. 246, 247.

Withey, S. B., et al.: *A Degree and What Else: Correlates and Consequences of a College Education.* New York: McGraw-Hill, 1971.

The World Almanac and Book of Facts, 1974. New York: Newspaper Enterprise Association, 1973.

CHAPTER

V

AFFLUENCE AND VALUES

And what happens when an economy in search of a new purpose seriously begins to enter into the production of experiences that blur the distinction between the|vicarious and the non-vicarious, the simulated and the real? One of the definitions of sanity itself is the ability to tell the real from the unreal.

Alvin Toffler

ECONOMIC GROWTH

The struggle of the American worker for increased affluence generally can be traced to our first settlers. More specifically, the struggle seems to have started with the gains made after the medieval guild system was overthrown in the mid-nineteenth century. This major change gave workers great freedom in choosing which occupations they would follow; no longer would they be locked into a given trade or mode of earning a living.

During the next hundred years or so, worker progress toward increased wealth and freedom was painfully slow. Most of the attempts made during this time centered around the rights of workers to organize and bargain collectively. The American courts viewed with suspicion organizations composed of individuals who possessed no property and received no grant from a state. When workers sought to organize to promote their interests, they were charged with violating the old common law prohibition against forming a conspiracy to restrain trade. Despite these problems, worker organizations grew, disappearing in depression times and reappearing in response to the need felt by American workers for better protection of their wages and working conditions. In 1836 labor at the Philadelphia Naval Base won a ten-hour day from the government, and by 1840 this ten-hour day was extended to cover all government workers and did not entail reduction in wages. The next gain, while largely illusory, did represent some limited progress in that the court in 1842 held that worker combinations by themselves were lawful and that only the actions or pursuits of combinations could be considered unlawful, depending on the individual case.

The turning point for employees regarding increased wealth began in the 1920s. The American worker and the country as a whole were no longer engaged in a struggle for survival; instead, a new era was starting to form, an age of consumer demand. In short, America was entering into an age marked by high labor productivity, mass production, mass distribution, and mass consumption.

The twenties saw consumer demand for passenger cars increase from 1¾ million cars in 1917 to 4½ million in 1929. In addition, the increased demand for vacuum cleaners, refrigerators, and electrical appliances of all kinds fostered increased production. The manufacture of the automobile and electrical products accounted for a large part of the economic growth during the 1920s.

This tremendous growth in the twenties saw productivity per man-hour increase from 44.6 to 74.3, and manufacturing production rose 38 points, from a low of 20 in 1921 to a high of 58 in 1929. The gross national product, which reached 103.1 in 1929 (base 1947 = 100 per cent), came to an abrupt halt in 1927 when Americans checked their buying habits. The country plunged into years of depression and mass unemployment. Upon reflection, the halting of growth was more a lack of market elasticity than a change in buying habits. Throughout the twenties the market growth in consumer products was largely caused by the demand of the wealthy, and when this demand was satisfied, the great mass of Americans could not provide an increased market. The lack of a mass market in America developed from the income inequalities and lagging wage improvements. While worker productivity per man-hour increased 36 per cent between 1920 and 1929, per annum wages increased from $1424 in 1920 to $1489 in 1929.

The American worker and the country left the twenties and entered the thirties deep in a depression— a depression that lasted until 1933 when a reverse trend was started with the inauguration of President Roosevelt. This reversal was spurred by a host of social legislation, such as Social Security, the National Recovery Act, and the National Labor Relations Act. Despite these "pump priming" efforts, the gross national product in 1935 was only slightly more than half the

1929 level. In addition, a new recession in 1937–38 brought the recovery and growth aspects of the Roosevelt era to the edge of disaster.
Deficit spending for Social Security, the veterans' bonus bill, and the
stimulus of the Spanish Civil War gave rise to a temporary business
spurt, but permanency was lacking and the economy fell backward. By
1940 increased European armament orders helped the gross national
product to reach its 1929 level.

If the thirties can be categorized as a decade of planning, then the
forties must be described as a period of growth. The growth of the
forties began with America's entry into World War II. America became
the "arsenal of democracy," producing equipment for its own needs
and that of its allies the world over. In the 12 months after the attack on
Pearl Harbor, the production of the United States outstripped the
combined production power of all Axis countries. Indeed, the labor
force by 1945 had grown to 65 million workers, as compared with 56
million in 1940. More than 5 million women entered the labor force,
and they, together with the young and the retired, accounted for much
of this increase in our work force. In addition, the work week was
increased from 40 to 48 hours. The result of all this increased production was a doubled gross national product—from $99.7 billion in 1940
to $211.9 billion in 1945. True, some of this increase was due to war-
time production, $62 billion to be exact, but the foundation was laid for
a mass consumer economy. By 1950 the gross national product had
reached $284.8 billion, with much of our postwar productive capabil-
ity being diverted into a gigantic consumer boom. Unlike in the twenties, this boom remained strong and continued for years. By 1950
median family income had also gone up, reaching a new high of $3319
per year.

The fifties may be described as a decade of continuing growth and
the sixties as some sort of harvest. The gross national product of the
United States increased to $503.7 billion in 1960, as compared with
$284.8 billion in 1950. Family median income rose to $5620 per year,
an increase of $2301 in ten years. An "extension of the market" had
been established which would grow through a renewed population
increase, large government expenditures, and higher family spending
power. The gross national product by 1970 had reached $974.1 billion,
with family median income growing to $9867 per year. Both of these
achievements represented almost a doubling of the respective 1960
figures. In addition, two new factors which have a much greater effect
on worker affluence must be considered. The first, disposable personal
income, increased from $350 billion in 1960 to $687.8 billion in 1970.
Secondly, personal savings jumped from $17 billion in 1960 to $54.1
billion in 1970 and $60.5 billion in 1971.

• *Impact on Management.* This economic growth has admittedly
taken us quite far, but its effect on management may not have been so

clearly beneficial. Managers are being challenged from both sides: the firms constantly push for greater profits and increased expansion, while the workers continually ask for more pay, better fringe benefits, and increased recognition as human beings, not cogs in a machine. Many managers are finding these pressures quite enervating and are seriously questioning their ability to function.

Corporations are faced with a prospective dearth of managerial talent because of an inherent change in values of those who are likely to join their ranks. Miner (1973) reports a disinclination among students to enter managerial careers because they strongly disapprove of the competitive spirit demanded of them and are against the strictly authoritative structure of organizations. In seeking greater personal responsibility in the place of work, they shun managerial positions which to them have become highly unattractive.

According to McWilliams (1964), a reflection of the managers' dilemma is to be found squarely in the community at large, where a serious conflict exists between private goals and social purposes. He maintains that existing principles of production are unethical and that there is a lack of moral doctrine permeating the whole workplace. According to McWilliams, we have followed the Calvinistic doctrine religiously, worked hard, measured our success in terms of our material well-being, and viewed money as the root of all happiness. In effect, we have created an economy of abundance in which we produce just to produce. We strive for growth and production as if they were ends in themselves and have created a "society of wealth" and affluence in which success means the acquisition of more material possessions. The whole process soon becomes self-defeating in an affluent society, for possessions become a bore and consumption becomes insatiable. As a result we end up producing frustration and disillusion at an extremely high rate.

Just how management will deal with these problems is a serious concern. At this point in time it seems clear that changes will have to be made in certain areas of management. The impact of workers' demands for satisfactions beyond pay will be felt, and a clearer understanding of higher human needs will emerge as a managerial requisite to ensure industrial peace and possible corporate survival. Human needs and motivations are the crucial items, and the satisfaction of these needs and the quest for a self-fulfilling life have encouraged men to struggle for an economy of affluence.

Segall (1972) predicts that by 1982, the 25 to 44 year old age group will increase 36 per cent and that managers in corporations, governments, and other organizations will become much younger. This will involve not only a shift in age but also a shift in values. The young businessmen and budding managers of the 1970s did not experience the Great Depression or ration their way through World

War II. Perhaps this partially explains why Miner (1973) found young managers lacking in characteristics traditionally internalized by them. Furthermore, the affluence of young people is predicted to increase, so that by 1982 over 300,000 nonmarried young people will be earning over $50,000 each year, and over 700,000 single people will be earning over $25,000 annually. As we shall see, increasing affluence necessarily involves changing value systems.

INCREASING LEVELS OF AFFLUENCE

American affluence has been increasing steadily since World War II and has been responsible for a standard of living unknown to previous generations. A study by the U.S. Department of Commerce (1972) shows that in 1971 more than half of all families had incomes over $10,000 for the first time in history. Although inflation helped to keep purchasing power pretty much the same, the median income of the 53.3 million families in the United States was $10,290, or 4.2 per cent higher than that in 1970. Moreover, in 1971 more people were making between $15,000 and $24,999 annually than between $10,000 and $12,000 (Table 5–1). Linden (1972) reports that roughly 12 million families, or 25 per cent of all families in the United States, have incomes over $15,000 a year. His study of supernumerary income (i.e., income in excess of $15,000 a year which accrues to families and represents the available resources for optional spending after all essen-

TABLE 5–1. Median Income of U.S. Families in 1971

Number of Families (in millions)	Below $5000	$5000 to $6999	$7000 to $9999	$10,000 to $11,999	$12,000 to $14,999	$15,000 to $24,999	$25,000 and above
	9,800,000	6,000,000	9,900,000	6,686,000	7,674,000	10,399,000	2,841,000

Annual Income

tial outlays have been made for everyday living expenses) reveals that, in the ten-year period between 1962 and 1972, the number of families with that kind of purchasing power increased 2½ times, while by comparison family population grew only 15 per cent. The number of low-income persons dropped from 39.5 million to 25.6 million (a 35 per cent drop) between 1959 and 1971, while the total population grew by 29 million people (U.S. Department of Commerce, 1972). Such trends seem to be rather permanent. Linden predicts that the number of homes with incomes of less than $10,000 a year will decline from 26 million at present to 20 million by 1980, even though the population may increase substantially.

As affluence increases so that the average family of four is earning over $15,000 a year, some significant changes will take place. The annual income of $15,000 is now generally assumed to represent the amount of money required by a family of four to experience a comfortable living standard. Families in this income bracket can improve their living situations by purchasing the better quality, higher priced goods and services. As these families continually move up the income hierarchy, increase their supernumerary income, and have all the daily necessities of life abundantly available, it becomes possible for them to reach for luxuries and services they never before could acquire. Although the $15,000 cutoff is relatively arbitrary due to variations in living standards and expenses in different parts of the country, the Department of Labor indicates that it provides a fairly realistic criterion for supernumerary income. Families of four who have an excess of this amount can generally spend more according to their own will and discretion and enjoy the spending freedoms provided by their "surplus income pool" (Meissner, 1971). It is important to note that both the number of families with supernumerary income and the amount of supernumerary income itself (both in dollars and per cent of income) have increased steadily over the 15 years between 1955 and 1970, and projections indicate enormous increases again between 1970 and 1980 (Table 5–2).

Linden cites some reasons for this increase in supernumerary income which could possibly have implications for managers. Because of a generally higher education level, there has been a 50 per cent rise in the number of people in technical and professional positions, and these complex jobs require greater compensation, usually in the form of higher salaries. There has also been an increase in the number of multi-paycheck homes. In 1950, 40 per cent of all families had two or more workers; in 1960, 45 per cent of the families had two or more workers; and in 1970, 55 per cent of the families in the United States fit into this category and the number is growing. In addition, it appears as though a large proportion of the upper-income families which achieve this status do so through the efforts of two or more members.

TABLE 5-2. The Rise in Supernumerary Income: Before and After Taxes, 1955–1974

| | Families with Supernumerary Income | | Supernumerary Income (billions of dollars, except percent) | | | | |
| | | | Before Taxes | | After Taxes | | |
	Millions	Percent of All Families	Current Dollars	1974 Dollars	Current Dollars	1974 Dollars	Percent of Family Income
1955	2.1	5.0	10.4	19.1	8.0	14.7	4.2
1956	2.6	6.0	12.2	22.1	9.4	17.0	4.6
1957	2.4	5.4	11.5	20.2	8.8	15.4	4.2
1958	2.7	6.2	13.0	22.2	10.0	17.0	4.5
1959	3.4	7.5	16.7	28.2	12.8	21.6	5.4
1960	3.6	8.0	20.0	33.2	15.2	25.3	6.1
1961	4.4	9.4	24.3	40.0	18.6	30.7	7.1
1962	4.7	9.9	23.7	38.7	18.4	30.0	6.7
1963	5.2	11.0	25.0	40.2	19.4	31.2	6.7
1964	5.6	11.7	27.3	43.4	21.3	33.9	6.9
1965	6.0	12.3	34.1	53.3	26.7	41.7	8.1
1966	7.4	15.0	39.5	60.0	31.0	47.1	8.6
1967	7.8	15.5	41.5	61.3	32.8	48.4	8.6
1968	9.4	18.5	54.2	76.8	41.1	58.2	9.7
1969	10.3	20.0	67.5	90.8	51.1	68.7	11.1
1970	10.4	20.0	72.8	92.4	55.4	70.4	11.2
1971	10.9	20.5	79.2	96.5	60.2	73.3	11.3
1972	12.8	23.6	100.7	118.7	75.3	88.7	12.9
1973	12.9	23.5	110.3	122.5	81.0	89.9	12.6
1974p	12.1	21.8	112.1	112.1	82.6	82.6	12.0
1980	20.5	33.5	—	213.6	—	156.3	17.0

* From Linden, F.: The arithmetic of affluence: Supernumerary income updated. *Conference Board Record*, Vol. 12, 1975, p. 15.

As Linden's study indicated, beyond a certain point income becomes surplus income, or supernumerary income. Once life's basic necessities are taken care of, an excess is left to be used according to one's own desires. It is beyond this cutoff point (e.g., $15,000 a year for a family of four) that we begin to see people looking in other directions, placing less emphasis on monetary raises and rewards and turning to other rewards to be gained from work. Basic needs no longer preoccupy the worker, and he begins to explore other facets of life, chief among which is the use of leisure time.

THE GROWTH OF LEISURE

Time has become an extremely important commodity, as DeGrazia (in his film *Of Time, Work, and Leisure*, 1963) has stated. We sell time. We get paid for the amount of time we spend working and often take on additional work loads, extra jobs, or overtime responsibilities in order to increase our pay. However, with increases in salary from one full-time job, a worker might be able to give up extra work and pursue more personal or self-fulfilling goals as more free time becomes available, and the question of leisure then becomes paramount.

What actually is leisure? Some people might see it as time spent away from work or duty, free time to do as you want. DeGrazia defines it even more specifically; he sees leisure as freedom in a self-perfecting context. Leisure has no bounds or parameters of time; it is not merely "free time." Leisure is an aspect of life that deals with freedom to do what you want and is concerned not so much with what you do as with how you do it. Leisure can perfect a man even though work may make him rich. It is important to look at leisure as something far greater than free time.

The fact that there is no clear-cut definition of leisure only makes this whole area more troublesome to delineate. Aristotle defined leisure as being occupied in something desirable for its own sake and made a distinction between idleness and leisure. Thus anyone can have free time, but not everyone can have leisure.

How many people desire true leisure in terms of Aristotle's definition? The modern definition of leisure is generally understood as time off the job. Galbraith (1971) puts this succinctly:

> In a society of high and increasing affluence, there are three plausible tendencies as regards toil. As the production of goods comes to seem less urgent and as individuals are less urgently in need of income for the purchase of goods, they will work fewer hours or days in the week. Or they will work less hard. Or as a final possibility, it may be that fewer people will work all the time.

However, as we move into the future it becomes fairly obvious that leisure time represents an opportunity for many people to grow personally and to fulfill needs that are not met in the context of their jobs. What is management doing to satisfy psychological growth needs on the job itself? In other words, why can't personal development continue to occur over one's working life at the place of employment? If managers deprive workers of this opportunity, they do so at their own peril, because this very deprivation forces workers to seek more time away from work to the detriment of managerial goals.

Harris (1974) reports that Americans have made a lifetime gain of 50,000 hours of free time in the last 100 years. Our average work week has dropped from 53 hours to 40 hours, and it seems extremely likely that the work week will shorten even more. Citing a report by the American Institutes for Research (AIR), the Harris article states that (1) from 1960 to 1969 the average vacation time for full-time workers rose from 1.8 to 2.2 weeks per year; (2) two-thirds of all workers in the private sector of the economy now enjoy paid vacations; and (3) by 1985 most businesses will be operating on a 35-hour work week, the average vacation time will at least double, education for workers will rise sharply, and most women will be in the labor force. The implications of these projections could be staggering. We will have twice as much vacation time, and a major organizational restructuring around work and vacation schedules will take place. Many more women will leave home and family to find a niche in the business world, and young employees with far more education than their immediate supervisors will enter the work force. Moreover, more people will be earning over $15,000 per year, and they are likely to make management aware that affluence alone will not be able to satisfy them.

A study by Nanus and Adelman (1971) lends further credence to the AIR report. It makes the following predictions about events that will occur before 1980:

1. The average work week will be further reduced to 32 hours.

2. The distribution of the average scheduled work week will generally be five days, seven hours per day.

3. At least one-half of all employees will be experiencing 30-day work vacations each year.

4. At least one-half of all employees will have 15 scheduled holidays each year.

5. The average retirement age will be around 60 years of age, increasing the lifetime amount of nonworking hours for every employee.

6. The number of voluntary part-time workers in the labor force will double.

Leontiades (1973) expresses the view that although free time will increase, it is very possible that its usage may vary according to a person's particular status. Young and old workers as well as married women seem to prefer shorter hours, while married men who have professional and managerial positions and are between the ages of 25 and 44 work considerable overtime, with over 4 million holding second jobs. The author contends that leisure itself is influenced by evolving changes and varying conditions, such as age, income, economic environment, and amount of free time. For example, as we get wealthier, our motivations change. As we get above a certain level of income (around $15,000 a year), many of us show a decrease in materialistic yearnings and our income is increasingly exchanged for time off from work in order to satisfy the desire for a more comfortable life, which is "indefinitely expansible." DeGrazia (1963), however, argues that the American worker now uses up the hours gained from work in moonlighting, greater job travel time, increased schooling, and other activities far removed from real leisure, and that the new free time is often an illusion.

The changing trends being fostered by increasing affluence are affecting people on various socioeconomic and occupational levels differently. It may be vital for managers to realize that all workers do not share the same enthusiasm for working overtime, that young unmarried men and married women, for example, usually prefer more time off. These trends are going to present new kinds of motivational problems for traditional "pay raise only" kinds of management. Management's creativity and imagination will be challenged to come up with motivational strategies designed to make work meaningful in an affluent society. Changing values regarding work will make this a managerial imperative.

The Effect of Work Experiences on Use of Leisure Time

Meissner (1971) reports that all workplaces generally vary in such things as the discretion which workers can exercise, the kinds and amounts of constraints that are imposed by factory technology, opportunities for social interaction, and the degree of social isolation on the job. More importantly, these work conditions can be regarded as having a profound influence and effect on the lives of workers both on and off the job. Wilensky (1961) has said:

> Where the technical and social organization of work offers much freedom—e.g., discretion in methods, pace or schedule, and opportunities for frequent interaction with fellow workers who share common interests and values . . . then work attachments will be strong, work integrated with the rest of life, and ties to community and society solid. Conversely, if the task offers little workplace freedom . . . then work attachments will be weak, work sharply split from leisure, and ties to community and society uncertain. (p. 522)

The roles which people play in their daily lives are commonly centered around their jobs, their families, or other institutions of society (i.e., church and schools) which they perceive as offering some meaning and value to the quality of their existence. Meissner (1971) postulates three hypotheses regarding workers' behavior: the "compensation" hypothesis, the "carry-over" hypothesis, and the "no relation" hypothesis.

The "compensation" hypothesis suggests that people basically have uniform preferences for such things as discretion, expression, and interaction. They therefore make the necessary efforts to balance each of these dimensions in their activities away from work. In other words, what they do not find in their jobs they will seek in their free time. For example, workers who occupy jobs with very little discretion—working in confined spaces, being paced by production lines, or serving as part of an interdependent system of tasks with limited choices—may compensate for this deficit by engaging in free time activities that have many choices and require great amounts of discretion (e.g., chairperson on community committees, volunteer tutor, or Sunday School teacher). Or workers might make up for the instrumental constraints of their work (like specially organized mechanisms of production for a particular purpose) by performing more expressive leisure activities such as those found in religious functions or art. They compensate for social isolation by engaging in leisure time activities involving social interaction.

The "carry-over" hypothesis assumes that no activity will be carried out unless the necessary skills have been learned and are regularly practiced and reinforced. Since the workplace is the most common source of regularly practiced skills, these work skills are presumed to diminish or be discontinued if opportunities for maintaining them cease. Furthermore, the incidence of nonwork activities requiring these skills is also expected to diminish. People who work at jobs with little choice or discretion also participate in discretionary free time activities. Moreover, the degree of isolation in the workplace carries over into situations off the job.

The so-called "no relation" hypothesis suggests that a person acts independently in his various roles, being flexible and adapting to the specialized functions of each. Thus work and leisure are seen as separate from each other, and such things as freedom or discretion on the job would bear no relationship to a person's discretionary activities during free time.

To date, there does not seem to be any evidence in support of one hypothesis over another or any particular data revealing specific behavior patterns associated with any one specific dimension of work and leisure. In fact, the effects of the job on a person's life are often as obscure as the individual's personality. Meissner's study, however, does lend credence to the belief that people's lives can become, and frequently are, influenced by their work situations. With the evidence provided by studies like Meissner's, we can begin to see the importance of managerial policies. If employees occupy boring, nondiscretionary jobs, then perhaps they will desire greater amounts of free time in order to find more meaningful, expressive activities which are lacking in their work. If the "carry-over" hypothesis is valid, a vicious cycle could develop in which the lack of growth in job situations could diminish a person's ability to grow during free time, and this stagnant life style could in turn engender all kinds of motivational problems for management.

Whichever way these hypotheses operate, managers are faced with a humanistic responsibility. Making jobs meaningful and interesting will afford employees an interesting and meaningful life outside the job. If managers continue to employ people in dull, soul-destroying jobs, the consequences for wage earners and society as a whole are grave. Many companies today realize this important managerial responsibility and are working to provide more growth experiences in the workplace in the hope that they will carry over into personal life.

JOB DISSATISFACTION

Given the growth of free time and employee affluence, the American worker's values now seem to be shifting toward self-fulfillment and the desire for a more meaningful existence. The desires of employees seem to be consistent with Maslow's hierarchy-of-needs concept, which states that after safety-security needs have been satisfied, workers are motivated by affiliation, ego, and finally self-actualization needs.

Terkel (1975) stresses the point that most of the 85 million workers in this country, both blue-collar and white-collar, hold jobs which make them physically or mentally ill. They apparently crave meaningful work, work which will accord them respect and recognition and give them a sense of pride in a job well done. When such satisfactions are out of their reach, their frustration mounts and they retaliate with sabotage, absenteeism, and substandard production.

A large-scale study by the Department of Health, Education and Welfare (HEW, 1972) confirms the growing trend of job dissatisfaction. The study points to the increasingly familiar blue-collar blues of bored, alienated assembly line workers. It also details widespread white-collar woes and serious job dissatisfaction at all occupational levels, including managerial. The discontent of trapped, dehumanized workers, the study states, is creating low productivity, increasing absenteeism, high worker turnover rates, wildcat strikes, industrial sabotage, poor-quality products, and a reluctance by workers to give themselves to their tasks. Work-related problems are also contributing to a decline in physical and mental health and a decrease in the quality of family life. This growing unhappiness with work is also producing increased drug abuse, alcohol addiction, aggression, and a delinquency in the workplace and in the society at large. Indeed, a correlation was found between job dissatisfaction and heart disease, ulcers, rheumatism, and mental illness. The study suggests that the nation's health priorities are misdirected, with too much emphasis on medicine and not enough on preserving health through such measures as improving the quality of work.

The report finds that the cause of blue-collar blues stems from the fact that workers have rising expectations of status and occupational mobility but cannot meet these expectations under the operating system. It is also stated that society's young graduates have taken the lead in demanding better working conditions. Young people are more affluent and better educated than in the past and, having been brought up more freely than their parents, tend to reject the authoritarianism of the workplace. In short, while the expectations and values of American workers are changing, the nature of work has remained mostly static.

The authors pay special attention to one special group of young workers—namely, the new graduates—and alert management to the need to extend special care to these people because of their unique qualifications. Management is urged to place them in challenging jobs so that they can use their talents and abilities. Managers in charge of these young people should also undergo special training to equip them better in the task of helping young graduates adjust more easily to their new jobs. Managers are also called upon to avoid the financial and social costs incurred by keeping an unhappy workforce and to design and redesign jobs so that they give workers more responsibility and autonomy at work.

The American Management Association (see Tarnowieski, 1973) studied a special group of white-collar workers to demonstrate their changing values and the resulting dissatisfaction with their jobs. There was a lack of synchronization between the existing situation in the workplace and employees' new ideas about earning a living. A total of 2800 middle management employees acted as subjects of the study, and they showed a decided trend away from viewing success in terms of money or promotions, neither of which was considered a factor in job satisfaction.

Of particular interest are the study's findings concerning the individual's assessment of his relationship to his workplace. Ninety-three per cent of the middle-manager respondents agreed that organizations should take an active interest in career-related employee objectives, and a majority also agreed that business should play an active part in assisting employees to attain overall personal aspirations, not only aspirations connected with a career.

In addition, when middle managers were asked to select their most important considerations in changing a job, "enhanced occupational status and authority" were the most frequent responses. Increased money was a secondary consideration in contemplating a move. Increased free time, i.e., time off the job, was given as sufficient reason to change jobs, by only 1 out of 12 respondents. This study clearly points out the changing desires of middle management and the high level of job frustration and discontent.

All of the aforementioned studies clearly lend support to the need for recognition by management of changing worker values. The current worker needs at many occupational levels seem to go beyond financial gain to include rewards of a strictly psychological nature.

The concept behind Maslow's hierarchy-of-needs is not new, although the method of formulation may be. Since the beginning of the Industrial Revolution, intelligent men have found fault with assembly-line methods. Adam Smith, a strong advocate of specialization as a precondition of productive efficiency, once wrote that "the man whose whole life is spent in performing a few simple tasks becomes as stupid and ignorant as it is possible for a human creature to become." Karl Marx devoted a good deal of his theory to the negative psychological consequences of capitalism and the division of labor, which were seen as vehicles for human degradation and alienation.

There would seem to be clear intellectual continuity between the ideas of Smith, Marx, and Maslow and the results of more recent studies. Truell (1973) attempted to compare nonjob activities and motivation with job behavior. He observed that those who appeared to be duds on the job suddenly came alive after work. These individuals exhibited a great deal of energy, took on increased responsibilities, and became highly committed and involved in many projects away from work.

As a starting point, Truell considered only one of many satisfying nonjob activities. He selected bowling and chose to evaluate a typical bowler's experience. In doing so he found that a bowler:

1. *Decides what he is going to do.* When the time is his own, he doesn't have to do anything. Thus he has some say about how he will use his time and energy.

2. *Is personally involved in doing it.* He puts a part of himself into the task. His effort, when he rolls the ball down the alley, is individualistic; no one else does it for him.

3. *Does something that is neither too simple nor too difficult.* The bowling lanes have been designed so that it is possible for him to get a strike, knock down only some of the pins, or end up with a gutter

ball. It is possible to get a strike some of the time but difficult to do it every time. Thus he feels he has achieved something significant when he does bowl a good game.

4. *Receives prompt feedback on how he is doing.* The feedback is prompt and easy to interpret; it helps him improve his performance during the course of the game.

5. *Receives rewards and recognition that relate to his achievement.* The scoring system directly reflects the degree of accomplishment, so he can clearly see the relationship between what he does and what he receives in the form of reward and recognition.

6. *Receives support and encouragement.* Teammates give encouragement to him while he is bowling. In addition, if he feels help is needed, there are instructors available.

Giving this example, Truell suggests that industry should build into work six elements found in the game of bowling. The elicited procedures will then increase worker satisfaction and give stimulus to greater productivity.

SOME NEW DIRECTIONS IN WORK AND LEISURE PATTERNS

Over the past 10 to 15 years, rising affluence has had an increasingly greater impact on the complex organization in terms of motivating employees to demand more than just earning an income from work. Lawler and Porter (1963) reported that the more pay managers received, the less important the pay was for them. The study indicated that satisfaction with pay increased with the actual amount of pay, but beyond certain levels pay in itself became secondary in importance to various other needs.

Many companies are modifying their structures and policies in attempts to cope with the changing demands of workers. Work schedules are being modified, recreational activities on the job are growing, and vacation schedules are changing. For instance, Faught (1970) advocated a three-day workweek with a four-day "timewealth" period for leisure-time activities to further accommodate worker demands. Faught points out that leisure can revitalize man's instinctive nature for craftsmanship by providing him with the time to create or build things which he would never be able to do working at a full-time job. Moreover, the leisure-time period could develop within the worker a creative spirit that might be carried back into the job situation. Leontiades (1973) cited the need for leisure industries to become increasingly cognizant of changing consumer spending patterns, which reflect not only increased affluence but also an increased demand for more leisure-oriented activities (e.g., air travel, boating, skiing, car rental, and so forth). Segall (1972) noted that the continuing increase in the number of affluent people has created enormous demands on the leisure-related market, and the tremendous demand for leisure activities has encouraged businesses to respond with things like indoor swimming pools, skating rinks, sports stadiums, and even surfing lakes in the desert.

Exciting alternatives to traditional work schedules and conventional work sites have been burgeoning in response to employee demands for more meaningful work experiences. Faught suggests that the problem of the "rat race of megalopolis" can be solved by letting people make their homes in "hinterlurbia" and commute into the city for a three-day workweek. Under this system, leisure would become available in the four-day "timewealth" period in which men and women would have a greater opportunity for personal fulfillment and suffer less exposure to crime, pollution, and massive traffic congestion. They would be free, then, to spend more time with their families and take command of their lives.

Some companies, prompted by research findings, have done a lot to ameliorate as many dissatisfactions as possible and to date have made substantial investments in changing the traditional concept of the workplace. *Business Management* reports that the tremendous growth in industrial recreation is "transforming many modern industries into 'veritable status factories.' " In response to the demands for more enriching and enjoyable work environments, the National Industrial Recreation Association (NIRA) evolved to help sponsor companies in developing and running recreational programs. By 1970, approximately 60 million workers in 50,000 companies were participating in employee recreation programs of some sort. The report states that people "bloom in the enthusiasm generated by recreation." Furthermore, managers have become elated over soaring productivity coupled with decreasing costs and absentee rates as a result of these innovations. Although the corporation's annual tab might be expected to inflate, companies reveal that they actually save money by having healthy, happy workers who come to work regularly. It is noted that the unfit employee is a liability and that physically fit employees lead "happier, more productive, and livelier lives." A. Carl Kotchian, President of Lockheed Missiles and Space Company in Sunnyvale, California, summarizes the effect of these ventures: "The aim of recreation is to create an opportunity for people to achieve meaningful involvement with other people." The creation of large recreational facilities within industrial complexes and parks has represented a rejoinder by management to the human needs of their workers.

MEETING THE CHANGING NEEDS OF EMPLOYEES

As our lifestyles continually undergo alteration, they pull relentlessly at the networks which have held society's institutions together for decades. What is it that really lies beneath these value changes? What encourages people to change their values, look in other directions, and reject older ethics and behavior patterns in search of new ones? Theorists like Abraham Maslow, Douglas McGregor, and Clayton Alderfer explain that it is the satisfaction of human needs. Hampton, Summer, and Webber (1973) express the view that all people bring to the workplace a supply of energy, or potential to perform, as well as "various needs or motives which predispose them to release their energy or behave in particular ways—ways which seem to them likely to satisfy their needs" (p. 3). Managers should be cognizant of these human needs and try to develop ways to handle or satisfy them. As people's needs change, so does their behavior. They will not be motivated or predisposed to release energies in the same particular ways. The acquisition of wealth, the accumulation of material goods and services, and the subsequent demands for more free time, more leisure, more time away from the workplace, all reflect a change in the perceived needs of the populace. In many cases the channels do not exist to meet these changing needs. This is industry's imperative—to recognize these new needs and adjust or grow to help employees channel them, so that industry can thrive.

Almost all of society's work is done in large complex organizations, be they public or private; managers must convert their organizations into channels or vehicles through which man fulfills himself through his work *in an organizational context*. If man cannot release his energies at meaningful tasks in his work environment, he will, like the disenchanted spouse, stray and seek to do so elsewhere. The United States can little afford this at a time when productivity is poor, quality of products and services is shoddy, and pride in one's work is all but nonexistent.

The so-called "needs theorists" have become fairly well-known in recent years, and names like Maslow, Herzberg, and McClelland have found their way into managerial vocabularies. However, a more precise understanding of the interrelationships and contingencies between the work to be done, the personal needs involved, and the rewards to be given may rank as one of industry's most crucial priorities.

Maslow's hierarchy is a model for the ordering of human motivational needs. Man strives to satisfy various levels of needs, which Maslow ranks as (1) physiologic, (2) safety/security, (3) love/belongingness, (4) esteem, and (5) self-actualization. It is his contention that as the physical and more basic needs are met new needs become activated to motivate the individual. Furthermore—and this has implications for effective management—a satisfied need does not motivate. Trying to influence behavior or arouse an individual's motive power by offering more of what is already possessed in abundance is a fruitless endeavor. Managers should consider this if they are to provide motivating and enriching work situations for employees whose levels of affluence have taken them beyond the struggle for material and physiologic needs.

A study by Alderfer (1972) offers some meaningful extensions to Maslow's theory and is composed of only three basic categories (Table 5–3): (1) existence needs (pay, fringe benefits, working conditions, and physiologic drives); (2) relatedness needs (acceptance, understanding, mutual sharing of thoughts and feelings with family, friends, and co-workers, and so forth); and (3) growth needs (those which impel an individual to be creative or productive for himself and his environment—finding wholeness and fullness as a human being).

The ERG theory differs from Maslow's theory in several basic ways. First, Alderfer considers pay to be an existence need. "Pay, per se," he says, "cannot satisfy relatedness or growth needs, but could be part of a process which results in these needs being satisfied (p. 13). For example, a raise can communicate various things to a worker. It may communicate a feeling of esteem or a sense of accomplishment. It may also be a way of "keeping him quiet." Increased income (and affluence) may provide a greater opportunity to obtain autonomy, but it will only do so if the person is able to use his increased income to create an environmental setting that is conducive to his being independent or self-directive.

Second, Maslow implies that an individual must satisfy needs in a prescribed order of potency. Consequently, if a man is hungry, he cannot think about his love needs until his hunger needs are satisfied. Alderfer finds this categorization to be too presumptuous. The ERG theory expresses interrelationships between human needs and components within each need area that have universal implications (e.g., the interpersonal vs. self-confirmed esteem needs of both employees and management which encompass both relatedness and growth

TABLE 5–3.   A Comparison of the Needs
Categorization of Maslow and the ERG
Theory of Alderfer

Maslow's Basic Hierarchy of Needs (with additional breakdowns)	Alderfer's ERG Theory
Physiologic Safety/material	Existence
Safety/interpersonal Love/belongingness Esteem/interpersonal	Relatedness
Esteem/self-confirmed Self-actualization	Growth

needs). Although certain basic physiologic needs must always be satisfied, the ERG theory does not imply that they are prepotent in the motivation of behavior toward any other need. It is conceivable that needs overlap and interrelate. It is possible for someone to have his love and relatedness needs fairly well satisfied, even though his existence needs leave much to be desired and drive him to work unceasingly for more pay. Sometimes the satisfaction of some needs can compensate for deficiencies in other areas (i.e., better relatedness need satisfaction could possibly compensate for little existence need satisfaction).

The following propositions are basic to ERG theory and should have great relevance to the manager who has motivational concerns:

P1   The less existence needs are satisfied, the more they will be desired.

P2   The less relatedness needs are satisfied, the more existence needs will be desired.

P3   The more existence needs are satisfied, the more relatedness needs will be desired.

P4   The less relatedness needs are satisfied, the more they will be desired.

P5   The less growth needs are satisfied, the more relatedness needs will be desired.

P6   The more relatedness needs are satisfied, the more growth needs will be desired.

P7   The more growth needs are satisfied, the more they will be desired.

It can be seen that an order exists in terms of need desires and need satisfactions, but the lines of demarcation are rather obscure (i.e., "more" or "less" relationships). Tremendous sensitivity and effort on the part of management are necessary if it is to successfully weigh desires and satisfactions, integrate salaries, vacation time, and work schedules, and make the work a vehicle for the achievement of human potential.

The question remains, "Does affluence affect people's values so that they demand more humanistic and satisfying strategies and policies from their work organizations?" This is certainly true according to Maslow, Alderfer, and others. Herzberg (1968) stresses the greater importance of achievement, recognition, and responsibility as motivational factors when compared with salary, work conditions, and supervision in modern complex organizations. His arguments substantiate the need for management to enrich jobs, not just increase salaries. When the head of an average family of four begins to make more than $15,000 a year, he starts to desire more personal achievement and recognition.

This is not to imply that pay is not important. Lawler and Porter

(1963) report that needs most frequently said to be satisfied by pay (e.g., esteem and security) are actually better satisfied for higher-paid individuals. Higher-paid managers showed greater satisfaction in the esteem and autonomy need areas of their study. However, the study also showed that higher-paid managers reported no greater satisfaction in social and self-actualization need areas than did lower-paid managers at equivalent levels of management. Apparently pay cannot buy every higher-level need; higher pay becomes less important as existence needs become abundantly satisfied. Something else is needed to provide for these growth needs, whether it be more leisure time, flexible time schedules, or human sensitivity on the part of administrators.

Laughlin and Kedzie (1972) point out that various problems arise when managers are faced with human relations problems. Especially in recent years, managers have become increasingly perplexed by the kinds of problems brought to the workplace by the so-called "new breed" of employees. These younger people represent an influx of new, inexperienced manpower, and they bring to the work force college degrees, ideas, and values that are loaded with conflict potential for older workers and managers. If predictions by Segall (1972) are correct and young people raise their membership in the business world from 49 to 66 million people in the next eight to ten years, then management had better devise personal as well as organizational models for dealing with this potential source of disorder.

The traditional forms of causing employees to "move" and the old ways of sparking motivation just do not seem to be working well in our affluent society. Some typical comments coming from managers illustrate this point: "I promised him a good raise if he did better, but it did no good at all. . . . I simply can't communicate with him. . . . He doesn't understand. . . . Looks to me like he's more interested in social service than in making money." Faught suggests that young people are, in fact, having an enormous impact on changing our values about time and money. Managers tend to view these changes as indicative of serious motivational problems for the corporation in the future.

Why does the problem posed by young people represent such a critical dilemma for managers? Does it relate to our affluence? Is it true, as Lorber (1972) suggests, that traditional management has not encouraged employees to bring their personal needs to the job and so has neglected to prepare itself to deal with the situation that is now upon them? Or could it be that managers have not attempted to understand the goals or values of the "newer generation"? Laughlin and Kedzie (1972) assert that "goal-congruence" is essential to industrial success, but it requires that both organizational and individual goals be synchronized so that employee satisfaction can both contribute to and benefit from higher levels of productivity. It is further suggested that managers be trained in human relations. Maslow's hierarchy of needs, for example, could be used as a guide for understanding motivational patterns better and to point out how values may differ between managers and their subordinates—"new" values are not necessarily "bad," and vice versa. The motivational model of Vroom (1964) would also be helpful.

Maslow and Alderfer both provide valuable sources of motivational information. Simplistic answers to many managerial problems just do not exist. McWilliams (1964) points out that our society of abundance and affluence has produced a whole series of new dilemmas. Laughlin and Kedzie (1972) proffer the needs hierarchy as a useful management resource. For example, it might be valuable to understand that not everyone has the same security needs: $1000 may be sufficient for one man and $1 million not enough for another. The meeting of certain needs ties in closely with a person's values and the effects affluence can have on his behavior. For example, a person who grew up during the Great Depression, having struggled for years for financial stability, might never have passed beyond the security stage. That same person possibly worked a lifetime to build a better life for his children—and he succeeded. He removed the pressure and worry over monetary security from their lives by always providing the financial stability that he himself lacked. This, of course, released the children to focus on other interests and higher-level needs (social or ego needs, or self-actualization and self-esteem). In fact, "success," in supplying families with various material possessions through increased affluence, has contributed to the managerial dilemma of decreased employee motivation. The newer generation is criticized for not being primarily motivated by money, yet it has not necessarily had to consider money a "need" in the motivational sense. In many cases it has always been there, supporting Maslow's point that a gratified need is not a motivator. Management is not going to be able to coerce or threaten new employees by constantly manipulating a variable that has lost a great deal of impact on them.

Lorber (1972) cites an interesting example of an industry which has noted similar motivational problems within recent years. Apparently the insurance industry has been a training ground for inexperienced, highly motivated college graduates to become Electronic Data Processing (EDP) professionals. However, after several years, these budding young men leave the insurance industry for higher paying jobs elsewhere. "Job hopping" has become so prevalent that the insurance industry is seriously worried. Is it that the industry does not pay enough, or is it just that the EDP specialist is no longer loyal to his company? Lorber suggests that "job hopping" is not the problem but rather the symptom, revealing the failure of management to analyze and handle human relations problems. Traditional company policies have failed to provide managers with human relations training so that they may communicate, understand, and empathize with the men under their authority. Consequently, the young employees soon come to the conclusion that they will not be able to fulfill their personal needs within the constraints of the organization. They also realize that management can only fulfill monetary needs, not social and esteem needs. So when they reach the top salary their company allows, they take their further dollar demands and skills to another organization. This is a classic example of the second proposition by Alderfer, which states that "the less relatedness needs are satisfied, the more existence needs will be desired." These young men are blamed for disloyalty or for being lacking in the "good old" traditional values; in actuality, their needs for relatedness and growth are not being met, causing disillusionment, frustration, and a desire for more existence-level compensation. John J. Cusack, Assistant Senior Vice President of Personnel and Labor Relations for Health and Hospital Corporation, sums up the situation: "These kinds of workers really long for and need 'high mental wages'—those non-monetary rewards a worker gets from his job like satisfaction in the sense of accomplishment, fairness, respect and consideration of his feelings, and other fulfillments which cannot be measured in terms of dollars and cents." Such cases will increase in number as long as our levels of affluence increase to a point where income loses its motivating influence and workers seek to satisfy higher-level needs which management is hard pressed to provide.

CONCLUSIONS

The effects of our affluent way of life are being felt by management. The problems are intricate and complex, and the responsibility to change many of the archaic industrial practices has yet to be assumed by management. Some changes are being made, but as long as we strive for productivity, abundance, and affluence, we will be required to strive equally hard for the creation of channels through which the workers can grow and satisfy their higher-order needs. Many authors predict tremendous increases in supernumerary income; others warn of the consequences of increased demands for flexible scheduling and more leisure time. Still others indicate that our consumer appetites have been satiated by our abundance and affluence, leaving us with an old-fashioned, fast-sinking, scarcity-oriented work ethic that does not seem to answer the complex questions of today.

Management has the awesome task of sensitizing itself to the workers' changing values that are born out of affluence and carried to the workplace in search of implementation. How well management handles this challenge remains to be seen. Whether or not it heeds the words of Maslow, Herzberg, and Alderfer, and how well it stands up to the pressures imposed by an increasingly affluent society can only be judged with time. It seems reasonably sure, however, that the future for industry lies in more human approaches, in participative management, and in management which cultivates trust and fulfills nonmonetary needs.

BIBLIOGRAPHY

Alderfer, C. P.: *Existence, Relatedness and Growth: Human Needs in Organizational Settings.* New York: The Free Press, 1972.

DeGrazia, S.: *Of Time, Work, and Leisure.* New York: 20th Century Fund, 1963.

Faught, M. C.; This man wants to put the country on a three-day week. *Sales Management,* Vol. 104, 1970, p. 37.

Friedman, M.: *The Worlds of Existentialism,* New York: Random House, 1964.

Galbraith, J. K.: *The Affluent Society.* New York: New American Library, 1971.

Hampton, D. R., Summer, C. E., and Webber, R. A.: Individual motivation. In *Organizational Behavior and the Practice of Management.* Glenview, Ill.: Scott, Foresman and Co., 1973.

Harris, L. C.: Work and leisure. Putting it all together. *Manpower,* Vol. 6, 1974, p. 23.

Herzberg, F.: One more time: How do you motivate employees? *Harvard Business Review,* Vol. 46, 1968, p. 53.

HEW: Work in America. Senate Bill 3916, Worker Alienation Research and Assistance Act of 1972.

Laughlin, T. C., and Kedzie, D. P.: Motivating the new breed or Maslow revisited. *Best's Review: Life/Health Insurance Edition,* Vol. 73, 1972, p. 102.

Lawler, E. E., and Porter, L. W.: Perception regarding management compensation. *Industrial Relations,* Vol. 3, 1963, p. 49.

Leontiades, M.: The concept of leisure. *Conference Board Record,* Vol. 10, 1973, p. 26.

Linden, F.: The arithmetic of affluence: Supernumerary income updated. *Conference Board Record,* Vol. 12, 1975, p. 15.

Lorber, R. G.: EDP staff loyalty costs more than money. *Best's Review: Life/Health Insurance Edition,* Vol. 73, 1972, p. 105.

McWilliams, C.: Ethics in an affluent society. *Wilson Library Bulletin,* Vol. 38, 1964, p. 473.

Meissner, M.: The long arm of the job: A study of work and leisure. *Industrial Relations,* Vol. 10, 1971, p. 239.

Miner, J. B.: The real crunch in managerial manpower. *Harvard Business Review,* Vol. 51, 1973, p. 147.

Nanus, B., and Adelman, H. M.: Work and leisure. *Business Horizons,* Vol. 14, 1971, p. 7.

The new bloom and boom in corporate recreation, *Business Management,* Vol. 38, 1970, p. 36.

Segall, M.: Travel and leisure in the 70's. *S.A.M. Advanced Management Journal,* Vol. 37, 1972, p. 79.

Tarnowieski, D.: Middle manager's new values. *Personnel,* Vol. 50, Nov.–Dec., 1973, p. 47.

Terkel, S.: *Working.* New York: Avon Books, 1975.

Truell, G.: Where have all the achievers gone? *Personnel,* Vol. 50, Nov.–Dec., 1973, p. 36.

U.S. Department of Commerce: *Commerce Today,* Vol. 2, 1972, p. 20.

Vroom, V. H.: *Work and Motivation.* New York: John Wiley & Sons, 1964.

Wilensky, H.: Orderly careers and social participation. The impact of work history on social integration in the middle mass. *American Sociological Review,* Vol. 26, 1961, p. 522.

CHAPTER
VI

TECHNOLOGY AND VALUES

||||||||||||||||||||||||||||||||||||||||||||||||||||||||||||||||||||||||||||||||||||||||||||||||||||||||||||||||||||||||||||||||||||||||||||||||||||

INTRODUCTION

Important factors that aided the development of technology in the United States include the American willingness to innovate, the absence of fixed traditions, the entrepreneurial spirit, and the desire to get ahead through monetary rewards. When social scientists speak of technology, they open the door to a host of accompanying economic, social, and political factors. The assumption that technology is constant, regardless of time lags between the idea and the actuality or between invention and innovation, simply sidesteps the problems of technological change.

Technology is known to be the dynamic force in modern economics, and it is a factor that brings desirable change and increased wealth. Even though technology can be defined as a way of producing goods and services, it has several meanings. The first refers to the quality of combinations of men and machinery. An individual with a shovel has less technical capital equipment to do a job than does one with a steam shovel. Second, it refers to changes in the principles embodied in machines. A steam locomotive has a different type of power, as well as less power, than a diesel or electric locomotive. Third, technology refers to vintages of machines which may work on the same principle; later models may be far more effective than earlier ones. The most recent computer is a faster, more productive instrument than its predecessor.

Not many authors try to define the concept of technology; most are content to associate the term with the idea of scientific advancement. Ferkiss (1969) perhaps defines technology best:

> Technology is more than tool-making. . . . [It is] a self-conscious organized means of affecting the physical or social environment, capable of being objectified and transmitted to others, and effective largely independently of the subjective disposition or personal talents of those involved. (p. 37)

When considering technology, one has to include an entire system of production, such as mass production, quality control, and research and development methods.

Schumpeter, the dean of economists concerned with technology, defined technology in terms of innovations. It is a popular idea that science provides the theoretical principles which later are embodied in practical inventions and innovations. There is some truth to this, yet science and technology can pursue somewhat independent paths. Especially since World War II there has been an increasing effort to apply science to technology. New technology based on the research and development process is a tremendous force reshaping the lives of modern men.

In regard to business, two major questions arise:

1. How will technological change affect the worker?

2. How can the organizational structure best adapt to this change?

In this chapter, some answers to these questions will be given, and some conclusions will be drawn therefrom. When the term "technology" is used, it refers to the application of scientific knowledge in an attempt to solve some problem perceived by those making the application. Thus technology can be used in a mechanistic, manipulative manner or in a humanistic, growth situation.

TECHNOLOGY AND SOCIETY

In the next 25 years, man is going to experience change more radical than anything he has lived through before. While some conservatives and naturalists would prefer that we turn back the clock to a simpler time, this can never happen. Merely to support the number of people that will exist in the year 2000, gigantic strides will have to be made, as Casserly (1967) states:

> It is obvious that without enormous technological change, we can neither feed, house, nor clothe the vastly increased population of the twenty-first century. It is perhaps equally obvious that without

a vast mushrooming growth of population, we shall probably not exploit our technological potential to the fullest possible extent. (p. 20)

We will have to advance technologically more than we ever have before. Depending on the values we bring to this process, we may attain new glories or vanish. According to Deutsh (1967):

> The relationship of science and values implies a double question: the mutual interrelation of science and the general values of a civilization; and the relationship of a specific state of scientific knowledge to the pursuit of specific purposes or policies. The first of these problems, the general relationship of science and value, and thus to some extent of truth and goodness, leads us close to the heart of every civilization within which it is examined. If conceived as mutually incompatible, science and values may frustrate and destroy each other, dragging their civilization towards stagnation or decline. As a mutually productive and creative partnership, science and values may succeed in strengthening each other's powers in a self-enhancing pattern of growth. (p. 37)

There have been periods in which rapid technological progress was accompanied by full employment, others in which a lack of innovation paralleled high unemployment, and still others characterized by the reverse of both of these situations. Increasing concern over the consequences of automation is based on the incorrect premise that it will lead to widespread unemployment; the evidence for this is still inconclusive. It is now a fact that technological progress, with or without automation, contributes to the creation of more jobs and higher living standards for workers. When labor-saving machinery is introduced in an operation, the resulting job dislocations may initially lead to a decline in employment. However, the continual growth in demand for the goods and services of the economy should restore the level of employment in the long run. Our new "industrial revolution" has been changing the composition of the labor force, causing special employment problems with respect to certain groups of employees as a result. Nevertheless, certain situations reveal that unemployment can occur due to structural transformation and to the introduction of new machinery.

Many distressed communities are located in the older centers of manufacturing, some of which have lost their earlier locational advantages. Several factors may have accounted for this: (1) the rise of new products and markets elsewhere; (2) depletion of the natural resources of an area; (3) population movements; (4) the changing structure of freight rates; (5) shifts in forms of transportation; and (6) the emergence of new technology. The areas most affected are those formerly dominated by a single industry that has declined or relocated.

Despite this unfortunate fact, technological improvement can re-store a depressed community with some promise of continuing job opportunities. If such improvements are not made, the plants will fall further behind the newer and more efficient operations in the industry elsewhere. Competition would eventually force the outmoded plants to shut down.

There is no question that, in interacting, both technology and society will undergo change in a cyclical-reactive fashion. Indeed, technological and cultural modification may be viewed as part of the same process, one of growing into a new cultural/technological relationship.

Technology admittedly has given us undeniable benefits. Bro-nowski (1972) states:

> What we have done, and should be proud to own, is to make the benefits of technology (in the sense of a high standard of health, convenience, privacy, and information) as much a human right as life and liberty. . . . With the step from privilege to everyday use, technology has become a moral and not a material demand; it is a visible expression of the drive for social justice. (p. 206)

It is now relatively easier to acquire the things that make life pleasant; in a very real sense, increased applications of technology have resulted in greater equality for the heretofore underprivileged.

Technology today tends not only to man's physical needs but also to his emotional needs. For instance, Slack and Slack (1974) report the development of a prototype psychotherapeutic computer based upon the premise that talk has a therapeutic value. The computer is modeled after a human analyst in the questions it asks; it stores the answers and follows up on problems indicated by the interviewee. In general, the subject is encouraged to talk. The experimenters found that subjects were willing to accept the machine as a listener.

> In sum, the large majority of our 32 subjects preferred to talk to human interviewers. But some did prefer talking to the computer, and almost all were willing to discuss intimate problems with it . . . [The computer] is programmed to treat each person as a unique individual, rather than just part of a mass audience. It lets everybody talk back to it, and it gives people the last word, which is much healthier than talking back to your TV set. (pp. 63, 64)

If the computer can succeed at present as an analyst, there is no limit to what can be achieved by the twenty-first century in the way of technology. This fact unfortunately lends special bitterness to the products of its abuse, as Bronowski (1972) points out:

> Every civilization has been grounded on technology; what makes ours unique is that for the first time we believe that every man is

entitled to all its benefits. That gives a special moral force to the
protest, a sense of revulsion in the face of abuse, when young men
see it used . . . in war. (p. 207)

While the application of technology to war instead of peace is perhaps
the most outstanding example of technological abuse today, there are
other less dramatic social costs involved in maintaining a high-level
technology. The increasing death toll due to automobile accidents,
lung cancer from asbestos inhalation, and emphysema and other lung
disorders from smog in our cities are just a few examples of this kind of
cost.

Our naive trust in technology has caused us to neglect crucial
social priorities, and this neglect will determine the structure of society for decades to come. We may have to pay an ever-increasing price
in the future for our present blunders. Any evaluation of technological
advances must also consider the resulting destruction and pollution of
natural resources, the alarming amount of dehumanization introduced
into our daily lives, and the rising amounts of frustration and violence
among the people who must cope with this disjointed new society. In
many cases the needs of men and the needs of technology may prove
to be irreconcilable.

Computer Technology.   Life with the computer is bound to be
different, but whether it will also be better depends on our ability to
anticipate and plan. It should be evident that in this day of nuclear
armaments, what may be technologically feasible may not be socially
desirable. The same qualities that make the computer an advantage to
the operation of the organization also render it a potential threat to the
privacy of the individual and his self-identity. The same is true for the
H-bomb, which is an effective deterrent for war while also being a
menace to the safety and security of humanity.

There has been a lot of discussion recently concerning the problems associated with increasing office automation and the resulting
construction of large, central files with the possibilities of emerging
impersonality, clandestine invasions of privacy by unscrupulous persons, intrusions by agents of the government, and criminal subversion
for illegal gain. These have received considerable attention and pub-
licity. We should note that the computer is not bad in itself, just as
atomic energy is not intrinsically bad. The resulting evils will depend
on how we use the computer and how we choose to use it in our
organizational structures.

The use of computers in education, as well as improving the average level of teaching, will also give the authorities a powerful influence over the minds of the future electors. The use of computers in
medicine could have significant consequences for improving general
health and for increasing longevity, but it will also provide a very
powerful means of remolding the human being.

In the United States in 1966 and 1968, Senate and Congressional subcommittees looked into the idea of establishing a Government Data Center which would bring together information already recorded on computer tapes held in various government agencies. We should try to realize that the proposers had no sinister motive. All they sought was an improvement of office efficiency, but the results are incalculable.

There has been a growth of private data centers, and in some ways these are considered more dangerous than government centers. A man seeking credit might be unable to avoid giving personal data which he would prefer not to. By having all information about an individual in a single file, users would tend to see more than they really needed for their purposes. The computer in this respect is a thing that never forgets and unforgivingly neglects our capacity for change and reform. Corrupted computer staff members could allow information to be removed or false entries made. There exist possibilities for blackmail that could attract the well-organized crime element.

What may worry people is the loss of privacy or the risk of inequity deriving from the improper use of information. These data may not even be known to the individual concerned, offering him no chance to challenge them as inaccurate. To be just and equitable, the individual needs to be aware of what alleged facts are being weighed for or against him. A more direct assault on privacy occurs at the nuisance level and comes from the flood of advertising circulars delivered to our doors as a result of computers processing name-and-address files that list our likely interests.

Advanced forms of automation using computers are penetrating industries with fruitful consequences. Valuable improvements have been made, especially those with the characteristics of continuous flow processing. Computers offer economic gains by maximizing the earnings of plant or raw materials; they also offer closer quality control by fast optimal use of plant controls in response to external disturbances. They are able to watch over the development of potentially dangerous plant situations and can relieve men of observation and control tasks in dirty, hazardous locations.

It is feared that because plants are automated they will need fewer employees. It has been argued that an automated plant, by de-skilling work, denies its workers the pleasure and the sense of achievement that a craftsman derives from exercising his skill. Automation breaks up work teams and restricts an individual to a narrow span of activity which detaches him from the productive result. Computers offer great benefits in efficiency, by relieving men of tiresome chores, and in insight, through greater control over affairs; yet these very benefits bring the risk of deprivation to some. Many people identify automation with unemployment and poverty.

Quality of Human Life.   What impact has technology had on the quality of human life in society? There are two opposing views to this question. At one extreme are the enthusiasts who see technology as the great liberator of man. New drugs, better medical attention, and improved health standards have more than doubled the average life span of man. Machines have released us from much of the back-breaking labor which in previous ages occupied most of man's time and energy. Our dreams of life free from suffering, famine, disease, and poverty are being fulfilled.

At the opposite extreme are those who view technology as man's enslaver. Here technology is seen as a threat to human existence, a power which man cannot control, a system with its own momentum. Technological changes have consequences which cannot be foreseen and which occur so rapidly that man cannot adapt to them.

Existentialist writers have all protested against the conformity of mass society and have defended human freedom and individuality against all forces which turn man into an object. Jacques Ellul (1964) has given one of the strongest arguments against the depersonalizing character of technological society. He describes the regimentation, standardization, and conformity which result from mass production of goods and mass media of communication. Within a uniform technological culture, differences among individuals and groups tend to disappear. The objectified and mechanized interactions between deadened individuals has been portrayed in the Theatre of the Absurd.

Here we see that the impersonality of power jeopardizes individual responsibility. Processes are segmented so that each person contributes only a limited operation with little or no chance to participate in decisions concerning overall goals. This even extends to one's relationships with other people. We become not the master of the machine but its servant. If consumers do not need a new product, the desire for it is created by high-pressure advertising. When such attitudes infect the political order, we are only one step away from Huxley's *Brave New World* or Orwell's *1984*.

We can say that the consequences of a particular discovery will depend on how it is employed. Technology has been an instrument of profit and power. Many times we have assumed that the pursuit of private profit would yield social benefits and that progress would automatically follow. The actual consequences of technology have been very mixed. A dominant technical elite develops with technology, since only a small group of experts have the knowledge necessary to make significant decisions. We assume that decisions will be more rational if they are made by those who are best informed. When computers play a role in decision making, their conclusions seem objective and unchallengeable, but their operation may conceal the judgments and values of the person who wrote the computer's program. Thus we will always need social controls over the controllers. We need new institutions of participative democracy in which the people most directly affected by policy decisions can have a more determinative voice in their own destiny.

There are nonphysical costs resulting from the new technology as well. Partially because of the recent and sudden rush of technological discovery, not much thought has been given to the selective application of this new knowledge. In fact, it seems evident that only two principles have been applied throughout:

1. If we have the technological expertise in a certain area, then we should apply it.

2. Output should be maximized.

These attitudes do not provide for any feedback of a humanistic nature; consequently, they are providing a poor solution to the problem of the satisfaction of human needs. There exists the danger, for example, that under these conditions a *Brave New World* type of society could evolve, in which humanity would in fact be subjected to the mechanistic aspects of technological advancement and "efficient" living—the kind of society that B. F. Skinner seems to consider ideal in *Walden Two*. Similarly, a culture that puts its chief emphasis on production and efficiency runs the danger of losing sight of the humanistic considerations that presumably were the reasons for the production in the first place. Such a culture will produce for the sake of production, resulting in a never-ending cycle in which means are mistaken for ends and production breeds the necessity for more production.

Increased knowledge concerning both our physical and social worlds is crucial for developing new cultural norms that avoid the entropy trap. From a practical viewpoint, an ever-expanding and widely disseminated body of knowledge is the most fundamental resource available for cultural advancement. Among the young and among highly educated persons there exists a feeling of revulsion toward science and technology, largely because both groups perceive these areas to be related only to defense and industrial pollution and as threats to biomedical technology. Science and technology are blamed for dehumanizing and depersonalizing culture, impoverishing the spirit of man, and stifling all that is spontaneous and creative in human life.

One value change which will affect the business climate is a new perception of the role of knowledge. This perception envisages knowledge as producing a more comprehensive understanding of human objectives in terms of new forms of measurement and the evolution of processes as well as products. In addition to establishing the Council for Environmental Quality, the law requires every U.S. government agency that is planning a project to file with the Council an assessment of its impact on the environment.

A power organization cannot long maintain itself unless it is supported by a more or less accepted system of ideas and values. People are now demonstrating that they want a higher quality of life. They want technology to be subjected to intelligent and informed assessment and control.

Technological and industrial accomplishments are at the core of our rotting cities. Widespread affluence dulls the sense of concern while sharpening the shame of poverty. The impersonality of industrial and urban society leaves in its path the crisis of identity and a sense of vague restlessness. There is a call in the 1970s for more responsibility on the part of business and the other major institutions of our society. There is a concern about the prevailing philosophy of capitalism as it is practiced today. A contradiction exists between our emphasis on work, on the one hand, and on high consumption and hedonistic pleasure, on the other. The Protestant Ethic is a code emphasizing work, sobriety, and frugality and discouraging personal indulgence. This definitely opposes an emphasis on high consumption. The counterculture rejects the bourgeois values of the U.S. business world. These values are criticized in the lifestyle, dress, speech, and sexual practices which reject the cultural mode that has existed for 60 years. This counterculture represents the acting out of liberal values espoused but not practiced by parents of the counterculture youth. In the 1960s we saw an interest in the social responsibility of corporations for the environment; choices facing, and informing of, the consumer; the use of natural resources and protection of values; and the quality, content, and truth value of advertising.

Mounting public concern about the impact of automation has led some people to conclude that the problems involved are too great for labor and management to handle and that what may be needed is government action. Many aspects of adjustment to the automation age go well beyond the confines of any single plant, company, or industry, and these are clearly in the province of governmental responsibility. One popular idea is that it would be possible for the government to anticipate the problems and to design programs to deal with the resulting dislocations of technological change if it had advance knowledge of such contemplated changes in companies. This has been endorsed by many labor leaders and political figures. This system seems rational, for it provides time to work out solutions to problems before the change is effected. The difficulty is that it is not always possible to identify when and where technological change will occur. Not all new technology is successful, and it usually remains experimental, even after being introduced.

In addition, technological change can have a disquieting effect. Employees resist the adoption of new production and operational methods because they fear the unfamiliar. Labor unions may try to prevent technological advances in many major industries when members react against these advances. Our educational system is in a quandary and is challenged by the need to restructure the curriculum in order to prepare the young for new and unique job opportunities. Today the call is for new ideas to cope with our new sweeping technological changes. Innovations have brought immediate adjustments and have left new problems with which we must deal. Change is an inherent part of a dynamic socioeconomic system. The business organization thrives on change, especially in a period of technological breakthrough.

It is very difficult to separate any particular change from the overall dynamics of an on-going enterprise. There are certain responsibilities which must be accepted by management, labor, government, and individuals. In exercising its responsibility to innovate, management must constantly bear in mind the importance of the job to the individual employee. Work provides his source of income; it is his attachment to society and is of value in and of itself. Technological change may disturb the deep and complex attachments established between the worker and his work. Thus it is important to provide information to employees to allay fears and to provide time for individual adjustment to change. Effective communication with management is necessary for the maintenance of satisfactory employee relationships.

Probably the greatest responsibility for adjusting to technological change rests with the individual. Frequently the individual affected, owing to his training and background, is the least able to shoulder that responsibility. Methods and techniques are changing, and these may threaten both the security of the job and the skills traditionally associated with certain work. With technological change, the individual, in order to adjust and grow with change, must broaden his horizons. The education he gets and the actions of his union and of his government will be the ultimate reflection of the actions he takes in satisfying his responsibilities to himself and his family. Each individual has a responsibility to reach out for new job opportunities, for retraining when his skills are no longer in demand, and for education as the basis of personal progress.

The attitudes and the role of organized labor are also put to the test in adapting to the realities of a dynamic economic and industrial environment. The industrial relations philosophies of companies, and management concepts of structural organizations, undergo modifications to meet the demands of a technologically progressive system.

Within the last decade, revolutionary forms of modern technology have materialized with increasing effects on jobs and people. Change itself is nothing new; it is the nature of change in terms of its qualitative impact on work that has been startling in recent years.

The individual's attempt to deal with the ever-expanding scope of technological change is not greatly different from that of society in general. It is plain that any incremental change in a technology has an effect upon the individuals who compose the culture in which the change took place, either immediately or in a delayed fashion. This effect is primarily one of disorientation during the readjustment process. McLuhan (1967) states:

> If a new technology extends one or more of our senses outside us into the social world, then new ratios among all of our senses will occur in that particular culture. It is comparable to what happens when a new note is added to a melody. And when the sense ratios alter in any given culture, then what had appeared lucid before may suddenly be opaque, and what had been vague or opaque will become translucent. (p. 8)

The contention here is that all technological changes are eventually extensions of our senses and abilities; consequently, confusion results from the restructuring of our sensory makeup.

A change in technology causes a change in one's perception of the environment. What is frightening to many individuals, however, is not the mere fact of technological change and the consequent environmental change but rather the rate at which this change occurs. Improved methods of transportation and communication have resulted in an incredible gain in the diffusion rate of new ideas in our society. While in the eighteenth and nineteenth centuries it could reasonably be said that an individual would die in the same culture into which he was born, such a statement today would be of doubtful accuracy. The following diagram postulates the development of a technological innovation and its spread into society:

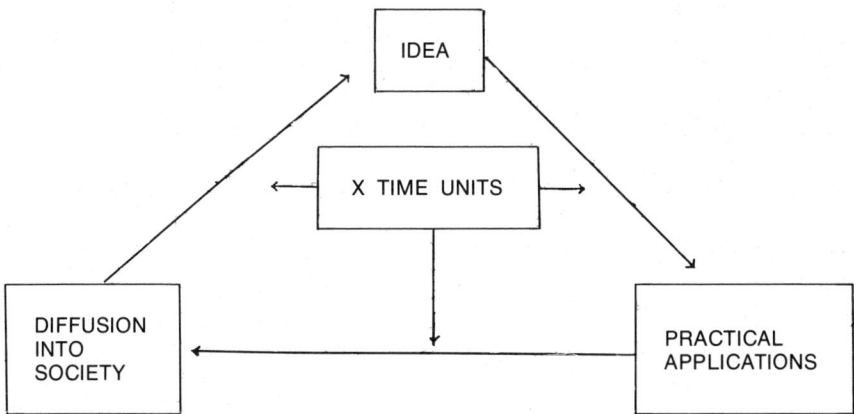

In other words, as new ideas are implemented and diffused throughout society, more new ideas and new applications develop. Whereas

Gutenberg's fifteenth century printing press took centuries to evolve
(and still had not been materially changed by the time of the American
Revolution), technology today has accelerated to the point at which we
get a new generation of computers every seven years or so. Thus the
relevant time unit for the technological cycle in Gutenberg's day
might be measured in hundreds of years; today, it could be expressed
in tens of years, or even months. It is no wonder, then, that many older
people feel a special sense of loss in a culture in which change is not
only rapid but also accelerating at high speed. McLuhan (1967) quite
reasonably points out that "innumerable confusions and a profound
feeling of despair invariably emerge in periods of great technological
and cultural transition" (p. 8). In fact, it seems safe to say that we have
transcended the "period of transition" as the term is ordinarily understood; rather, we are entering into a period of *permanent* transition
with fewer and fewer identifiable states of constancy. Toffler (1972)
states:

> While we tend to focus on only one situation at a time, the in-
> creased rate at which situations flow past us vastly complicates the
> entire structure of life, multiplying the number of roles we must
> play and the number of choices we are forced to make. This, in
> turn, accounts for the choking sense of complexity about contem-
> porary life. (p. 33)

These choices are not limited to the individual's working life;
they extend, in fact, to the most fundamental aspects of life in all its
complexity. For instance, a critical topic now is the inability of many
people to make use of radically increased leisure time, as put by Reisman (1966):

> For many people today, the sudden onrush of leisure is a version of
> technological unemployment; their education has not prepared
> them for it and the creation of new wants at their expense moves
> faster than their ability to order and assimilate these wants. (p. 191)

Clearly, new approaches to the socialization aspect of education will
have to be examined in order to rectify the confusion.

Well-adjusted living in this kind of society calls for a specific type
of individual—one who, among other characteristics, has been able to
internalize the norm of constant change. "The individual who has
internalized the principle of acceleration—who understands in his
bones as well as his brain that things are moving faster in the world
around him—makes an automatic, unconscious compensation for the
compression of time" (Toffler, 1972, p. 43).

Clearly, then, as the technological culture progresses, more will
be required of the individual in terms of exercising his own autonomy;

his choices will be richer and his environment more complex than ever before in the history of mankind. With this prospect before him, however, there exists the very great and real danger that the individual will abdicate his power of choice, whether by accident or by design. This danger is magnified by the inability of many people to perceive themselves as a relevant part of the technological/cultural system in which they live. This breeds frustration and eventually alienation in the individual, who comes to regard himself as passive and ineffectual. According to Walker (1968), a population of consumers results, not because they prefer to think of themselves in this somewhat less than noble role, but because they are no longer able to think of themselves in the role of shapers of their own destiny. In a disoriented world of this sort, we "seem to lose control over our own system. We execute the decisions which our computer calculations make for us. We as human beings have no aim except producing and consuming more and more. We will nothing, nor do we not-will anything" (Fromm, 1968, p. 1).

Technology itself, therefore, does not present a threat to our well-being but induces man's willingness to be passive, to let the system make the decisions for him. Self-actualization has always been man's right in our culture; once abdicated, however, it is not easily won back. In the words of Weizenbaum (1972), the situation looks even more complex:

> What is wrong, I think, is that we have permitted technological metaphors and technique itself to so thoroughly pervade our thought processes that we have finally abdicated to technology the very duty to formulate questions. Thus sensible men correctly perceive that large data banks and enormous networks of computers threaten man. But they leave it to technology to ask the corresponding questions. Where a simple man might ask, Do we need these things, technology asks, What electronic wizardry will make them safe? (p. 611)

We must also consider the impact of the technological mentality upon human attitudes. First, the environment has been exploited. Our forests have been cut and burned, our rivers polluted, and much of our wildlife exterminated. Second, power is dangerously relied upon. Technology is a potent instrument of man's purposes. We too readily assume that it can deal with all problems. Third, our exclusive dependence on the technological approach deadens our imaginations and thus our emotional lives.

The problem is not technology but preoccupation with technological goals. The scientist, engineer, or computer specialist may be oblivious of the social consequences of his inventions and totally unconcerned about the relation of knowledge to life. Every specialist is

tempted to reduce reality to fit the categories of his own field. Technical solutions and increased efficiency become ends in themselves.
There seems to be neither time nor inclination to reflect on their implications for the quality of human life. For individuals, what should be a
legitimate concern for material needs becomes a frantic pursuit of
comfort—a dedication to self-gratification. Our industrial society awak-
ens false needs through the deliberate creation of new cravings. Advertising stimulates our appetites as consumers and creates an insatiable drive toward greater affluence. Man then ends as a slave to his
own desires. Such an obsession distorts our basic values.

It seems that man is developing an unqualified devotion to
technology. We are developing the belief that all problems are solva-
ble by technical analysis. Earlier generations spoke of understanding
nature, whereas ours speaks of conquering it. Technology should be
redirected to help improve the quality of man's life in this world.
Technological innovation should proceed more cautiously, with
greater attention to environmental repercussions and social consequences. Our task should be the humanization of the technological
revolution. We should strengthen the social institutions which shape
and control technological forces. Only then will technology serve man
and not man serve technology.

New biological and technological knowledge will yield increasing power to control man and his future. Genetic control, such as
through eugenics and artificial insemination, presents new problems.
We are at a point at which we cannot simply be guided by ethical
advice. We are treading new paths.

Ellul (1964) feels that technique has not always been the master of
man. At the start, techniques were employed to help the culture. Now
we have come to the stage at which technique is the master and society is the means for technique. In the past man used his own talents to
achieve efficiency. Now man uses the machine as a means of attaining
real efficiency.

Ellul foresees for man certain unexpected developments. He believes a stable population will exist in which disease and famine will
be eliminated. Artificial insemination may be employed in the future.
The reproductive cells used will be of those of good genetic content.
Eventually scientists will be able to shape human emotions, desires,
and thoughts.

The scientific and technological revolution is changing people's
values in profound ways. Business leaders need to understand how
these values are changing and why, since business succeeds when it
produces what people want. In this decade people have grown more
concerned about the quality of their lives. Changing national priorities
interacting with changing values and growing capabilities resulting
from technological advances will reshape the business climate. The

knowledge brought by science has refashioned man's commonly held
principle concerning the earth and the cosmos and is now shattering
ancient and cherished beliefs about God, the universe, the origin of
life, and the appropriate means of survival of the human species on
earth.

If we do not control our culture, it devours us. Jacques Ellul
(1964) warns against the dangerous belief that what is technically possible should therefore be done and is thus morally and socially desirable. Appropriate technology depends upon the economic niche in
which it is employed. An increasing concern in industrial societies is
that technology, far from creating a livable environment, is actually
destroying it. The growing concern is that ordinary people have too
little to say in the technological process. All this amounts to a crisis in
Western cultures. The Renaissance belief system is being challenged.
The efficiency of the scientific-technological enterprise is being questioned. The fitness of the present industrial system in relation to the
survival of the human species is also being questioned.

The idea that artificial intelligence might overtake man threatens
his self-image. The traditional view of human nature is challenged by
the reductionistic image of man as a complex machine. There is also a
fear that the computer will develop a mind of its own and possibly
become man's master rather than his servant. Thus far, computers
have displayed amazing achievements. A computer that can play
checkers consistently beats the world's checkers champions. Computers may eventually surpass man in all fields of thought.

A computer receives information as discrete units and processes it
serially in well-defined sequences of steps according to formal rules.
The human brain is able to receive information which is global and
continuous in character. That brains and computers process information in such different ways gives us more confidence that machines
will never be able to do everything that man can do.

There are some ethical problems which arise from applications of
cybernetics. One immediate effect is technological unemployment
and the need to retrain displaced workers for new kinds of jobs. Automation is increasing the productivity of each worker and will undoubtedly shorten the average work week. Thus automation creates
new patterns of work and leisure for which traditional ethical norms
are inadequate. Luther and Calvin spread the belief that any useful
occupation could be a service to God and to man. They emphasized
individual virtues, such as honesty, thrift, and hard work. A man used
to be able to make his own ethical decisions in the course of his work.
Today it is the machine and the total organization which are productive. Most of the important decisions about work are made by men in
groups, not by individuals. Responsibility here requires not individualistic virtues but awareness of the social implications of one's work

and intelligent participation at those points in industry and government where decisions are made.

Over two centuries of technological innovation have changed our workers from artisans and craftsmen into machine-minders. Before the Industrial Revolution a skilled workman was a craftsman. He was always conscious that he was a member of an honored craft. He took legitimate pride in the excellence of his work. Today, we are far removed from that state of society.

The growing popularity of do-it-yourself kits and craft hobbies is evidence of an attempt to recapture something of the deep satisfaction enjoyed by the craftsmen of old. The sad thing is that such hobbies can only be briefly enjoyed after a day's work instead of being the daily work itself. Presently our technological expertise and our overriding concern for efficiency lower the satisfaction of the workers with their job performance.

We must be aware of some incongruous and inconsistent attitudes toward work. Most of us are inheritors of the belief that work is worship. At the same time we spend many of our days in desperation, planning for vacations and retirement which seldom fulfill our expectations.

In earlier days when there was so much work to be done, leisure was viewed as a time to recuperate from work. In the Puritan Ethic of hard work, the idle were looked upon as sinful. Our age of automation requires a new philosophy of leisure. Today, it is considered not just a departure from work but also an opportunity for service, growth, and enjoyment. With less hours required on a job, Americans often work overtime or take a second job. Free time seems to lead only to boredom.

It is possible that leisure can provide new opportunities for voluntary service. It is also an opportunity for self-fulfillment. In the past, work has been the main source of personal identity.

Computers have already been a boon to almost every branch of industry, government, and education. Defense missiles, space launchings, and even lunar landings are controlled by radar and computer systems. Before too long computers will be used for medical diagnosis and for legislative and legal reference. The ends to which technology should be directed are matters of human choice. Computers enhance the power of the technical elite who know how to use them. In turn, the control of the computers can only be accomplished through the political process.

The poor have benefited least from technology. Unemployment from automation hits the unskilled the hardest. A freeway is seldom used by the ghetto residents whose houses are torn down to make room for it. It seems that technology tends to increase the gap between the rich and the poor. Technology has become a major instrument of profit. Often the financial rewards have gone to those who could find new ways to exploit our natural resources cheaply. Today the social costs of these exploitations are very high, and new forms of taxes, fines, and incentives are needed so that the person who really contributes to the general welfare is rewarded.

Technology should be redirected to reduce the gap between the rich and the poor. We should use technology to abolish poverty and hunger, not to produce more luxury goods. Space and military technology is highly developed but little effort has been given to the technology of urban housing. We have in our power the technical ability to fulfill man's dream of peace and plenty, once we seriously consider our ideals of justice and equality. Science and technology have placed in our hands the power to create a world in which everyone has the opportunity of leading a meaningful life—one free from starvation, deprivation, and misery.

One of the prices we have paid for rapid technological advancement has been rapid technological implementation without an adequate amount of forethought. The purveyors of the technological society have not yet made the leap from the mechanistic idea of "we have it so we'll use it" to a more humanistic philosophy. Such a change must come, however, if the society is to survive in any recognizable form. Lee DuBridge (1962) has pointed out some of the more pressing problems the technological system must face in providing for the individual's welfare.

1. The avoidance of war.
2. The maintenance of a free society.
3. The dissemination of technological benefits.
4. The minimization of distress from adjustment to technological change.
5. The regulation in the public interest of large agencies of technology and the economy.
6. The creation of an educational system to help people adjust to the changing world.
7. The evolution of new social mechanisms to achieve the above.

Thus technology must be perceived as a means; the end to be achieved is the preservation of an individual capable of autonomy. Hopefully the individual will evolve as society evolves; as technology takes more and better care of his mechanistic needs, man will be able to develop more fully toward the satisfaction of his human needs, but he will have to have the corporation's help to do so. Fromm (1968) sees this as follows:

> Man's development requires his capacity to transcend the narrow prison of his ego, his greed, his selfishness, his separation from his fellow man, and, hence, his basic loneliness. This transcendance is the condition for being open and related to the world, vulnerable,

and yet with an experience of identity and integrity; of man's capacity to enjoy all that is alive, to pour out his faculties into the
world around him, to be "interested;" in brief, to *be* rather than to
have and to *use* are consequences of the step to overcome greed
and egomania. (p. 135)

If we use it with insight and care, technology has a tremendous
capacity for making man more free than he has ever been before.
Unfortunately, such potential has not, in the main, been realized. Especially in the working environment, outdated and mechanistic concepts and organizational structures are still being applied; it is to these
concepts and the search for a viable alternative that we now turn.

TECHNOLOGY AND WORK

We have already seen that the new technology has brought about a
restructuring of the labor force within plants. In some cases, plants
were laying off machine operators at the same time that they were
hiring skilled craftsmen. The displaced operator lacked either the
qualifications or the desire to get the jobs which were available.

It is difficult to isolate the total employment effects of technological change. Such innovations usually have these effects: (1) a shift
from blue-collar to white-collar employment; (2)within the blue-collar
group, a shift from direct production to maintenance work; and (3) the
elimination of unskilled jobs. These shifts have occurred regardless of
whether total employment was increasing, decreasing, or stabilizing.
This restructuring of the labor force has occurred in all industries,
though it is more or less pronounced depending on the amount of
automation involved in the technological change.

In a great many cases, short-term, on-the-job training was sufficient to equip employees for the new job requirements. The content of
the operator's job changed so that it required less machine skill and
manual dexterity and more attentiveness, quick thinking, and alert
action, as well as adaptability and the educational background for
training.

Certain groups of blue-collar employees, such as the less skilled,
the inadequately educated, the very young, the aging, and blacks,
present special employment problems. These groups have been ad-
versely affected by the shifts in labor force composition. It has been
said that a high proportion of displacement was attributable not only to
skill deficiencies but also to the lack of appropriate background for
learning the needed skills. Younger employees are usually more willing to relocate, and this heightens their chances for transfer to job
openings rejected by their seniors.

Companies have recognized the importance of having employees
accept change and have therefore given much attention to reducing

the extent of these problems before new technology has been introduced. Being aware of the fact that employees react negatively to change, managements have applied their efforts, before introducing the technological innovation, to changing the current manpower situation to fit their projected needs. The objective has been to decide upon ways in which the companies could shape their policies to accommodate the dislocations from technological change.

The normal process of attrition among workers must also be considered. In the Kaiser Steel Corporation established in 1943, more employees have been lost through resignation, death, and other natural causes than through discharge owing to technological change. By limiting the entry of new employees as replacements, companies have used the incidence of labor turnover to creat vacancies for members of the work force who would otherwise have faced layoff when technological change became a reality. Moreover, the retirement of many employees before their normal retirement dates is becoming a standard form of attrition in companies. Provisions in pension plans for early retirement are now more common than before, but unethical practices in not providing pensions are also all too common. Early retirement is encouraged for employees who are prevented by age, health, or job attitudes from keeping pace with pressures of new times.

The ability to introduce intraplant transfers smoothly is highly dependent upon a sensitive management implementing humane and astute recruitment, job training, placement, transfer rights, and seniority practices. A great effort is required to minimize job loss through intraplant transfers.

Despite a company's willingness to relocate employees, a relatively small percentage of them will take this opportunity. Frequently, employees will accept inadequate retirement benefits or will prefer being laid off to being transferred to another area. In some cases management has taken action to help the displaced find alternative employment in their home communities. These actions have helped employee morale during the transition to new technology.

With technological innovations comes a demand for entirely new skills, the new jobs going to specially trained technicians. A need also arises for en masse retraining programs; some have been launched under the Federal Area Redevelopment Act of 1961 and the Manpower Department and Training Act of 1962. Various state governments and local communities have also undertaken independent programs. The hazard of setting up broad training programs unrelated to specific needs is that a disparity between the kinds and quantity of available skills and the needs of industry may result.

It seems that the skills demanded by the technological change are not fundamentally different from former job demands, and they are therefore within the learning capacity of the regular work force. Both management and unions have tried to protect the jobs of employees in the face of new technology. The compromises made on both sides to accommodate employee training in the operation of newer and more complicated machinery have helped maintain job security.

Modern technology could take new turns and make greater demands on employee talents. Greater capacities for concentrated attention and process conceptualization are needed than ever before. There are also changes in the work environment which may be more significant than job requirements for worker adaptability to advanced technology.

Despite company training and utilization of employees from the established crafts, it has been difficult to secure an adequate supply of craftsmen. More skilled employees are needed to maintain and repair automated machinery. Some companies have tried moving production workers into skilled maintenance jobs, but with little success. For skilled work, production men have lacked either the basic qualifications or the desire to transfer to maintenance jobs.

Since workers must continually bring new skills and better educational backgrounds to their jobs, much of the training responsibility lies with educational authorities. Educators must reexamine present school programs to ensure that they are providing youth with the types of skills that will be required in our times of rapid technological advancement. Industry must also give encouragement and guidance to the educators.

Automation has frequently made old job classifications obsolete. Greater skill and responsibility are required to operate expensive machines. The mental fatigue involved should justify demands for higher rates of pay. Revisions of such systems are required to take into account factors which at the present time are given little or no weight.

Some automated operations do not lend themselves to realizing the usual benefits of conventional incentive plans because the speed of production being built into the machinery is outside the worker's control and his output cannot be measured. One new method of rewarding employees which has been adopted by management involves merit wage increases. This method is based on the capacity of employees to master more than one kind of job. In automated operations, group incentives may be an important means of motivation for greater output. This system might integrate an entire plant into the type of social unit needed to achieve high levels of efficiency. Adoption of a Scanlon-type group incentive plan encourages worker participation in production problem solving and permits a sharing of the gains of automation.

The impact of automation on supervisors is even more critical than its impact on workers. Automation requires that the supervisor make decisions at the work level that were formerly made at higher levels in the hierarchy. Increasingly his work will resemble that of middle management. The supervisor has to uphold his prestige as leader of his group and must maintain a mood of camaraderie with members of the group.

Fear of the possible deleterious effects of technology upon the work situation goes back in time farther than many analysts suppose; even Adam Smith expressed the apprehension that work in a too highly mechanized environment would stultify the worker's intellect.

> The understanding of the greater part of men is necessarily formed by their ordinary employments. The man whose life is spent in performing a few simple operations, of which the effects, too, are, perhaps, always the same, has no occasion to exert his understanding, or to exercise his invention in finding out expedients for removing difficulties which never occur. He naturally loses, therefore, the habit of such exertion, and gradually becomes as stupid and ignorant as it is possible for a human creature to become. . . . His dexterity at his own particular trade seems, in this manner, to be acquired at the expense of his intellectual, social, and martial values. (Quoted by Heilbroner 1962)

Thus, even as far back as the eighteenth century, it was understood that technological innovation and specialization has the power to change the working environment to such an extent that the worker could be affected far beyond the point which the innovation meant to achieve initially.

Basic changes in the technology of a job mean that concomitant changes will occur in the division of labor around that job and in the actual content of the job itself. In the minds of most people the direction of such change has meant more specialization and less meaningful jobs. In the factory as well as in the office, this may imply greater efficiency presently, but it exacts upon the workers a toll, which in the long run can become very costly to the employer as well.

The changes that result alter the existing patterns of work organization, the numbers and kinds of jobs, and the distribution of work. In other words, they disrupt the established relationship between management and labor. When employees are represented by a union, technological change will involve the furthering of the collective bargaining process.

Unions may be committed to the necessity of technological change for the health of an enterprise, but they also view union interests and roles as being at variance with those of management. Management perceives its primary responsibility as maximizing the profitability of the company by increasing its efficiency and its effectiveness. The role of the union is to protect the job security and income of its members. These two goals may be in conflict when major technological improvements do occur.

Opposition to change by employees can hamper management's ability to introduce new production processes. This is accomplished by making the undertaking exceedingly costly or by erecting numerous roadblocks to effective utilization of the new technology. In one situation the unions did not resist technological improvements but insisted on maintaining outmoded work crews which nullified the anticipated savings (Beaumont and Helfgott, 1964).

The most frequent line of disagreement between labor and management has been that of establishing rates of pay for the new jobs that emerge through technological innovations. Unions adopt the attitude that with the introduction of labor-saving machinery, workers should get higher rates of pay, regardless of whether actual job requirements have expanded or not.

Technological changes in an industrial environment are not, of course, harmful per se. Working conditions, job safety, and pay are usually better in the technologically advanced plant. However, there are some major sources of dissatisfaction in this type of automated situation. In some systems, there is a high degree of man-machine interdependency, leading to a necessity for constant alertness; this increases on-the-job tension. Such would be the case even in more highly automated systems, in which machines do a large part of their own monitoring and control. Since system integration generally means fewer workers on the job and increased responsibility, opportunities for interpersonal interaction among workers (in a nonformal sense) decrease. The technologically advanced plant puts workers "on their own" to a higher degree than formerly. Since workers are likely to have a negative view of the benefits of automation to begin with, they may choose not to notice actual advantages. In one newly automated tube mill plant in a large steel corporation, it was found that workers perceived their jobs as physically easier but mentally more exhausting. When the men were asked if the new mill was of benefit for the worker, two-thirds of them answered in the negative, claiming that new automated mills in the steel industry were "a real threat to the working man." Despite the fact that their own jobs were secure and the pay was better, the net result was a reduction in the number of workers, and this was seen as a real danger to the stability of their employment. Thus the worker in a highly technical situation may not perceive his environment in the same way it is perceived by those who shape it for him. More importantly, the influence of the work itself may have serious consequences for the worker's self-identity, reducing him to a dial-watcher rather than a doer (Beaumont and Helfgott, 1964).

In the assembly line situation, the worker must regard his fellow workers in the light of two different structures—the informal organization and the formal organization. Informally he may be cognizant of others as individuals, whether friends or enemies. However, the formal organization demands that he see others as anonymous, inter-changeable persons without identities. In any situation in which an individual is denied the opportunity to identify with someone or something, he may become alienated from that situation.

This alienation is a result of the mechanistic application of technological innovation commonly found in work today. It is not lim-ited to the plant; man's identity has been so split up and differentiated in every area by the plurality of the roles he must play that it is not surprising if he eventually begins to lose sight of himself in these roles. When this occurs, he becomes alienated not only from others, but also from himself. In a sense, modern man has a permanent iden-tity crisis precipitated by more social differentiation than he can han-dle. This is the kind of alienation C. Wright Mills talks about in *White Collar,* but with a new twist. Instead of being lost only in the bureau-cratic shuffle, man may be lost in the technological/social shuffle as well.

We have said that this alienation is a product of the mechanistic society in which we live. Such alienation can be fatal to a society if it is present to an overwhelming degree; even in its present stages, it con-tributes to the feeling of hopelessness and passivity with regard to the technological/social system that is prevalent today. All this is suc-cinctly described by Mann (1962):

> Life can be experienced only in its individual manifestations, in the individual person as well as in a bird or a flower. There is no life in the "masses," there is no life in abstraction. Our approach to life today becomes increasingly mechanical. . . . People love me-chanical gadgets more than living beings. The approach to men is intellectual-abstract. One is interested in people as objects, in their common properties, in the static rules of mass behavior, not in living individuals. . . . Briefly then, intellectualization, quantifi-cation, abstractification, bureaucratization, and reification—the very characteristics of modern industrial society—when applied to people rather than things, are not the principles of life but those of mechanics. People living in such a system become indifferent to life and even attracted to death. (p. 51)

Clearly a society based on principles inimical to life cannot survive.

The dangers inherent in the denial of the individual should be apparent. Because such denial breeds alienation and passivity, the very essence of being human can be lost. An antihumanistic culture "can only lead to the perfection of a completely autonomous technol-ogy in which the human is a slave and not a master. It promises us a pursuit only of what is technologically feasible to the bitter end; an antiseptic world in which spontaneity is a gross crime" (see Berger, 1973). Too many individuals have already abdicated their powers of discretion to the system; when this happens a crisis eventually occurs.

Whereas the "scientific" managers of sixty years ago would generally express the motivation for work in one word—pay—today it is recognized that this is clearly not the whole answer. "When we are inquiring into the philosophy of value, or trying to foresee the future of value, the one kind of value we are not considering is cash value" (Fromm, 1968, p. 57). The job must satisfy symbolic or higher-level needs as well as biological or lower-level needs. Fromm (1964) makes it quite clear that rejection of this dictum may lead to dire consequences.

> There exists the danger that the sense of powerlessness which grips people today—intellectuals as well as the average man—with ever increasing force, may lead them to accept a new version of corruption and original sin which serves as a rationalization for the defeatist view that war cannot be avoided because it is the result of the destructiveness of human nature. (p. 21)

Structural alienation and passivity, the twin products of the mechanistic view of man, must therefore be avoided in constructing the new world of work.

If we try to evaluate a system without taking into account the human value of the jobs within that system, or by assigning only monetary measures to those jobs, then we are only misleading ourselves as to that system's effectiveness. We could compare mechanistic management to operating in a two-dimensional universe, the humanistic element being the third dimension. In a humanistic technological society, the jobs which a person would value most would be those in which he is regarded as an individual, not just an adjunct to a technologically sophisticated process. In other words, a role that can be internalized easily and without conflict is sought. "The young today reject goals. They want roles—that is, total involvement. They do not want fragmented, specialized goals or jobs" (Fromm, 1968, p. 35).

The great transition in the U.S. economy is evident in the labor force. We are approaching a time when only 20 per cent of the labor force will suffice for producing all agricultural and manufactured goods. In the future, the labor force will experience sharp changes. We will see a dramatic increase in the 25 to 44 year old group of workers who are better educated than the corresponding group in the 1960s. They will bring higher expectations, more innovative interests, greater mobility, and a greater desire to participate in the decision-making process. This will bring a greater competition for the jobs in middle management. The 45 to 54 year old group will diminish in size, creating a shortage of senior managers. Over the next 15 years, the labor force will include more highly educated people.

The role of work in society is changing in significant ways. Employee benefits by 1980 will expand to include longer vacations, more holidays, and five or six long weekends. Hours of work will decline to average 36.8 hours per week, and more companies will have four-day weeks. By 1980, almost all employees will work at salaried rather than hourly rates.

The labor market and our attitudes toward it will change. In the future, it will be possible to give more guidance concerning career choices. Upward mobility will depend more on education, and professionals in management will be more numerous and powerful. Women will be playing a bigger role in the labor force.

There is an obvious change in the values of workers. Better educated, more knowledgeable, less rigid workers—male and female, black and white, technical and managerial—are challenging job definitions. People seek broadened responsibilities, job rotation, better choice of hours, and the four-day week. Their disillusionment with present conditions is evidenced by lower productivity, higher absenteeism, product sabotage, plant vandalism, alcoholism, and drug addiction. Workers often feel like they are mere cogs in the machine.

During the 1970s two-thirds of the growth in the nation's work force will be occurring in the 16 to 34 year old age group—a group bred on television, better educated, and with greater expectations for job satisfaction. As we saw in our discussion of education, these young people have been taught to think independently in school. They have lived in a social environment based on controversy and have existed in a dehumanized, affluent suburban world. Some would say it is wrong to view this job malaise as a decline in the work ethic. It may be another indication of the declining power of Cartesian analytical and perceptual modes of design for the human environment.

Work as the financial and psychological center of life is declining, according to many sources. Cited as reasons are the growth and depersonalization of corporations, longer paid vacations, longer weekends, more education, more discretionary income, and fewer working hours.

We have just begun the Age of Leisure. There will be more government support in the years ahead for leisure, recreation, and cultural activities. There will be more leisure services for the young, elderly, ill, and handicapped, more commercial leisure time activities, and more stress on leisure activities to maintain physical and mental health.

The successes which we experience are accompanied by serious social problems. We have been able to prolong the life span of individuals, the result being overpopulation and problems of the aged. With the machine replacing manual labor, we have developed an unemployment problem. Advances in communication and transportation have caused urbanization, increasing complexity, and the risk of societal breakdown. We have developed greater industrial efficiency, and with it work has become dehumanized. As our knowledge has expanded, we have threatened people's privacy. Through affluence, we have created environmental decay, mounting pollution, and an energy shortage. There has developed an increasing concern for a need-level hierarchy, and now we have a rebellion against meaningless work. If people feel that they are not needed in a society which knows about Maslow's hierarchy of values, if they feel that they can be replaced by a machine, if they feel that they have nothing to offer, the arbitrariness of our prevailing reward system is being felt.

Seniority standards will undergo a change. The development of a work force willing and able to adapt itself to the changing needs of an evolving work process will mean more than an application of seniority protections to broaden units of work. Ability to learn might eventually replace ability to do the job.

Technology, because it influences the roles defined by the formal organization, must therefore influence industrial behavior, for how a person reacts depends as much on the demands of his role and the circumstances as on his personality. There can be times when the behavior forced on the individual by his role is in conflict with his personality. If so, role considerations may lead him to alter or modify his personality, or to leave his employment and seek a job that is more in tune with his personality structure.

We are now living in a more educated society. Fifty years ago, education was called nonwork, and intellectuals on the payroll were considered overhead. Today, the survival of the firm depends on the proper utilization of brainpower. There will also be an ever-increasing job mobility. Employees will be shifted from job to job, even from employer to employer, with much less fuss than we are accustomed to. Much of this is the result of lowered expense and ease of transportation, as well as the needs of our environment.

Firms will be relying even more on intellect than on muscles. New tasks will be too complicated for one person to handle or for individual supervision. Moreover, there will be more conflict over effectiveness criteria. The reason for this is the number of professionals involved who identify more with the goals of their profession than with those of their managers or their companies.

Many feel that a push-button world would be a good thing. However, with the inevitable elimination of human purposefulness and pride of accomplishment, it may not be the best of all possible worlds. Education could hold the answer to a better life in which man is master of automation and not mastered by it. Just as education equipped man for the challenge of the race for space, education will help man to meet the challenge of leisure.

Man must take effective action in planning for the Age of Automation. As the shorter working day creates more and more leisure time, man will think more and more about continuing his education, developing new skills, and retraining to channel his abilities. By preparing for automation and technological advances as soon as possible rather than surrendering to it and compromising the human spirit, man stands on the brink of a new and fuller life with greater dignity. Education is needed because there is no room at the bottom for those who are illiterate, unskilled, undereducated, or unable to become meaningful members of our society. To the best of our ability, we must cultivate a receptivity to change, for change is certain.

The technological environment is a consequence of the application of intellect to man's environment. It is a result of the spirit of rationalism and inquiry whose development is a vital part of Western liberal thought. It seems that we are constantly searching for new knowledge. The result of change is that values are shaken. The norms which should guide us in choosing our ends and in moving toward our objectives are dissolved. Our society spends much time and energy on researching and developing new methods to make things different from what they have been. The premise is that change is good. We must now question this basic premise by asking if *all* change is good.

We have always said that if a man wants to work, he can always find work. This notion has played a central role in our society and even in recent presidential elections. One hundred years ago, we saw that human muscle was disengaged from the productive process. Now the human nervous system is being disengaged. Many of us shudder at the notion that machines can make more sensible decisions than human beings. Many simply reject this idea as being too awesome.

The fact that the computers of today are still high-speed morons, capable of doing nothing beyond the scope of the instructions carefully programmed into them, has given many people a spurious sense of security. Many agree that a machine cannot be more intelligent than its makers, even though it may be a million times faster in operation. This argument could be completely fallacious. Even machines less intelligent than men might escape from our control by sheer speed of operation. There is a good possibility that machines will become much more intelligent than their builders, as well as faster.

THE NEW STRUCTURE OF THE ORGANIZATION

We must realize that an organization is a system that is open to its environment and its interaction with society. Society puts constraints on an organization, and the organization puts constraints on society. Society is made up of people with values. It is impossible to neglect man's values if we see the organization as being open to society, for each person is influenced by those things which occur in society.

Organizational alternatives in the face of effective change in the environment can be illustrated in terms of the following chart:

```
                    ┌─────────────────────────────────────┐
                    │   STIMULUS FROM THE ENVIRONMENT      │
                    └─────────────────────────────────────┘
        Minimal               Optimal                    Drastic
                    ┌─────────────────────────────────────┐
                    │      ORGANIZATIONAL RESPONSE         │
                    └─────────────────────────────────────┘
        Tenacious             Elastic              Self-Determinative
        Conservative          Adjusting                  Extensive
                    ┌─────────────────────────────────────┐
                    │      EFFECT UPON ENVIRONMENT         │
                    └─────────────────────────────────────┘
```

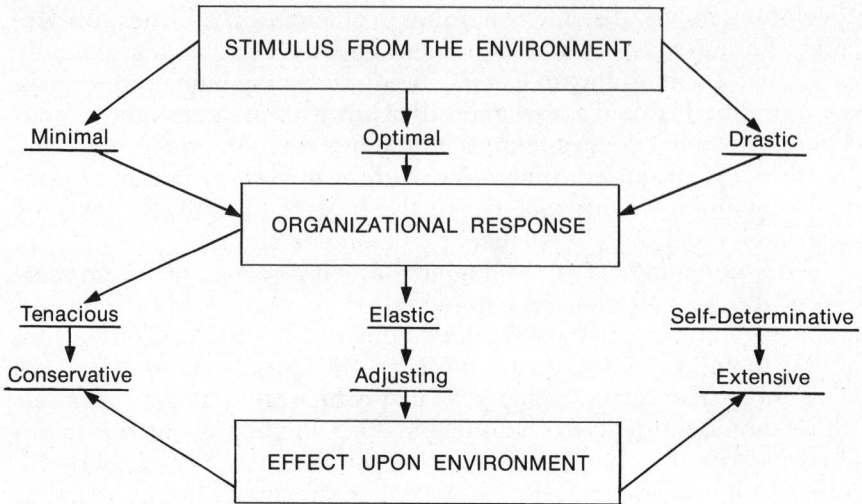

A self-determinative orientation within the organization means that the organization has the ability to change with its environment and yet retain its identity by transforming elements of the environment to meet its own needs. In management terms, this means that we should structure the organization by situation rather than by goal or job description. This not only would facilitate the speed of decision-making but also would increase the relevance of the decisions made in order to match the vitality of the organization as a whole. "If the organization is structured to be organic rather than mechanistic, as adopting spontaneously to its needs, then decisions will be made at the critical point and roles and jobs will devolve on the 'natural' organizational incumbent" (Casserly, 1967, p. 68). Bennis (1970) calls such a structure "organic-adaptive." Toffler (1972) calls it a "throw-away" organizational structure and points out that, at least in part, it has always been with us.

Change has become too powerful for management to resist, even in token form; management must learn to adapt to such change in an interactive manner. Examples of this kind of management are already prevalent. Perhaps the example providing for optimal contrast in the area of organizational structure is the concept of chief programmer team management recently developed by IBM.

In the past, most programmers have been in charge of all duties related to the program they are currently writing. This means that in addition to the design, coding, and testing of the program, the programmer must punch his own decks, make his own corrections, set up his own runs for testing, and prepare his own documentation. The lack of standardization between programmers often leads to serious problems in subsystem integration, system testing, and documentation. This inevitably leads to a lack of control and a general loss of effectiveness throughout the project. Because such clerical work is added to the programmer's job, more programmers are required, and there are also many more oppuntunities for misunderstanding when there are several personal interactions. Graphically, we may represent the situation of the programmer as follows:

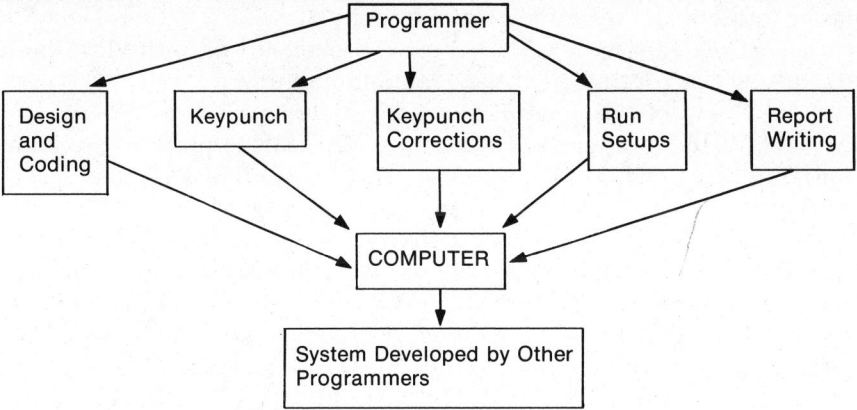

Thus the programmer must maintain activities that do not bear directly upon his task. The fact that he does not interact with the rest of the system developers at the design stage also creates confusion and inefficiency.

The team programming concept frees the programmer from the burden of clerical tasks. When these are divided among a programming team, the sources of conflict and job dissatisfaction are minimized. The team consists of a chief programmer, a backup programmer, who assists rather than works independently, and a librarian, who is not necessarily a technician. The team concept is presented graphically as follows:

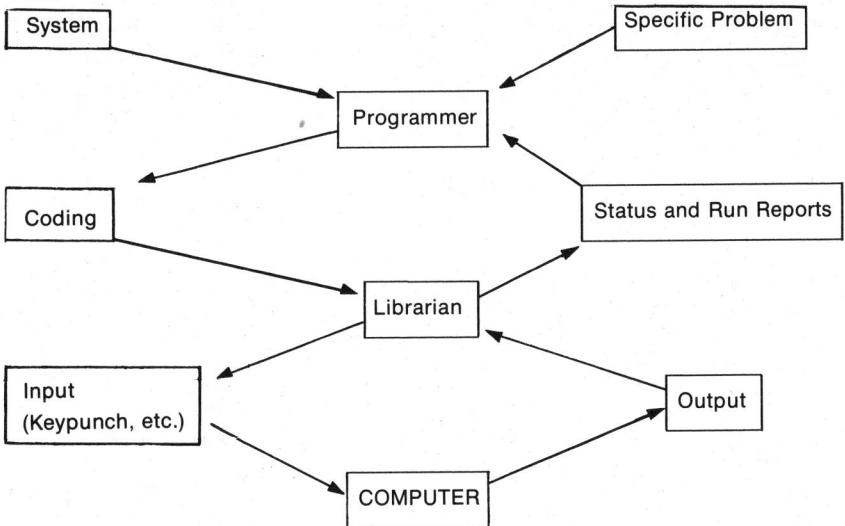

Under this concept several beneficial results are obtained:

 1. The programming effort is more modular and more directed to the problem.

 2. The programmer need not worry about essentially clerical tasks, traditionally a source of discontent.

 3. The team as a whole can be broken up or shifted without disturbing the continuity of the programming effort.

 4. Complete documentation is facilitated.

Not only is the programmer as an individual left to perform the more unifying tasks of his role, but also the organizational structure as a whole can handle change more effectively.

In a less highly technical environment, the question still remains as to how we can provide for both organic adaptiveness and humanistic management. Erich Fromm (1968) gives us a possible solution in the development of decentralized business organizations within a single business entity to handle functions that must respond to change. At the same time power and responsibility flow in both directions instead of unilaterally, as in the traditional business organization.

> While in alienated bureaucracy all power flows from above downwards, in humanistic management there is a two-way street; the "subjects" of the decisions made above respond according to their own will and concerns; their response not only reaches the top decision-makers but forces them to respond in turn. The "subjects" of decision-making have a right to challenge the decision-makers. Such a challenge would first of all require a rule that if a sufficient number of subjects demanded that the corresponding bureaucracy (on whatever level) answer questions, (and) explain its procedures, the decision-makers would respond to the demand. (p. 100)

To function effectively in the business environment, such an organization would depend on intralevel communication to a much greater extent than is now used. Such communication saves the time normally required to "go through channels" in the traditional bureaucratic form, consequently rendering the organization more effective in dealing with its environment.

CONCLUSIONS

As we have noted, Alvin Toffler (1972) suggests that we will become a "throw-away" culture, and because of the speed of technological change, society will become entirely modular. He cites three reasons for this development:

 1. The manufacturing process will become cheaper than repair.

 2. Models will become increasingly subject to change.

 3. There will be increasing uncertainty concerning future needs.

This concept undoubtedly has great significance for the future development of work—and of the individual—in areas in which change has occurred. However, this concept applies equally well to both mechanistic and humanistic cultures. More crucial to the benevolent development of mankind is the humanistic development of the technological attitude. Erich Fromm (1968) suggests four basic steps in such a process.

1. Planning which includes the system Man and which is based on norms which follow from examinations of human beings.

2. Activation of the individual by methods of grassroots activity and responsibility, by changing the present methods of alienated bureaucracy into those of humanistic management.

3. Changing the consumption pattern in the direction of consumption that contributes to activation and discourages "passivation."

4. The emergence of new forms of psychospiritual orientation and devotion, which are equivalents of the religious systems of the past.

It seems that he has identified the problems and their solutions. Emphasis should be placed on systems for people instead of systems for machines, but people must also evolve a new orientation, a new confidence, that can shape the designing of that system. As in the past, people—and that includes working people—may not hope to overcome their problems by retreating from them; we must grow to meet them.

All growth, whether it be technological or scientific, means that we must abandon our familiar positions and change our values. Our environment is so viable that there will constantly be a need for change. We as individuals must realize this and must be prepared to adapt to these changes. Today there is a need for new knowledge among high-level executives and administrators of work organizations as we move into an epoch in which our values are changing, affecting our daily lives.

BIBLIOGRAPHY

Baker, F. T.: Chief programmer team concept management of production programming. *IBM Systems Journal,* Jan., 1972.

Barbour, I.: *Science and Secularity–The Ethics of Technology.* New York: Harper & Row, 1970.

Beaumont, R., and Helfgott, R.: *Management, Automation and People.* New York: Industrial Press Inc. 1964.

Bennis, W. G.: Organizational revitalization. *California Management Review,* Vol. 9, Fall, 1966, p. 51.

Bennis, W. G. (Ed.): *American Bureaucracy.* Chicago: Aldine Publishing Co., 1970.

Berger, P.: *The Homeless Mind.* New York: Vintage Books, 1973.

Bertalanffy, L. von: *Robots, Men and Minds.* New York: George Braziller, 1967.

Brickman, W., and Lehrer, S. (Eds.): *Automation, Education and Human Values.* New York: School and Society Books, 1966.

Bright, J.: *Automation and Management.* Boston: Harvard University Press, 1958.

Bronowski, J.: Technology and culture in evolution. *American Scholar,* Vol. 41, Spring, 1972, p. 197.

Burke, J. G. (Ed.): *The New Technology and Human Values.* New York: Wadsworth Publishing Co., 1966.

Cappon, D.: *Technology and Perception.* Springfield, Ill.: Charles C Thomas, Publisher, 1971.

Casserly, J. W.: *In the Service of Man.* Chicago: Henry Regnery Co., 1967.

Computer—problem solver, problem maker. *Business Week,* Oct. 17, 1970, p. 184.

Deutsh, K.: Some problems of science and values. In Burke, J. G. (Ed.): *The New Technology and Human Values.* New York: Wadsworth Publishing Co., 1967.

DuBridge, L. H.: Educational and social consequences of technological change. In Dunlop, J. T. (Ed.): *Automation and Technological Change.* Englewood Cliffs, N.J.: Prentice-Hall, 1962.

Dunlop, J. T. (Ed.): *Automation and Technological Change.* Englewood Cliffs, N.J.: Prentice-Hall, 1962.

Ellul, J.: *The Technological Society.* New York: Vintage Books, 1964.

Emery, F. E. (Ed.): *Systems Thinking.* Baltimore: Penguin Books, 1969.

Feibleman, J., and Freind, J. W.: The structure and function of organizations. In Emery, F. E. (Ed.): *Systems Thinking.* Baltimore: Penguin Books, 1969.

Ferkiss, V. C.: *Technological Man.* New York: New American Library, 1969.

Ford, A. B.: Casualties of our time. *Science,* Vol. 167, Jan. 16, 1970, p. 256.

Friedmann, G.: *The Anatomy of Work.* New York: The Free Press, 1961.

Fromm, E.: *The Heart of Man.* New York: Harper & Row, 1964.

Fromm, E.: *The Revolution of Hope.* New York: Harper & Row, 1968.

Galbraith, J. K.: *The Affluent Society.* Boston: Houghton Mifflin Co., 1969.

Gruber, W., and Marquis, D.: *Factors in the Transfer of Technology.* Cambridge, Mass.: The M.I.T. Press, 1969.

Heilbroner, R. L.: The impact of technology—The historic debate. In Dunlop, J. T. (Ed.): *Automation and Technological Change.* Englewood Cliffs, N.J.: Prentice-Hall, 1962.

Kaplan, M., and Bosserman, P. (Eds.): *Technology, Human Values and Leisure.* Nashville: Abingdon Press, 1971.

Lawler, E. E.: How much money do executives want? In Bennis, W. G. (Ed.): *American Bureaucracy.* Chicago: Aldine Publishing Co., 1970.

McLuhan, M.: *The Gutenberg Galaxy.* Toronto: University of Toronto Press, 1962.

McLuhan, M.: *The Medium is the Message.* New York: Random House, 1967.

Madden, C.: *Clashing of Culture: Management in an Age of Changing Values.* Washington, D.C., National Planning Association, 1972.

Mann, F.: Psychological and organizational impacts of technological change. In Dunlop J. T., (Ed.): *Automation and Technological Change.* Englewood Cliffs, N. J.: Prentice-Hall, 1962.

Miewald, R. D.: The greatly exaggerated death of bureaucracy. *California Management Review,* Vol. 13, Winter, 1970, p. 65.

Miles, J. A.: The wife of Onan and the sons of Cain. *National Review,* Aug. 7, 1973.

Mills, C. W.: *White Collar: The American Middle Classes.* New York: Oxford University Press, 1951.

Mishan, E. J.: *Technology and Growth—The Price We Pay.* New York: Praeger Publishers, 1969.

Reich, C. A.: *The Greening of America.* New York: Random House, 1970.

Reisman, D.: Leisure and work in post-industrial society. In Burke, J. G. (Ed.): *The New Technology and Human Values.* New York: Wadsworth Publishing Co., 1966.

Rose, J. (Ed.): *Technological Injury—The Effect of Technological Advance on Environment, Life and Society.* New York: Gordon and Breach, Science Publishers, 1969.

Slack, C. W., and Slack, W. V.: Good! We are listening to you talk about your sadness. *Psychology Today,* Vol. 7, January, 1974, p. 62.

Spencer, D. L.: *Technology Gap in Perspective.* Rochelle Park, N.J.: Spartan Books, Hayden Book Co., 1970.

Toffler, A.: *Future Shock.* New York: Bantam Books, 1972.

Walker, C.: *Technology, Industry and Man—The Age of Acceleration.* New York: McGraw-Hill, 1968.

Weiner, R.: *The Human Use of Human Beings.* New York: Avon Books, 1967.

Weizenbaum, J.: On the impact of the computer on society. *Science,* Vol. 176, May 12, 1972, p. 609.

CHAPTER
VII

CONCLUSIONS: VALUES AND THE FUTURE ORGANIZATION

VALUES AT ODDS

It has been shown that the value changes of American workers are having an impact on the organizations in our society. This impact will become greater as the twenty-first century nears. More importantly, the impact may become more negative as the motivation, productivity, and satisfaction of the worker steadily declines. The consequences for the organizations are obvious. Management will increasingly find itself paying more and more for less and less. It will have to pay more in terms of fringe benefits, not the least of which is a shorter work week. Can the business corporation survive if it becomes nothing more than an aggregation of disinterested, disloyal, and disenchanted robots? Will government bureaucracy and business corporations become repositories for "legions of dead men" so alienated from their work and from themselves that their organizations will find it almost impossible to be effective?

We have seen that, as a result of major societal forces, American workers' values are changing. We also know which values are held by business executives (Sikula, 1971; Guth and Tagiuri, 1965; England, 1967a, 1967b). These values call for profit, efficiency, and productivity, and reflect economic, political, and organizational concerns. These differ from the value orientations discussed in the earlier chapters of this book. Finally, and perhaps most importantly, managerial values do not seem to be undergoing any dramatic changes (Luck and Oliver, 1974).

As managers increasingly must interact with subordinates who do not share their values, we see the potential for conflict increasing accordingly. The resolution of conflict, nothing new to the managerial task, may be taking on a degree of significance heretofore unknown in our organizations.

THE CONCEPT OF COMMUNITY

Although conflict and its resolution are not new to organizations and the management of them, we may have to change our perception of business and government organizations in order to minimize the destructive influence that unresolved conflict can have on effectiveness.

The "new perception" of these organizations is *community.* The concept of community has defied precise definition among sociologists and social philosophers. For our purposes, community is an aspect of common life. When people work together in an organization, this "common life" begins to take on characteristics of its own such as patterns of behavior, speech, and functional interests. This notion of *interest* is important because human beings relate to one another in a psychological way, and social relations are motivated by the desire of human beings to achieve for themselves some particular goals or objectives. Maciver (1970, p. 98) points out that social relations are relations of minds. What binds one person to another in society are what he calls psychical laws. These are the spring-board to understanding the concept of community, which is created by the activity of men's minds. Maciver goes on to say that it is

> . . . on the objective side the *interest,* that for the sake of which we will the relations of community, on the subjective side, the *will,* the active mind for which the interest exists. It is as men will in relation to one another that they create community, but it is by reason of, for the sake of, interests. (p. 98)

What we now begin to see unfolding in our discussion is that "community comes into being because interests are realizable only in common life" (Maciver, 1970, p. 102). The question now is whether modern business and government organizations, by virtue of their structure, leadership style, job design, and lack of authentic human relations, have ignored and neglected the interests of the many for those of the few. We have already seen that management's values run counter to those of the many non-managers. The approach of *organiza-*

tion as community may be the direction taken by organizational analysis in the future. It may well be more than a matter of intellectual exercise for academicians—it may be a matter of practical necessity for managers who are interested in organizational survival in a turbulent society.

If this seems a bit drastic, managers should consider the logic of the following: If, as we have seen, the interests of human beings provide the basis for social activity, then *changes* in their interests provide the basis for social evolution. Is it too far-fetched to consider that when the interests of the many become greatly differentiated from the interests of the few, new social forms may evolve? These new social forms may be organizations that will carry on the activities of the business corporation but not resemble it as we now know it. The business corporation is one of the most significant and important institutions in our society. It has made tremendous contributions to America. As society changes, however, so must the business corporation. Managers may ask why they should be concerned with changing American society. What has that to do with making cars, televisions, radios, toasters, computers, soap, toothpaste, etc.? The answer is obvious, given the types of products mentioned.

But managers of business and government organizations may have been misled by fashionable words like "business and society," "government in an open society," "the corporation in a post-industrial society," or "medicine and society"; misled because society tends to be thought of as some faceless, amorphous mass. This is a major sociological error. Maciver (1970) warns of this when he states:

> There are no individuals who are not social individuals, and society is nothing more than individuals associated and organized. Society has no life but the life of its members, no ends that are not their ends, and no fulfillment beyond theirs. There is no conflict between society and the individual, between the welfare of society and the welfare of the individual. The quality of a society is the quality of its members. There is no social morality that is not individual morality, and no social mind that is not individual mind. (p. 69)

The critical importance of this for the manager is that those who make up a government organization or business corporation are not only its workers but also members of society. And if values in our society are changing, then the values of organizational constituencies are also changing. Society is *not* greater than the sum of its parts. This is a fallacious trap into which many have fallen. Society is not just some set of social relations. It is human beings and their individual relationships. Society is *in* the person.

With this in mind, the business corporation and government agency must see to it that they serve society. Earlier, it was noted that the business corporation has made tremendous contributions to our society. It is hoped that this will continue. No brief is being made here for socialization of business. A healthy, vibrant, and dynamic free enterprise system composed of private business corporations is one of the major cornerstones of a free society. The business corporation must make a contribution, however, to the quality of life in our society. Since the mid 1970s, and increasingly so in the future, this contribution has meant more than providing jobs. The expectations for business corporations in 1977 America are vastly different than they were in 1907 America. The ethos that provided the foundation for the American business corporation has greatly changed in 70 years. This shifting foundation requires a changing edifice so that the business corporation can survive as a free institution in society, an institution that contributes to the well-being of American society, and this, as we now know, means the well-being of its workers. Here is the rationale for the organization as community thesis.

At this point it is important to understand that, contrary to what many writers and scholars suggest, essentially there is no *antagonism* between the interests of society and the interests of the individual. When the business corporation helps to enhance the quality of life in our society, it enhances the quality of life of the members of society, whether these be workers, consumers, vendors, or any other constituents. This is a key point for the survival of the business corporation in America. As we begin to understand community more clearly, we realize that the interests of the individual *are* the interests of society, or individuality and sociality are interrelated.

What does this mean for the practicing manager? Simply this: If the manager takes into account that the values of his workers are changing he must realize that outmoded managerial styles are inadequate. The sophisticated manager will consider the interests of organization members as a means of optimizing effectiveness. A means-end relationship between individual interest and organizational effectiveness now begins to emerge. Furthermore, as noted earlier, we can take this one step further by extending the path-goal connection to include "societal effectiveness" or, putting it another way, the well-being of society. In other words, the manager must look at this "individual interest–organizational effectiveness tandem" not as two separate things but as two aspects of one thing. The business corporation must be effective and efficient in order to survive, but can it survive in a society that is not conducive to its very existence, let alone survival? The society that is responsive to and provides support for the business corporation is a society that benefits from the existence of the free enterprise system and its corporate members. Any societal benefits or any social ideal can only be realized in the lives of individuals, i.e., members of work organizations such as business corporations and government agencies. For the modern manager this has further implications with respect to his concept of management. More and more often, the evolving definition of management will have to include the part played by managers in the development of individuality within the organization. Values are changing, and ultimately all values are personal. They are values of individuality and personality. It is not an exaggeration to suggest that organizations and institutions, public and private, find their raison d'être is the service of individuality and therefore of society.

' If this seems to be a distorted justification for the existence of organizations, consider that this nation was founded on the principle that government should serve the people. Government is an organization, and if our government reflects the philosophy of freedom and democracy, is it not logical that our democracy's constituent institutions likewise reflect such a philosophy? For our purposes, the major institution in our society is the business corporation, and since we are now rethinking our perception of the corporation, we must ask whether the corporation serves the interests of its members. The "interest of its members" may be thought a meaningless and vague phrase because there are, of course, conflicts of interest. We are looking at the corporation as community, however, and this means the manager must break loose from traditional and, in many cases, dysfunctional modes of thinking about the business corporation. Therefore, it is suggested that the primary interest of organizational members is *survival,* but not economic survival, as it was in the early days of this century. This is a new age, an age in which changing human values have spawned a concern with survival of the human being psychologically, spiritually, and emotionally—physical survival is no longer the problem. In an affluent society economic impoverishment is not a pressing problem. The question to which American managers must address themselves is "can the American worker survive psychologically?" This is the new type of survival for which most members of American society are fighting. What is the mode of survival? It is personality. And now we have come full circle. All values relate to personality, and individuality, and the existence of institutions has been justified, because they serve personality, individuality, and therefore survival of the *total* human being. This is a worthy service, because there is nothing more important than the human being and the fulfillment of his capabilities.

We may have been confused by extreme philosophies regarding this matter. One extreme drowns and suffocates the human being in his social organizations. The other extreme places man above social relationships and suggests that the laws and institutions of society are inventions of the weak to shackle the strong. Each of these philosophies is fallacious. "Social relationships are not external things, not nets in which personality is enmeshed, but functions of the personality of each, the fulfillment of which is the fulfillment of personality" (Maciver, 1970, p. 95). Is the American work organization a place in which personality fulfillment is possible? This is a question for the modern manager to consider seriously. It is not ludicrous. We are concerned with organizational goals and objectives. The primary goal of the business corporation is survival. Can it survive if it ignores the survival of its members? The function of personality is to provide an individual with the means of adjusting to his environment—a means of survival. If the American worker finds the continued development and fulfillment of his personality impossible, given the nature of the organization, then the business corporation and the government agency are in trouble. But critics will say, "the business of the corporation is not to promote and enhance human development." We submitted here that insofar as such action promotes and enhances corporate survival (free of government control) it *is* a pressing concern of business organizations and for that matter every organization in which human beings enter into social relations to achieve organizational goals and objectives.

Managers have always been inclined to look favorably upon the notion of individuality. The history of capitalism is replete with the feats of entrepreneurs and managers who were not afraid to act in unique, venturesome ways. Have modern managers lost sight of the fact that all individuality finds realization in society and its organizations? Precisely because this is the case, however, individuality must somehow be given up to society. The failure of individuality is in its detachment from social service. For organizations to achieve any sense of community, managers must expand their role to include social service. This social service is of a new type, however, a type that most business and society texts or social issues books have by and large not recognized.

"Social responsibility" has corporate managers discussing the problems of pollution, consumerism, equal employment opportunities, and the like. These are important, certainly, but they are old hat—volumes have been written on these issues in the past decade. America has reached a critical point in its development. Corporate social responsibility must take on an expanded meaning in our society, and "corporate social conscience" must be redefined. As one of American society's greatest and most influential institutions, the business corporation must play a central role in improving American civilization. This means that corporate managers must lead society by playing a more active role in the direction this nation takes. Managers must learn to see that many workers are frustrated, alienated, and disenchanted by a meaningless society in which institutions have helped to break down much of what they once built up—the individual who possessed dignity and worth and who made this country great. Now managers of our business and government organizations must transcend themselves and make a commitment to establishing a sense of community in their organizations. The sophisticated manager must understand the organization in this new light. He must identify himself with the purpose of the organization as community. It is a lofty purpose but not an idealistic or unrealistic one. It cannot be idealistic if organizational survival is tied to it, and it cannot be unrealistic because it involves the fruition of individuality, without which the work of the corporation or government agency will not effectively and efficiently be accomplished.

Personality development is most at home in community. The highly developed, complex organizations in our society can help individual workers to achieve their potential by having a farsighted management that sees the organization as a community. In so doing the manager is serving society. Why? Because the self-determination, initiative, and sense of responsibility so crucial to organizational success are hallmarks of a fully functioning, emotionally healthy personality. This is the *new* corporate social responsibility: to provide an organizational climate that accommodates fulfillment of the new personal values and is conducive to the development of personality to its fullest potential. This is the *real* social issue for business organizations and government agencies, because only this type of fulfillment and development can create and maintain those deep and authentic social relations so vital to the survival of the individual, the organization, and society. The corporation that recognizes this is truly socially responsible, for it has greatly contributed to the high quality of society. As members of society develop personality and individuality at work, so society becomes the better for it.

IMPLICATIONS FOR MANAGEMENT AND ORGANIZATIONAL BEHAVIOR

What does an analysis of the organization as community mean for top management? The literature of organizational behavior has contributed much to management because it has provided insights, information, and knowledge regarding individual and group behavior. Organizations have been analyzed in terms of open systems and human behavior has been explored from the standpoint of workers' motivation. Managers have been provided with concepts of leadership, which, since they stress contingency and situations, have given them guidelines for effective behavior. These points, of course, do not do justice to the contributions made by the disciplines of organizational behavior and organization development. The intention here is not to give a complete history of these disciplines nor is it to minimize their importance for managers.

What is intended, however, is an attempt to illustrate that what is needed for the future is a more all-encompassing philosophy of work organizations and the behavior that takes place within them. This was the rationale for introducing the concept of community. Looking at the bureaucratic structure as a vehicle for the accomplishment of work and various other organizational goals and objectives was a result of the industrial revolution. It was a most appropriate model for the organization of work and people. It is still useful, but we are no longer at the threshold of the industrial revolution. Organizational analysis has not kept pace with the realities of our society and management has not fully grasped the effects of these realities on the worker. The impersonality of modern life has taken its toll on all of us, but what is most important for management to understand is that the predicament of man in modern society affects the business corporation and the government agency.

We said earlier that the most fruitful way to view human personality is as a method for survival. We also said that psychological survival is of paramount interest to almost every person who is aware of feelings of dislocation, alienation, and psychological discomfort brought about by modern life. If the human being suffers from these feelings in our very complex technocratic society, what does the manager suppose the effects have been for human personality? For the most part, the effects have been negative, creating a lack of integration among the parts of the personality system. Peter Drucker's description of our time as an "age of discontinuity" prompts us also to consider it as an era of the disintegrated personality.

The fully developed human being is considered by most personality theorists as one who has harmoniously integrated the various structures of his personality. The component parts of the personality should not be in conflict with each other. The sine qua non of a well developed personality is considered to be internal consistency. Richard Lazarus (1963, p. 44) says: "In this view, a person strives to harmonize every brush stroke in his picture of himself, so that all are put into perspective by some common principle or set of values." Note the use of values as an integral part of this harmony. The social forces we have identified in the previous chapters are causing human values to change. This means that the "age of disintegration" can, with enlightened management leadership, be an exciting era. With managerial help, the worker can relate his values to work and to the organization. The manager needs to understand that what a human being does in one part of his life should not be in conflict with what he does in other spheres of his existence. Otherwise, there is no consistency, and we have already seen the harmful effects of this on personality development.

We said in Chapter One that values dispose a human being to behave in certain ways. It will also be recalled that values determine our choices and that the choice of a given course of action (mode of behavior) is made in expectation of improvement of the quality of one's life. Workers are making new and different choices in the various spheres of their lives. They are striving for those modes of behavior and those interpersonal relationships that will make a favorable difference in their lives. The bureaucratic model for organizational design is inadequate to the task of helping the worker integrate his personality. Organization as community, however, can go a long way in this direction.

The modes of behavior and the interpersonal relationships toward which the value changes are directing humans can be best described as *authentic,* meaning awareness of one's self. We saw in Chapter Three that a major societal force is man's increased understanding of human behavior. More and more members of society are gaining an insight into and an awareness of the dynamics of human behavior. There is a good deal of searching going on in our society—aimed at gaining knowledge about the human being. In this search we also gain some knowledge of ourselves. As a result, one of the important value changes taking place in America involves the desire for greater self-understanding as well as the understanding of others.

We spoke earlier of Carl Rogers' concept of owning one's feelings. This is important, as it is a step toward being a congruent person. The *congruent* person is an *authentic* person, because after being *truly* aware of one's feelings, one takes conscious possession of them—one owns them and *accepts* them for what they are. The congruent person then can communicate these feelings openly and honestly to any other person. This is authenticity, and in a society that contains so many phoney, shallow, and plastic people, a move toward authenticity is refreshing. This movement away from the superficial to the authentic is a goal sought by many persons in today's society.

Soren Kierkegaard (1941, p. 29), the great philosopher, best described what we are talking about here when he used the phrase "to be that self which one truly is." This is the goal to which we should all be striving. This is what management should seek to promote, because we are living in an age of "partial people." They are not whole, but segmented owing to the tremendously complicated lives most Americans live.

As a psychotherapist, Carl Rogers has devoted a great part of his life to this question of searching for and discovering one's true self. His years of experience with clients have led him to suggest that Kierkegaard's words have a definite meaning. To Rogers (1960) it implies:

1. A movement away from facades and towards being what one is without fear of "exposing" oneself.

2. A movement away from a compelling image of what one "ought to be."

3. A movement away from living according to what others have defined as "meaningful" for you.

4. A movement away from constantly trying to please others and having to "hide" oneself and one's feelings from oneself.

5. Movement away from some fixed goal and toward a realization that authenticity is "being a process, a fluidity, and changing." Putting this in terms of Maslow's concept of self-actualization, it means one never "has arrived." One is never self-actualized but is self-actualizing. It is a "force for growth" that should extend over one's entire life.

6. A movement toward being all of oneself at any given time. In other words acknowledging one's total spectrum of complex, changing, and sometimes contradictory feelings in each moment of one's life.

7. A movement toward openness to experience. This involves a person "listening to himself" in the sense that one tries to hear the messages and meanings being communicated by one's own physiological reactions. It means not being afraid of one's inner experiences or the messages of one's senses.

8. A movement toward the acceptance of others. It means one values and appreciates the experience of others for what it is, without trying to change others into one's own image and likeness.

9. A movement toward trust of self. This is a matter of thinking one's own thoughts and not what others (who are supposed to be "experts" or the "best" in their profession) think. It involves becoming significant and creative in one's own profession, vocation, or trade, and not being afraid to express one's own feelings. It also means living by values one discovers within and expressing oneself in one's own unique ways.

By now we should have a clearer understanding of what authenticity means. To make this concept more relevant to the world of work, organizations, and management, we can refer to Martin Buber, as we did in Chapter Two when we discussed the new morality. We saw that finding one's authentic self and owning one's feelings can best be done through "meeting." This means the personal *I* meeting the personal *Thou*. It is another way of saying that authenticity is achieved only through human relationships. Buber says that "actual presentness" is the source of reality, and the present comes about only when *Thou* becomes present. When a human being relates only to things he uses or to objects he possesses, the relationship is between man and *things.* This keeps man from being authentic, because he always exists or lives in the past; there is no present. The world of the past is the world of *It,* because there is no sharing of experiences with, or relating to another human being. There is only a relationship with inanimate objects. It is this kind of relationship that prompts people to describe themselves in terms of what they *have* and what they *own* rather than *who* they are. Man's values are changing, however, and we do not want to relate to things but to one another. Since values are choices, and man is free to choose, we are witnessing a movement toward the *I-Thou* meeting. This is where *I* becomes a person who is aware of himself in all his individuality, unique from anyone else. The *I-Thou* meeting, therefore, is a sharing of experiences, values, beliefs, and ideas. Buber, as we saw in Chapter Two, says no sharing means no reality. Only to the extent that the personal *I* shares in reality does it become an authentic being. We cannot share with things or objects.

To further summarize Buber, we must restate his point that sharing is achieved through genuine dialogue. What is the goal of genuine dialogue? It is to establish a vital and dynamic relationship with another person. The essence of this is that both persons keep each other in mind as particular, differentiated beings, with no judging and full acceptance of each for what they are, not what one would *like* the other to be. Now we begin to see why this is reality. Many of our relationships, especially those between management and workers, are monological. Conversations are superficial and artificial. It is not truly dialogue, even though two persons are involved. Each person speaks to himself only. He does not really listen to the other. There is no intention of establishing a reality-centered relationship. The monological person is not living in reality and, therefore, cannot hope to "become that self which one truly is"—an authentic person. In monological encounters, the other person is never "allowed to be." The other person is perceived through one's own perceptive filter, which can distort reality. Managers too often do this. They promote and reward mirror images of themselves. They look upon others who are not "just like me" as weird, strange, or odd.

In the last chapter, which dealt with technology and values, we saw the problems that the misuse of technological advancement can cause. It is appropriate at this point to recall Buber's third type of dialogue—technical. This type is made necessary by the need to become familiar with and understand objective facts. In our technocratic society we find ourselves trying to keep up with the tremendous explosion of knowledge in whatever profession or field we specialize. The task is awesome. But so are the negative effects on human relationships. Depending upon our specific field, we relate to things (computers, balance sheets, production schedules, sales quotas, engineering drawings) or to so-called *facts.* We are enthralled with facts, data, and information. Managers are mesmerized by numbers. If something cannot be quantified it is not considered "scientific," realistic, or objective. Managers must have hard, cold facts! One of the negative side-effects of this technical dialogue is that we can easily tend to look at another person merely as a source of information or data. Individuals are not seen for what they are, i.e., unique, human beings who have values, feelings, and beliefs worthy of consideration. Furthermore, persons are considered only for what use they can be to us. The technical dialogue, then, is artificial, and the person whose working life is comprised of these dialogues is not living in reality and, therefore, can never become an authentic person. Anyone who perceives another human being only in terms of that person's usefulness is incapable of sharing in reality. The new understanding of morality to which we addressed ourselves in Chapter Two rejects such relationships because they are not moral. Our service-oriented society has had its effects on human relationships inasmuch as these relationships (if they can truly be called that) are conducted in terms of one person providing a "service" or being of some use to the other and in return being paid a fee, wage, or salary. It is not unrealistic to suggest that relationships in work organizations such as corporations and government agencies are of this nature. To the extent they are, there is little hope for the future of highly motivated, productive performance. Managers have spent a lot of time and money in seminars, conferences, and literature trying to find the answer to the motivational problem. The development of congruent persons whose individuality is nurtured by authentic relationships is not usually discussed in the typical management development conference.

The question now arises as to how realistic it is to suppose that genuine dialogue and reality-centered relationships can take place in the bureaucratic organization, the structure of which has not changed for nearly 200 years. To behavioral scientists, "structure" means the pattern of interpersonal relationships that take place in the organization. This includes communication networks, information systems, and the human relationships inherent in the planning, organizing, and measuring (controlling) activities. Structure should not convey a static notion of organization. The attitudes toward interpersonal relationships in organizations have not changed very much because organizational designs have not changed very drastically. Organizational analysis has advanced a bit but not to the point at which managers have equated the configuration of interpersonal relationships with organizational configuration.

The pattern of interpersonal relationships we call organizational structure must be reconsidered at this point in our organizational history. This reconsideration requires a new analysis that conceptualizes the organization as community. It is only with this analytical framework that we can hope to assimilate the human values that are being reaffirmed in America and that are discussed in this book. As we have seen, the position taken here is that the value of individuality is to be very much prized and cherished because of its relationship to the congruent, fully functioning personality. Authentic, reality-centered relationships between human beings contribute greatly to their development as emotionally healthy people.

This in turn enhances our society and the quality of life in it. Healthy people make for a healthy society, and the part American business corporations and government agencies can play in this very worthwhile endeavor is very important.

Because the concept of community views man in his wholeness, it should be the new "model" for organizations. The person is perceived in all his facets, rather than in a partial or fragmented way. When the industrial revolution ushered in the specialization of labor, the disintegration of human personality began. In some twisted way we reached the point at which we perceived man-in-organization as less than whole because he did not do the whole job. Since man did only a small part of the total job, he was perceived in the narrowest sense, i.e., in terms of the specialized function he performed in the manufacture of a product or the delivery of a service. Man became "partial man" because he only performed partial functions. The development of interchangeable parts was paralleled by the development of interchangeable persons. Individuals became expendable because no one person was necessary for the total performance of any job or the completion of any mass-produced product. In other words, no human being in the work organization need be considered an integral part of the organization or its work processes. The individual was on his way to losing his integrity, his wholeness, and ultimately, his importance as a human being. Scientific management analyzed work in terms of the time and motions necessary to perform a function. Man was timed and his movements were observed, just as machines were analyzed, for his efficiency in cutting metals, drilling holes, or whatever function a particular machine was to perform.

One major objective of the scientific management school was the efficient integration of man and machine. Man was perceived merely as an adjunct to the machine on which he worked. The optimal work situation was seen as one in which there was perfect coordination between the machine operator and the machine itself. The two were part of a *system*. In this man-machine model of management it might even be said that the machine was the more important part of this system because it represented a greater capital investment and, if taken care of, could last a long time, during which it could be financially depreciated.

This segmentation of the individual has been one of the more tragic results of the industrial revolution and the organizational vehicle designed to carry it along—bureaucracy. In redirecting bureaucracy toward community, the total person comes to the fore. In his book, *The Sociological Tradition,* Nisbet (1967, p. 47) discusses the concept of the whole man as an essential aspect of the idea of community: "Community is founded upon man conceived in his wholeness rather than in one or another of the roles taken separately that he may hold in the social order." Modern mass society as a "social order" is like a beehive, where individuals are regarded as means to ends. The individual suffers from estrangement due to the impossibility of identifying with mass society because relationships are functional.

We play many different roles in our modern society. These roles are, for example, a function of one's job or profession (electrician, manager, plumber, engineer); one's marital status (father, husband, wife, mother); one's leisure interests (bowling team member, country club member); and one's church affiliation, with all that implies in terms of religious denominations and sects. The end result is that we act out each role in a very specific way, given the boundaries of permissible or acceptable behavior, which are socioculturally determined. Each role holds expectations to which the individual must conform with little deviation. We relate to one another not as whole persons but as role players. Members of society meet one another, not in Buber's I-Thou manner, but in monologic encounters that do not allow persons to be fully human—only functional.

There are additional reasons why community as an organizing force should be considered by managers. One of the most important is that the bureaucratic structure of organizations has contributed to the estrangement of the employee. In a community the individual feels he is an integral part of the life of the organization. He does not perceive a gulf between his attitudes and values and those of the others who make up the community membership. He sees himself as a *member* of the community because he shares in its life. But is this the way most employees of our work organizations feel? Any discussion with large numbers of workers on this issue shows otherwise.

Our bureaucratic organization structures are centralized in terms of power, authority, and influence converging at the top of the pyramidal design to which most work organizations conform. The result has been a singular lack of involvement on the part of the vast majority of employees. Because of specialization of labor and departmentalization of organizational functions, no one worker can really see his part in relation to the whole. The only thing the worker shares with others in the same predicament is a feeling of alienation. The worker does not feel a part of the organization because he has no influence in its decision-making or goal-setting processes. Notice the use of "processes." It is not intended here to take decision making away from managers nor inferred that the planning function is not to continue as one of management's major tasks. What is being suggested very strongly, however, is that most workers are not even able to participate in the processes that culminate in a decision or a goal, objective, or standard that they will be held responsible for implementing or accountable for achieving. Is it any wonder, then, that the motivation to work is something less than optimal? Should it come as any surprise to managers that a conspicuous lack of initiative exists in our work organizations?

This lack of involvement becomes a major problem. The attitudes and values of management prevail to the exclusion of what most of the nonmanagers value. It is not an exaggeration to say that given the organizational ethos that pervades much of our thinking, more and more lower- and middle-level managers are feeling the same estrangement hitherto felt only by the rank and file. When there is no participation or involvement it is very difficult to feel responsible. The goals and objectives of the organization do not become internalized by employees. There is no feeling by the rank and file that "these are *my* goals and objectives," or that "I can identify with these goals and objectives." When this is a predominant feeling, organizational effectiveness is impaired.

Many managers have said that they decry the worker's lack of initiative, his unwillingness to get involved, and his attitude of no commitment. The response to this complaint is to ask the managers how often they actively seek participation and involvement. How much do they solicit the employees' input, advice, and suggestions? The managers' answers to these questions quite often turn out to be "very little." One of the more sorry consequences of this has been "class warfare" in our bureaucratic organizations. The nonmanagerial employee says "it's us against them." If there is any sense of community in our present day organizations it is only among the nonmanagers and it is not contributing to overall organizational effectiveness. How could it, when the formal organization's goals and objectives, indeed its very mission, are not the concern of the nonmanagers or many of the managers.

As a result, nonmanagerial employees demand more and more pay, fringe benefits, and security but fewer working hours. They feel no obligation to an organization that does not promote their involvement and participation in a community sense. They feel no loyalty to an organization that wants only their skin surface abilities and sees them only as means to ends, only as the functions they perform. The security that workers gain may be financial if their jobs are practically guaranteed (federal civil service workers). What about psychological security, however, which comes from a sense of belonging, rootedness, and solidarity? The modern complex work organization does not offer these, and therefore there is very little psychological or emotional security. Only the organization as community can satisfy these very basic needs in the employee, which are quite normal and positive for the human being.

Organizations are very much political entities, and business corporations are no exceptions. Political involvement refers to participation in decision-making and goal-setting processes. It is concerned with the influence process, and where community members feel they have no influence, full potential will not be realized. The lack of political involvement on the part of most employees is a sorry predicament to which policy-making executives must address themselves. If a worker feels he has no impact on actions of the organization, he feels unimportant. His opinions are not solicited; his suggestions are rarely sought—he has no voice in the organization. His job is so specialized that he doesn't even have any influence over his *work*. Because of the way most jobs are designed, he has few or no options regarding how his work can be done. His choices are limited. The worker clearly has no control over his work and no influence in the political sense. It is highly improbable that feelings of self-esteem can result from this situation. If the worker gets no recognition from management that he is a worthwhile human being, his self-concept takes a beating. If his work is so boring and meaningless that the worker gets no *psychic* income from it, his motivation for high-quality performance is drained.

What is left? Exactly what we have—workers going through the motions, barely performing, at levels necessary to keep their jobs—movement not motivation. Managers who are upset by this are naive and unrealistic regarding human behavior. In fact, this is a tragic flaw in the managerial character. As a class, professional managers are intelligent, pragmatic, clear thinking, tough-minded, and realistic individuals. This is good. But there is one area in which they are unrealistic—human behavior and all that it encompasses. Managers think that the attitudes, beliefs, and values of their employees should not be brought into the workplace—they should be hung up at starting time, like their hats and coats, and left in lockers and cloakrooms. When quitting time arrives workers can pick them up again as they leave. Workers are supposed to stop having feelings from nine to five.

Earlier in this chapter the well-integrated personality was discussed from the standpoint of personality theorists as conducive to emotional health, maturity, and psychological development. It was suggested that community promotes this and traditional organizational structure does not. At this point, it is relevant to mention the life-cycle theory of leadership (Hersey and Blanchard, 1972, pp. 138–139). This theory suggests that the maturity of workers has an impact on leadership effectiveness, inasmuch as the leader must adapt his style to the maturity level of his subordinates. The leader of immature workers would be most effective if he structured the task greatly and if he gave little socioemotional support to his workers.

The question now is: Will this managerial behavior ever change if it becomes very difficult for workers to grow and develop in traditional bureaucratic organization structures? Hersey and Blanchard call this theory life-cycle; but aren't we in a vicious cycle of manager-worker relationships? Workers find little opportunity for continuing their maturation process in bureaucracies. Hence managers deem it necessary to structure tasks even more, assign less responsibility, and maintain their psychological distance from workers. The cycle continues. Workers act in more childish ways, become disinterested, disloyal, and disenchanted with work, the organization, and its managers. The fact that our productivity increases at a paltry rate of little more than 2 per cent a year is evidence that whatever increased performance we achieve at the workplace is not coming from our human resources but from our technology. With prices increasing more than productivity, inflation seems an inevitable part of life. However much inflation is detrimental to the quality of life, the stagnation of psychological development and the poverty of the spirit are even worse. Since these latter two processes, which are occurring at rapid rates in America, cannot be quantified like the inflation rate, however, we pay little or no attention to them. They do not make the nightly news nor are they mentioned in the popular press.

A SUMMARY

We saw in chapter one that America is faced with a serious problem in its workplaces. An *Industry Week* advertisement has noted: "American business and industry are plainly in trouble." Business is under attack from almost every sector of our society. Each sector, of course, has its own axe to grind and therefore bases its attack on a specific problem that it perceives business has created. This book has taken the approach that whatever problems we are facing in America with reference to work, business and government organizations, their management, and policies, all of society is affected, not just any one segment of it. It has been argued that "society" must not be considered some faceless mass. On the contrary, it must be defined in terms of the individual, who with other human beings, composes "society." The argument, therefore, puts man at center stage in society. Workers make up society, and whatever occurs in work organizations to affect them affects society, not only the employees alone but also their families.

Symptoms of the problem were outlined in the first chapter. Some of these include absenteeism, turnover, alcoholism, drug addiction, mental illness, and deliberate sabotage by workers. The literature of organizational behavior is not without reference to these symptoms, however, and organizational behavior has addressed itself to the problems of work and motivation. It has discussed the necessity for understanding man and organizations to modify the behavior of each in order to make them more compatible. Organizational behavior, as a discipline, has endeavored to find an optimal mutual adjustment between man and organization so that the goals and objectives of each can be simultaneously achieved.

This approach is a bit myopic and does not go far enough—it is not as all-encompassing as we need in the latter part of the twentieth century. Most of the literature does not seek this mutual adjustment through a genuine understanding of man's changing values *as a member of society*. The present focus is on man's needs as they are exhibited within an organizational context. The organizational approach of today fails to recognize adequately that man moves in and out of organizations as a member of society. Man's behavior is very much shaped and influenced by his *values*. Organizational behavior has not given adequate attention to societal forces, as they are affecting human values and, indeed, changing them. Man's values are not affected by the corporation only. Major forces are at work in our society, and they have an impact on human values.

This book has taken a different, and hopefully more encompassing, approach to the problems of work as they are manifested as the symptoms noted. Understanding the intimacy of the relationship between organizations and society is stressed. The starting point is man, who is at the center of society, and his values as they are shaped in society. The important role played by values in our lives must be brought into clear focus because the failure of American corporations and government agencies to allow a fuller expression of human values in the world of work has placed the corporation and other work organizations at a crossroads. If management hopes to induce people to participate in and truly identify with work organizations, this becomes an absolutely essential item on its agenda for the future.

Values have been defined as choices. These choices, of course, can be made about anything. One can choose a product, a form of entertainment, a life-style, a set of religious beliefs, or an ideology to live by. The important point is that human beings make choices that they *perceive* will improve the quality of their lives. In other words, an individual makes certain choices in order to make a positive difference in and enhance his total existence. The phrase *quality of life* must not be considered only from a materialistic point of view. It must be considered in terms of the social, psychological, physical, spiritual, emotional, *and* economic dimensions of one's life. Work is an important part of life and it is an important factor, which affects the quality of life. To the extent that managers ignore this link between work and quality of life they run the risk of contributing to a poor quality of life for their organizations' employees. Since there is a connection between man and society, i.e., the workers also *are* society, business corporations and government agencies can have a deleterious effect on our quality of life.

The thrust here has been to suggest that this is the new corporate social responsibility—it is the new social issue for business and government organizations. These organizations are socially responsible, as far as enhancing the quality of life of their employees *at the workplace* (not outside it) by sponsoring bowling leagues, softball teams, picnics, etc. These are fine, but they do not address the issue of what work means and the relationship between a human being and his work. This is a critical issue for managers, their organizations, and for America. The symptoms outlined in the first chapter point up the problem of work in our society. Superficial applications of bandaids are not going to cure the sickness of the work ethic in America. If there is no psychic income from work, if psychological growth and development are thwarted, if the satisfaction of socioemotional needs is frustrated by the organization, all the bowling leagues, softball teams, and company picnics in the world will not prevent apathy, disinterest, lack of motivation to high quality performance, and negative attitudes towards the managers and the organization.

How can managers get to the roots of the problems faced in their organizations? How can they treat the problems and not just the symptoms? The answers to these questions lie in the heightened awareness managers should have of their employees' values, the major societal forces causing a shift in these values, and how these values or choices will affect workplace behavior and therefore the management of organizations.

One force at work in America that is causing value changes is what has been referred to in chapter two as "the new morality." This phrase implies that we are witnessing a new understanding and a different interpretation of the standards, doctrines, and principles that serve to guide and regulate the behavior of human beings. It can also be stated in terms of the development of alternative means for evaluating human conduct. Central to the concept of morality is the notion that there is a set of ideas or customs of a given society that regulates relationships and prescribes modes of behavior to enhance society's survival. Two points must be emphasized here. First, it is the "set of ideas or customs" that is changing, and it is in this sense the word "new" is used when discussing morality. Second, "enhancing society's survival" is a crucial aspect of this discussion because we are all interested in survival—in the physical sense but also in the psychological, socioemotional, and spiritual sense. Corporations are of necessity interested in survival, and it cannot be emphasized too strongly that as society goes, so goes its constituent institutions, such as business corporations and government bureaucracies.

Since World War II, American society has experienced one traumatic event after another—the Korean War, the civil rights movement, the Cuban missile crisis, the Vietnam War, assassinations of national leaders, and Watergate, to name just a few. Moral confusion, nagging doubts, and even despair followed in the wake of these events. Many Americans were losing their "anchors." They were experiencing the feeling of helplessness. They began to feel alienated from society's religious, economic, political, and academic institutions, to which they had looked for a leadership that proved to be nonexistent. The kind of leadership Americans were yearning for was essentially moral. The credibility of many of society's leaders who spoke in "classic" moral terms was at a low ebb—hypocrisy seemed the order of the day. Could classic concepts of morality prove adequate in reconciling man to his fellow man and to the institutions to which he had to belong. Obviously, many Americans did not feel that way. The mood of the country was conducive to an exploration, a searching for something that could help answer the question "what's it all about?" Much of this searching has led to a change in values, i.e., new choices regarding which ideas should regulate human relationships and prescribe modes of behavior—a new definition of what it means to be moral.

One of the newer ideas chosen was situationism, an approach to behavior that has great utility for the making of moral decisions. It stresses agapeic love, which is an unselfish type of love that does not consider the benefits accruing to the giver or the cost to him. The concept of agapeic love is not calculating in its consideration of whether the recipient deserves the love. There is certainly nothing morally or ethically lax about this concept. On the contrary, it is quite challenging. Situationism takes morality out of the legalisms of the medieval period, in which rules, codes, and regulations were the bases for human conduct and the prescription for interpersonal relationships. With agapeic love as the only absolute, there is a new definition of what is moral and ethical. Questions of organizational relevance now have to do with whether this love is put into action and practiced. Is it the criterion for one's decision making? In today's complex organizations, decision making is one of the manager's most important functions. The integration of financial, economic, marketing, production, and engineering data is crucial to deciding upon a course of action. However, the ultimate level of this integration should be at the human level. This is where the individual emerges as the unique, all-encompassing gestalt. In the situational context of the decision, human values must be considered by the manager. When Fletcher said that "love is using its head," he was suggesting that love must be the motive force for rational decision making. The new morality advocates, just as managers always have, that the consequences of one course of action vis-à-vis another must be carefully calculated. This new understanding of morality, however, says that love must do the calculating through the use of prudence, as managers try to cope with the complex problems of business and government. Managers must see that justice for all employees should be a paramount goal. If justice is the same as agapeic love, then purposeful, calculating rational love will guarantee moral decisions. To say that our governmental and private institutions have lacked moral decisions in the last 10 or 15 years is not an exaggeration.

The new morality is not what the mass media in America has suggested—sexual license, "do your own thing," and no inhibitions. On the contrary, it is a deep, honest, and continuing commitment to and consideration for one's fellow human being. The legalism of code ethics is being replaced by the law of love—agapeic love. One enters a specific situation in an open, nonprejudicial manner. What is moral or immoral becomes a matter of whether one has hurt another human being. This harm or damage to another person is not considered only in the physical sense but, more importantly, in the psychological, socioemotional, and spiritual. The question is whether the organizational climates of business and government are conducive to this new set of ideas, which regulates relationships and prescribes modes of human behavior. The concept of organization as community does just that.

In chapter two we saw that more and more members of society are gaining a greater understanding of human behavior; knowledge of "what makes people tick" is not the sole possession of the M.D./psychiatrist or the Ph.D./psychologist. Certainly, they are more sophisticated and have an in-depth understanding of behavior that nonprofessionals do not possess. A larger number of individuals have gained insights into how people behave, however, and why they behave as they do. These large numbers are represented by high school and college students who take courses in the behavioral sciences; college students who major in one of the behavioral sciences; students at the master's level, and so on. To this number must be added all those adults who are taking courses in continuing education programs on a part-time basis, an ever increasing trend in our society.

In addition to the numbers taking courses in a formal setting, there are those taking correspondence courses, attending sensitivity group sessions, encounter group sessions, and seminars in transactional analysis or e.s.t., for example, as well as the great numbers who do not attend any courses or seminars but read. To get some notion of the current interest, we need only look at the best seller list published weekly. The books on this list are not necessarily representative of the quality of output, but are merely indicative of the *numbers* sold. In the past several years there inevitably have appeared on the list books that deal with human behavior, e.g., *I'm O.K.—You're O.K.; Journey to Ixtlan; Beyond Freedom and Dignity; How to Be Your Own Best Friend; Tales of Power; When I Say No I Feel Guilty; TM; Winning Through Intimidation; Power!; The Relaxation Response; Passages.* These 11 titles represent books on the best seller lists of the past four years. This means that almost three behavioral books per year sell enough to make the list. What of the many books dealing with human behavior that sell large amounts but not quite enough to appear on the list? And how many would be on the list if we would go back ten years?

What of the great numbers who are involved with transcendental meditation, yoga, biofeedback, and other such endeavors that have as their goal inner peace, self-understanding, and control of one's mental and biological functioning? Americans are searching. Just as they are developing new concepts and standards of what is right or wrong, so too are they seeking to *understand* themselves and others. In this search for greater understanding, many Americans are beginning to gain more control over their stimulus-response cycles, and in so doing they have the potential for improving their decision-making processes.

As individuals increase their knowledge of human behavior, they begin to make high-quality decisions regarding interpersonal relationships. In other words, these individuals have rather precise ideas with respect to what constitutes a good and meaningful interpersonal interaction. This means that the individual who understands himself and others makes certain choices regarding the kind of interpersonal relationships into which he enters. Those relationships are chosen or "valued" to the extent that they maintain or enhance feelings of self-worth. Ego-destroying relationships are not chosen. If found in such interpersonal relationships, the individual makes every attempt to disengage himself.

Note the use of the words "choices" and "valued." We are back to our main theme—that major societal forces are affecting and changing human values. The increased understanding of human behavior among many members of our society is another force affecting human values and is thus directing their choices toward interpersonal experiences that are psychologically rewarding. The individuals whose awareness of human behavior is now heightened, understand why they feel tense, frustrated, angry, depressed, or anxious in certain situations. They understand the stimulus-response cycle of their behavior. By understanding themselves, they are better able to understand others. They now can exert greater control over their lives and their environments. It should not be forgotten that the major component of an environment is individuals acting in concert with others in group situations. Since these individuals are also employees of organizations, their values affect their behavior at work.

One of the most important ways in which this happens is through the psychological contract, a set of mutual expectations between management and its subordinates. This set of expectations is largely non-verbalized. An important part of the psychological contract is the *perceptions* workers have of management and the managerial perception of employees. These expectations include matters such as working conditions, hours of work, and performance standards. They also include the all-important matter of manager-worker relationships. Since an individual's perception is in part influenced by his values, managerial perceptions of employees have not changed very much because, as we saw earlier in this chapter, management's values have not changed. Employees' values are changing, however, and so are their perceptions and, therefore, their part of the psychological contract. Their expectations for management are vastly different from those of workers of 50 years ago. The contemporary American worker does not like interpersonal relationships in which the manager treats him as though he were a machine or just another piece of equipment. The worker does not like relationships in which his feelings are trampled.

The worker's increased understanding of behavioral dynamics makes it more difficult, if not impossible, for management to "psych him out." The American worker is not a psychiatrist or psychologist, but he is not stupid. The days when managers could psychologically manipulate workers are over. In the search for understanding of self and others, workers are more sure of themselves. They have a heightened sense of identity because of the trend in our society toward personalism that emphasizes man's capability for self-determination. This, coupled with man's inherent human dignity, prompts workers to opt for high-quality interpersonal relationships at work. To the extent that management creates the kind of organizational climate within which such relationships are impossible, the worker will be turned off, unmotivated, and even hostile toward the organization. The impact on organizational effectiveness will be negative. This is an accurate description of what is going on at work today.

In chapter four we discussed the relationship between education and values. We saw that education has grown dramatically in recent years. The median level of education of the American labor force is almost 13 years. By 1985, 20 per cent of the labor force will have had a college education.

Since the reader has been bombarded with enough tables and statistics in chapter four, it is not the intent in this summary to present any more. However, the two figures cited here with reference to the education of the labor force make the point: as management is confronted by more highly educated, articulate, and thinking workers it will have to re-examine its position regarding motivation, leadership, organizational design, and work itself.

What does the educational process do for the individual? One of the important goals of an education is to instill a spirit of inquiry—a questioning attitude. As one goes through the process of becoming educated one learns to look at both sides of an issue before jumping to a conclusion. One learns to "weigh the evidence," to look at the facts, and to marshall these facts in support of an argument or point of view. The educated person has learned to be analytical. This allows the individual to separate an issue, a problem, or data into constituent parts and to examine these parts critically, so as to get to the essence of whatever is being analyzed. The parts are then brought back into a synthesis about which the educated person now has some opinion, some conclusion, some "answer."

Now we must ask: "How does one manage individuals who are capable of thinking like this?" One answer is certain: "Not in the manner of 50 years ago." It is a new ball game. The educated workers' values are changing. They are not afraid to question why something is being done in a certain manner. They are not afraid to express their beliefs. They are not afraid to disagree with management, and as a matter of fact, they do not hold managers in awe. The authority of managers, while it may not be challenged, is not enough to get a manager through a sticky situation. Educated workers do not easily accept answers like "We've always done it this way," or "Because I said so" when they ask the reason for an order, a procedure, or a policy.

When an individual goes through the educational process, his personal values come under the same questioning, the same analytical inquiry, and the same dissection as do organizational and managerial practices. Organizational and managerial behavior actually is questioned precisely *because* human values are changing. As an individual becomes more educated, he is exposed to a whole new range of ideas. Armed with more information and knowledge, the educated individual enters into a new realm of thought. He therefore has more alternatives from which to make his choices; i.e., he can affirm new and different values.

These changing values affect individuals' choices regarding the kinds of jobs they consider meaningful and which offer opportunities for self-development, creativity, and individuality. Organizations need talent; they depend on it. Management's inability to understand the link between education and values could endanger its chances of getting its share of this pool of talent. We are living in a knowledge-oriented society. The work organizations of our society, most especially the business corporation, deal in the currency of brainpower, not muscle power. This is not a new or startling revelation. It may be revealing to managers, however, to suggest that they cannot have their cake and eat it with reference to the educated manpower they sorely need. They are naive to think they can entice well-educated people

into their organizations and then expect those individuals to stop questioning, or being critical (in the best sense of the word) or analytical.
These are all attributes of a mental process that goes on all the time in
the educated person. It does not occur only in relation to a specific
problem one has to solve in doing a job. It "spills over" into every area
of working life. Thinking people continue to use their minds, considering such matters as organization leadership, the mutual trust and
confidence existent, the ethics of management, and the opportunities
to participate in decisions that affect them. Is it realistic for managers
to expect educated individuals, who have been encouraged to think
for themselves, to stop thinking because they have entered the organization and the world of work? Business corporations and government
agencies, no less than universities, must support and foster intellectual
freedom.

The phenomenon of affluence—a societal force discussed in chapter five—is affecting human values. The economic growth of post-
World War II America has been spectacular, and it is now commonplace to refer to this country as the "affluent society." As we have
seen, however, this affluence has not been an unmixed blessing for
work organizations and their managers. It is ironic that the American
business corporation, which has been the single most important reason
for our society's affluence, is now experiencing negative side effects of
the very affluence it created. No doubt many a manager sees this as
unfair and unjust, but it will do no good to dwell on ironies and
injustices. Management must deal with the problems of affluence if it
is to get on with the task of enhancing organizational effectiveness.

Without repeating the statistics and the figures of chapter five, we
want to summarize the major points expressed there: As individuals
become more affluent, the pressure and anxiety of "keeping body and
soul together" begin to diminish. As material benefits increase, workers begin to look at their work in terms of what else it offers. This is
especially true of more educated workers and of those workers who
understand human behavior. These factors are related to each other
and in turn are related to the new definitions of morality that workers
have been developing. Together they interact to prompt a rethinking
or re-evaluation of work. If work provides little or no psychic income,
workers begin to question its value and also whether it makes any
sense to work harder or more conscientiously. They settle into a groove
of only working and producing at a level that will keep them from
being fired. The productivity figures for America graphically illustrate
how inadequate a level this is.

Organization members must have that psychic income so necessary to round out the quality of life. Where do they seek this psychic
income? Away from work. Now they have the affluence to engage in
activities that they perceive will make life somewhat more meaning-

ful, enjoyable, and rewarding. However, the individual must have the necessary time to play golf or tennis. He must be free to go fishing, camping or boating. This is the current trend. Affluence has played its part (an important one) in changing peoples' choices, or values. They are choosing leisure because such activities provide them with opportunities for the satisfaction and growth needs that most work in America does not provide. Is this "bad"? Certainly it is not bad for individuals to seek the satisfaction of very real and pressing higher order psychological needs. What is sad is that an employee cannot fulfill these needs in the context of a work organization. We spend many of our waking hours at work, and it is unfortunate that most jobs are merely tolerated, with workers just marking time until they can leave at the end of each workday. Eventually they begin to mark time until they can retire. Managers can attest to the fact that many workers already have "retired" on the job.

It should be emphasized here that boring, monotonous, routine, and overly specialized tasks are not a recent phenomenon. The scientific management movement, in designing jobs, separated planning from "doing" and contributed in large part to this type of work. This means that much of America's work has been like this since the early days of this century. Now that affluence is a more recent phenomenon, work that conforms to these characteristics is looked upon from a different perspective. Where management in America is failing is in the realization that organizations and the work done in them must change to the extent that they adapt to changes in lifestyles, values, attitudes, and needs. This is not a matter of managers giving the organizations to the workers. It is not a matter of letting workers "do their own thing" and thereby neglecting organizational goals and objectives. It is a matter of winning back workers that management has "lost." This is not meant in a physical sense—they still come to work (high absenteeism notwithstanding)—but managers have lost many workers psychologically. The will to work is waning, if not lost. Organizations have lost the commitment of their employees. The affluence, which has been well documented and enumerated in chapter five, has enabled these members of work organizations to become active members in other organizations that offer full participation as "first class citizens." They can have the voice, the involvement, and the influence on goals and objectives that they have not been able to obtain through membership in work organizations. This increased affluence has provided them with the financial means to acquire skis, golf clubs, boats, campers, second homes, memberships in country clubs, and airline tickets to hitherto only dreamed-of places. As noted earlier, these things require free time to enjoy them.

Many more working people, therefore, will choose to have free time, and what they can do with this free time, rather than more work. In its negotiations with the major automobile manufacturers in 1973,

the United Auto Workers Union made it a matter of contractual obligation that management could not force union employees to work overtime. If the worker chose to work, fine, but if he did not, no action
could be taken against him. This is interesting, considering the high
hourly wages in the automobile industry and therefore the very high
overtime pay a worker would receive. The choices (values) are
clear—more emphasis on leisure, less emphasis on work; more value
placed on the satisfaction of higher order needs with less importance
given to lower level needs that are already satisfied in an affluent
society. There is no more poverty of the flesh, only poverty of the spirit
and the psyche. There are those who argue that when we talk about the
modern worker and the quality of his life we should ask questions like
"compared to what?" and "compared to when?" We are living in the
present. We have to think existentially. It would be very difficult to
motivate the worker of today, one who is doing a meaningless, boring
task in a very hostile organizational climate, by reminding him that he
is materially better off than his predecessor of 50 years ago. He can't
relate to that.

In chapter six it was seen that America has been going through an
era of technological development unparalleled anywhere in the world.
That this development has brought with it heretofore undreamed-of
benefits can hardly be questioned. These benefits have been realized
in the fields of medicine, transportation, and communications, to name
just a few. Technological advances have clearly improved man's lot.
Its benefits to mankind have been impressive. But there is an aspect to
this that must be considered not only for its importance in this latter
half of the twentieth century but also for the critical nature this issue
has for the twenty-first century and its people.

The critical issue is that technology has increased our choices by
making available a wider range of alternatives than we have ever had.
For example, before the development of the airplane and the automobile there were two fewer options open to us with respect to
travel. As we are faced with more and more new alternatives in every
aspect of our existence, we must weigh these new options against
those we already have. Thus there is a questioning of the old vis-à-vis
the new. Technology influences man's values. Questioning becomes
an ever more deeply imbedded part of the technologically complex
society in which we live. However, society must ask the right questions. To what ends is technology put? Who in our society will control
the direction technology takes? Who will control the controllers? What
kinds of institutions will we need to insure that technological change
does not sweep us into a state of slavery?

These questions cry out for answers. It is suggested here that the
answers must always be given in terms of the human being and what is
best for him because, as we saw earlier in this chapter, there is no
society apart from its individual members. So, what is best for the

person is best for society. The following passage from an article by Harvey Wheeler in *Center Magazine* is frightening in its implications:

> John Wilkinson, a mathematician at the Center, estimates that the complexity of our social and political problems is of such an order that we need an I.Q. of 140 to understand and cope with them. If that is true, the prospect for democracy is very dim and we are fated for a future dominated by an intellectual elite, unless scientists throughout the world can help us. . . . (p. 50)

It is obvious that the new technology, with all its ramifications, is not very well understood by many people. However, this should not deter us. We cannot give ourselves over to a scientific elite because they think they "know what's best for society." Technology is producing social and cultural changes and with these changes come a shift in values, a shift in choices. Technology has liberated individuals from muscle tasks but not from new values. New choices must be made, but these choices must be made actively not passively. In the past, choices were made by individuals in order to achieve economic efficiency as defined in the marketplace. The market does not account for social costs in its transactions, however, and so technologies have been implemented with a positive private benefit but a negative social benefit. In effect, the market mechanism has inefficiently assigned no value to costs incurred by society as the result of technologies that cause pollution and cancer and create a uniform culture of regimented, standardized, deadened individuals.

Applications of technology primarily have been biased in favor of efficiency, cost savings, labor savings, convenience, speed—"the better life," in which man is freed from the burden of backbreaking, time-consuming work. What kind of work has man been "liberated" to do? Boring, monotonous, purposeless, mind-deadening work created by automated technology which has no challenge, no intrinsic worth, and offers no opportunity for human development. When the worker goes home he turns on television, which tells him he should like what he is getting. Television drugs the individual with opiates like cars, stereos, tape recorders, great varieties of after shave lotions, and other products whose uses promise "the good life." The big bureaucracy makes man's work routine, organizing its human resources en masse the same way it organizes the work of the enterprise—function is substituted for person; then mass media take over and, as has been pointed out, tranquilize the individual into submission.

A change in values is producing a revolution of the mind, however, a reassertion of man as the center of his own reality. This mental change, through which the individual is going within the context of this task-organization-technology triad, results in a loss of awe and reverence for technology. Managers of bureaucratic work organizations must see that it is their new social responsibility to create organizational climates in which technological innovations are implemented in the service of man and not just to maximize profits. Managers must exercise wisdom and philosophic knowledge, not just rational, economic knowledge. This type of knowledge is no longer enough, because man is not just rational-economic man but complex man. The life of the mind—the life of the spirit, these are the essence of the good life. Can the work organization contribute to the good life? Work is presently designed and its organizations structured in such a way that it cuts most people off from life. The mass electronic media continue this process of divorcing man from reality.

Man is fighting to get back to center stage. His values are changing so that he is going to assess technology in terms of its ability to improve the quality of his existence. So far the scientists, the business corporation managers, and electronic media managers in the communications industry have arrogantly decided what is best for the individual. They have treated human beings like undifferentiated idiots. Man doesn't need an I.Q. of 140 to *experience* and *feel*, in an existential way, a sense of alienation, powerlessness, and disorientation caused by a dehumanized technology in which man is reduced to a number on a computer card. To the extent that this continues, the damage done to the human beings in our society finds its way into the institutions of our society, not the least of which are the business corporations and the government bureaucracies.

A Plea to Managers

Managers must take their place as leaders in our society. They are intelligent, well-educated, and highly motivated individuals who, as a class or profession, know better than other groups about goal achievement. As leaders in society they must first realize the tremendous obligation they have to improving the quality of life. This can best be accomplished by the manner in which they manage their work organizations and the human resources in them. Being a good manager is not necessarily being a good leader. Leadership is an influence process comprised of three factors—the manager, the followers, and the situation. Two of these three factors are quite different today than they were 50 years ago. The followers have changed and the "situation," with all that this concept means, has changed. The managers who continue to march to the beat of the old music will certainly be out of step. By becoming effective leaders *within* work organizations, managers will contribute to the satisfaction of those higher order psychological needs that are latent and waiting to be satisfied. These needs must be given opportunities for satisfaction at the workplace.

This book has suggested that if workers can continue their psychological growth and development while doing their jobs, management will be a causal factor in promoting a society of emotionally mature, psychologically healthy human beings. These individuals will be able to move continuously toward realization of their full potential. The achievement of human potential thus becomes one of the major reasons for work. Managers must make their organizations places in which the fullness of personality can be realized. Work and the organization in which it is done must become the means by which human beings can realize their individuality in its most complete way.

The time has come for managers to make the work organization a *community* in which these things can happen. Then will work organizations be the bulwark of a healthy society because they will be places where individuals find purpose and meaning in their lives. This is how management contributes to the quality of life in our society; this is how managers become the leaders of our society. This is management's *new social responsibility*. It is only in this way that managers and the business corporations and government agencies can regain the credibility they have lost.

To take on this new societal leadership role that our times demand, however, managers first must transcend themselves. They have to rise above and outside of their own "worlds," which they have created owing to the manner in which they perceive themselves. All the "data" and all the stimuli with which they have been presented have been "filtered" to form a view of their environments that has not been the most all-encompassing. It has been a view that is too narrow, too limited, and therefore not adequate in the era in which we now are living. It will certainly be inadequate for the future. Managers are increasingly discovering that their perceptions of a given situation are not shared by many of their subordinates. They are finding that their perceptions of work and the organization are not shared by many of those individuals who have to do the organization's work.

What are some things that managers can do to manage the "new work force" with its changing values? What can managers do to recapture the lost motivation, the vanishing commitment, and the indifferent worker? Participative management is a very misunderstood concept that managers must not only understand but also employ as a leadership style. It is not giving away the organization to the workers. It is not letting the workers do their own thing, and it is not giving up managerial prerogatives. It is simply soliciting the advice and counsel, the participation, and involvement of one's subordinates in the various processes of planning, organizing, and controlling. An example is the decision making process. Those subordinates who have to implement or execute a manager's decision ought to participate in the *process* of making this decision. The process is not the decision, however. The final decision is still made by the manager—this hasn't changed—and the manager gives up no managerial rights. What is involved in the *process* of making a decision is (1) determination of viable, feasible alternative courses of action; (2) identification and enumeration of the consequences that will occur for each alternative course of action; (3) determination of the probabilities of each of these consequences happening. This is the input a manager should solicit from his group. After this process has been accomplished, the manager takes all the data represented by the inputs and at some time thereafter makes his choice (decision). He then announces the decision to his group with an explanation of why he chose the course of action he did. This explanation is an important follow-up because invariably some members of the group would make a different decision.

The benefits to organizational effectiveness that come from using this approach are many. Obviously, the manager gets more input, and data upon which to make his decision. This information is coming from individuals who should be knowledgeable about the situation under discussion. After all, they are working at the tasks in this situation on a day-to-day basis. In addition the potential for motivation is great. This style of leadership taps the latent needs noted earlier—needs we all have. For example, when the manager calls his group together to involve them in this decision-making process the need for affiliation and relatedness is being satisfied *in the process of getting an organizational task accomplished.*

When the manager calls his group together he is according the individual group members *recognition.* He is in effect telling them he thinks enough of them to solicit their input. He values their counsel. The individual subordinate should be able to take away from these kinds of experiences a heightened sense of self-esteem. Although no one can give another person self-esteem, managers can create organizational climates in which individuals can have increased opportunities for achieving greater self-esteem. The more managers relate to their subordinates in a manner that recognizes them as worthwhile individuals, the greater are chances that the individuals can enhance their feelings of self-worth.

This participative management approach can also be used in the goal setting process. Once again, individual subordinates are not setting their own goals and objectives (though this has enough merit for management to consider) but are involved in the *process* whereby these goals and objectives are set by management. As human values change, people want some degree of participation in the process of setting these goals and objectives by which management will judge and appraise their performance. In other words, if management is going to hold subordinates responsible for the achievement of certain goals and objectives and will appraise their performance according to whether these goals and objectives are accomplished, then the subordinates want the opportunity to participate in the goal setting process by giving their input. This input involves the circumstances or conditions faced by subordinates that should be considered when goals and objectives are determined. This is especially useful in setting sales quotas for organizations in which salesmen operate in different parts of the country, each with unique economic and financial conditions. This example can be extended to any function of organizational management—production, research and development, engineering, finance, etc. The idea is not revolutionary, but it is not very widely implemented. It is an idea based on common sense—it is suggesting that human beings will be more motivated to execute decisions and will work harder to accomplish goals and objectives that they have had a part in setting than if these decisions, goals, and objectives have been perceived by subordinates as having been arbitrarily imposed. When this perception of arbitrariness is made and when employees are shut out of the processes described here, they more often than not "drag their feet," "go through the motions," or even sabotage decisions, goals, and objectives.

Another example of enlightened leadership is rethinking, reanalyzing, and re-evaluating the nature of work. Management is long overdue in this regard. The scientific management movement revolutionized the manner in which work was done. Sixty years later we are still designing tasks in the same way. Little or no thought has been given by managers, engineers, and production specialists to the fact that the *people* have changed. Their values, attitudes, and beliefs have all shifted. Their priorities have also changed, as has the definition of a good job. The worker of today is not the same as his predecessor of 60 or 70 years ago, but the work has not changed very much nor have management's values.

What is needed is a new revolution regarding work and how it is to be done. Workers, especially the "new breed," who are younger, more highly educated, more assertive, and more articulate, just are not "producing" when they have to do a task that was designed for an uneducated and more compliant individual whose options regarding the kind of work he wanted to do and the mobility for exercising these options were virtually nonexistent. It makes no sense for management to bemoan this state of affairs and to long for the good old days. This accomplishes nothing. No brief is being made here that managers should *like* what is happening. It is not a matter of liking or not liking but a matter of organizational survival. If organizations are not effective they have no chance of surviving, and if they are not adaptive to this changing and turbulent environment we live in, they will go the way of the dinosaurs.

Work must be conceived in terms of the human being. Tasks must be structured and designed with the individual in mind. It is inconceivable that in a nation which has many brilliant, energetic, and creative people—people who have sent rockets into outer space, landed astronauts on the moon, created life in a test tube, and performed other fantastic feats in various fields—we cannot find ways to design jobs that provide meaning, purpose, and a sense of self-esteem and achievement.

What of the kind of organization in which this work is carried out? Just as we have to rethink the nature of work, we must likewise rethink the nature of organizations. The bureaucracy, which was the organizational vehicle for getting work accomplished, has not changed much since Max Weber gave us his model about 50 years ago. We must revolutionize our thinking about the kind of organizations we need in order to promote the emotional health and the psychological growth alluded to earlier. The "revolution" is really only a matter of changing our ideas about organizations. Nothing very drastic is required if only managers realize that organizations are not *structures* made up of bricks and mortar. Organizations are nothing more than patterns of human relationships. We have to perceive organizations in this way. When we do, we start to see how much more beneficial it is—to the workers, to management, and to organizational effectiveness—if we conceive of the organization as *community*. In this way we offer opportunities for human beings to work at their newly designed tasks in the fullness of what it means to be human. The business corporation and the large government agencies will then be providing society with work organizations that become the cornerstone upon which a higher quality of life can be built. It is then that corporate and government managers will be leaders in society, not just in their organizations. No less than this will secure their future because the administration of organizations in society must be consonant with the changing human values in that society.

BIBLIOGRAPHY

Wheeler, H.: Technology: Foundation of Cultural Change. *Center Magazine*, Vol. 5, No. 4, July–Aug. 1972, p. 50.

Nisbet, R.: *The Sociological Tradition*. London: Heinemann, 1967.

Sikula, A. F.: Values, Value Systems, and Their Relationship to Organizational Effectiveness. *Proceedings of the Thirty-First Annual Meeting of the Academy of Management* 1971, pp. 271–72.

Guth, W. T., and Tagiuri: Personal Values and Corporate Strategies. *Harvard Business Review*, Vol. 43, Sept.–Oct. 1965, pp. 123–32.

England, G. W.: Personal Value Systems of American Managers. *Academy of Management Journal*, March 1967, pp. 53–68.

England, G. W.: Organizational Goals and Expected Behavior of American Managers. *Academy of Management Journal*, June, 1967, pp. 107–117.

Luck, E. J., and Oliver, B. L.: American Managers' Personal Value Systems—Revisited. *Academy of Management Journal*, September, 1974, pp. 549–54.

Maciver, R. M.: *Community: A Sociological Study.* (Fourth Edition). London: Frank
    Cass & Co. Ltd., 1970.
Lazarus, R.: *Personality and Adjustment.* Englewood Cliffs, N.J.: Prentice-Hall, 1963.
Kierkegaard, S.: *The Sickness Unto Death.* Princeton, N.J.: Princeton University Press,
    1941.
Rogers, C. R.: *A Therapist's View of Personal Goals.* Pendle Hill Pamphlet 108. Wal-
    lingford, Pa.: Pendle Hill, 1960.
Hersey, P., and Blanchard, K. H.: *Management of Organizational Behavior.* Englewood
    Cliffs, N.J.: Prentice-Hall, 1972.

AUTHOR INDEX

SUBJECT INDEX

197